"THEY HAVEN'T GOT ME YET!"

a life history of

PETER DASHWOOD

17th April, 1928 - 10th June, 1990

by

Peter and Janet Dashwood

Published privately by Janet Dashwood.
Available from JANET'S 1, Gallow Tree Road,
Rotherham. S65 3EE. 0709 377084.
Price £7.00 + £1.50 pp.

ISBN 0 9525074 0 4

ACKNOWLEDGEMENTS
To Derek Schofield, who inspired me to start
this book; Graham Potter, who encouraged me
to continue; John Osband, who suggested I put
a copy in the Vaughan Williams Memorial
Library, EFDSS, which made it a different
document from the one I started and Doc Rowe
for advise. I am particularly grateful to John
Dowell, who prepared the whole for printing in
his spare time and to Giles and William for
their patience.

For photographs: Kit and Derrick Dashwood,
J & P Grimshaw, Thames Valley Morris Men,
Roger Wolfe, Hartley's Photographs, Peter
Davis, Derek Schofield, Handsworth
Traditional Sword Dancers, Janet Dashwood,
Cambridge Evening News.

Typeset by Interface. 0392 444045
Printed by Brightsea Press. 0392 360616

Cover photo – Boxing Day 1988
© Derek Schofield

DEDICATION

"This is dedicated to all those volunteers who made it worth while.
I'm just grateful for having known you."

Peter Dashwood

and

For Peter

CHAPTERS

INTRODUCTION

Peter Dashwood grew up in the New Forest. After National Service he joined the Civil Service. In 1964, he gave up his pension and half his salary to work for the English Folk Dance and Song Society. "The EFDSS exists to collect, research and our preserve our heritage of folk dances, songs, music and customs so that they can continue to bring enjoyment." Peter was one of eighteen members of staff who were building upon Douglas Kennedy's ideas of popularising folk music. Douglas, a charismatic man even in his eighties, had taken over from Cecil Sharp as Director in 1924 to retirement in 1961. Without his innovative ideas it is unlikely that Peter, and many more men, would have been attracted to dance.

In the sixties and seventies EFDSS staff and members started Sidmouth, Keele and Whitby Festivals, Folk Camps, a residential Folk Centre at Halsway Manor, Folk Centres, Workshops, Training Days, Newsletters, Morris and Display teams. They collected in the Field; organised, called and sang at Ceilidhs, Dances, Festivals and Folk Clubs and provided training and work for bands, callers, dancers, musicians and singers. All this influenced a generation and was copied.

In 1986 Peter was made redundant. In 1987 he started limping and, a year later, was diagnosed as suffering from Motor Neurone Disease. MND causes paralysis and is fatal. As Peter's body succumbed to the disease he used a word processor to write about his childhood, for his own satisfaction; his work, in notes for a magazine article and citation for an award; and his life, for research into MND. He died in 1990.

Later that year Derek Schofield, of the EFDSS NEC, wrote a paper on the Future Organisation of the English Folk Dance & Song Society, in which he asked, " When the 60s wanted to organise Ceilidhs and the 70s discovered its folk dance and music roots, where was the Society?" Reading this two months after Peter's death, written by one of those who had sacked Peter, made me angry. I went to the work Peter had left

on the word processor for reassurance and started to amalgamate all his writing into a booklet, adding bits of my own. I did it mainly for myself and our boys, but John Osband suggested I put a copy in the EFDSS Library and it "just grew".

When I came to the diagnosis I remembered Peter had requested that I write an Ideal Care Plan for MND. Much has changed in Community Care in the last few years so I decided to describe what it is like to live with MND. This was the hardest part to write, so much happened in a short time. Although I found writing about the redundancy therapeutic and our life together enjoyable, the MND sections were frustating and annoying. We had lived through MND and survived, I did not need or want to do it again! However, MND dominates this book, as it did our lives.

A similar number of people develop MND as Multiple Sclerosis, 1,200 per year, yet it is little known by the general public, or, worse, the Caring and Health Services. This is mainly because people with MND die within a few years of diagnosis.The effects of MND are terrible and individuals have different ways of combatting them. Some seem to give up and die quickly; others refuse to succumb to using technology; at least one did not have any choice as he was missed by the Services who should have cared for him. We chose to do battle with whatever was available. It was not an easy option. There is nothing easy about coping with MND. I hope that by writing of the effects MND had on our family it may help others. We learnt an awful lot from MND.

Should you be moved at all by this book the MND Association urgently needs money for research, equipment and care. The address is at the back of this book.

The sections in normal print are by Peter, those in italics by Janet.

A VILLAGE CHILDHOOD 1928-1944

I was born 17th April, 1928 at Pennington, Lymington in Hampshire, the youngest of five children.

Peter's father was Charles Henry Dashwood, a steward in the Merchant Navy from Southampton and his mother Annie Frances, nee Boyce, of Bootle, Liverpool. She was the youngest of four children born to Richard Boyce and Sarah Ann, nee Kelly, who both came from Ireland, meeting in Liverpool. Sarah had six brothers, all over 6 feet tall, who went to America. She was born in County Sligo in 1855 and died 2nd June 1937. Richard Boyce came from Dublin or Wexford, born in 1852, died 9th April 1912. Both are buried in Kirkdale Cemetery, Lang Moor Lane, Liverpool. Peter was taken with the fact that there is 130 years between four generations, Richard Boyce, Peter's grandfather, born in 1852, Annie Boyce, born in 1895, Peter, born in 1928 and William Dashwood, born in 1982.

I can't remember when I was very young. I know that I played with a teddy bear which had come to me after my three brothers and sister had grown bigger, I am the youngest in my family. I discovered that if you are the youngest in the beginning you are the youngest throughout life and always treated as such. Teddy had been hugged by Bobby, Kitty, Charlie and Derrick and now me, Peter. I think that he must have been tugged and chewed by everyone too, because for me he had no ears, one eye, one arm and a gammy leg.

I do remember sitting up in my pram one day outside, "Isn't he shy?" said a lady neighbour to my Mother. I remember those words then and I remember the same words being said time and time again as I grew bigger.

I have heard tales of the time I was lost near to the river and the sea at Lymington more than 2 miles away. How I came to be there is not explained but it is said that our local District Nurse found me and returned me safely on the back seat of her bicycle. Otherwise, at age 3, my normal world was the garden, which to me was enormous, full of grass like a field and apple trees at the bottom. Everybody remembers the time I fell and hit my head on the doorstep. The scar on my forehead remains with me to-day, a continual reminder never to walk about with shoe laces untied.

There were a lot of children in our road and with having brothers and a sister I was soon playing in the road and down on the Green or around the little pond. There was no escape for me as the smallest and youngest when it came to the real challenges of life — dropping from trees or crossing the river on a log and smoking woodbines!

Miss Rixton's ducks waddled to the pond every day and I was frightened of them and expected them to peck at me as they went by. The little pond also had tadpoles which we were told would turn into frogs. There were thousands of tadpoles but we didn't see many frogs.

As far as I can remember I had all the usual childhood illnesses. In my very young days Diphtheria was still a killer and one heard a lot about TB. When I was a bit older the scourge of Polio hit the country and I knew of several young people in the area who were affected.

Peter aged 4 – 1932

THE LITTLE SCHOOL

I think I remember the first few days at the little school and I don't think I liked it. It seemed a long way from home, down to Yondy Corner, across the big Common, past the big pond, past the Churchyard and the Church and then the Big School and the shops to the Little School. In the early days I would sit on the back seat of Mum's bicycle and on rare but special occasions I would get a lift with Mrs Metcalfe in her pony and trap. More often I walked with my sister Kit and I believe that I was often the cause of her being late at the Big School.

I have few early memories of the little school of any significance except that it was next door to the bakery and the delightful aroma of newly baked bread wafted over. We met our class mates at age 5 and in general were with the same children at age 14 when we left the school. I didn't really identify with those around me until we moved up to the big school and then boys and girls became individuals.

You knew who was brighter than you and who was less so, who was good at football and cricket and generally who you liked. I always regarded some of the girls as brighter but I think my judgement was based on the fact that they seemed to be able write more composition.

I will try a memory test of those who were in the first class which was taught by Mrs Torah:- Billy Webb, Gerald Waters, Harry Stote, Spencer Phillips, Charlie Elford, Doug Huntington, Ken Brown, Brian House, Des Orman, Billy Joyce, Douglas Ayling, Robert Bradshaw, William Pink, Peter Metcalfe, Doug Rendell, Dorothy Letts, Phyllis Rickman, Elsie Goodman, Margaret Boyle, Margaret Whatley, Florrie Blatchford, Pearl..... Muriel Ednie, Margaret Plumbly. There's a few more I can't remember.

My only Folk recollections was of holding the Maypole, if I was lucky, at school while others held ribbons and danced around it. Later, I danced the Sailors Hornpipe with the Sea Scouts; we also had a good line in Sea Shanties.

THE GREEN, STREAM and BOG

There was much to be discovered not far from Hazel Road. We learnt to play rounders, cricket and football on the Green, the bumpiest Green you could ever wish to meet. The balls were often lost in the ditch banked by stinging nettles or in the gorse on the other side. There were lots of expeditions to be made towards the river. From the Green, follow the stream down and alongside the copse. It was boggy further down and we had to step carefully to avoid sinking down in the mud. It was not just boggy; there were dire warnings from older boys that you could disappear forever in one particular spot which was oozing soft mud and water from a spring. Perhaps it was the same spring which had been piped from the copse bank into the stream. We drank from this pipe on occasions. The journey towards Wainsford Road was full of hazards but it was all pleasant on the other side of the road where the stream ran under the road. This was where we raced our sticks through the big pipe, in the minds of young boys they became speedboats, racing cars or whatever else moved fast. This is where we also gathered watercress and nearby was a tree which grew sloes, but boys soon found out that they were unpleasant to eat.

TO THE RIVER

These were big expeditions. Follow the road past King's Huts to the farm to face the first hazard.

Geese guarded the whole of the road and it was frightening to pass the gander who hissed and stretched his neck towards us smaller kids. His beak was on eye level to us but somehow we had to brave it and run past to reach the Common. Another 100 yards or so and here was the rubbish tip, always an interesting diversion to discover what others were throwing away. No matter which Common we were on there were always gorse (fuzz) bushes and blackberry brambles to negotiate as well as bogs, not so pleasant in short trousers. The river was not far away and our favourite spot was 'Plank', because there used to be a plank across the river. This marked the end of the Common and there was barbed wire across to stop cows from wandering down river from the field. It was a fascinating spot and we spent many happy hours paddling on a sandy bottom and on rounded pebbles in the shallower water. Here we could also catch minnows in our jam jars and get an occasional glimpse of a trout. On a very big trip we would climb through the wire and follow the river and fields to Gordleton Mill and then walk back through Ayles Farm and across fields to Ramley and then home on the proper road.

THE COPSE

Climbing trees and dropping from the lower branches was the most favourite activity of all. Easily the best climber was a fir tree which to us was an enormous height but once you reached the top you were rewarded with views across to the Isle of Wight. The oak trees with long lower branches were best for dropping from and the height challenges were considerable to a small chap like me. Every oak tree we knew could have been the hiding place of King Charles 1st when trying to elude the forces of Cromwell; but then probably every old oak tree in England has similar claims.

THE PONDS

If every summer was long and hot, then I'm sure every winter was long and hard. We had a number of ponds around us but the big one where everyone gathered was halfway between home and school. The pond was completely dry in the summer but it filled up during the Autumn and with some hard winter frosts we were often fortunate to have ice, sometimes for weeks on end. A good run from the bank and a slide on the ice was our competition. To travel far it was essential to have good boots preferably with metal tips. When word got around that the ice was good lots of youths came from other villages and they were not always welcome. Not many people had skates and the few who did seemed to belong to an upper class. Messing about with ice was also dangerous, especially when it was not quite strong enough to bear weight. If the ice broke beneath you it was easy for your little piece and you to slip underneath the bigger surface. I recall having to reach out and give a hand when needed.

THE COMMON

By any standard the Common covered a big area, but to a child it was an enormous stretch. The Common separated the village from Upper Pennington, where we lived but for any formal journey to Church, school or shopping at Lymington it meant crossing the Common or travelling the road which ran alongside. For much of the time it was a walk. The luxury of a bicycle, later, did not always mean a comfortable journey as the vicious South Westerlies swept in from the coast, just a few miles away at Milford and Keyhaven.

Much of the Common was covered by gorse and there's no finer sight than a springtime carpet of deep yellow bloom from the young shoots. In fact the fuzz, as we called it, never had a chance to grow old or high because it was burnt regularly. I suspect most boys would confess to setting fire to the odd patch now and then and I was no exception. After a good burn up there followed a bleak period when the blackened earth and and charcoal sticks of the old gorse presented a eyesore, but it was not long before green grass sprouted and new young shoots of gorse appeared.

THE GREEN

Despite all other attractions we spent most of our early childhood on the tiny Green at the end of our road. Parents knew of our whereabouts and we could hear Mr. Stone's whistle which called Ray back for mealtimes. It was on the Green that I learnt my football, emulating Stanley Matthews and other heroes of the day. It was here too that I was inspired by Len Hutton when he made that record breaking score against Australia at The Oval in 1938. It was this same Green, which had bumps all over the place which killed off my cricket potential. Ray could always bowl fast and was still bowling for the village team in his fifties. Had I and others been able to cope with the pace then perhaps our cricket careers might have been

pursued with more enthusiasm. I recall too being invited along with other boys from the Green to listen to the broadcast of a cup final; Huddersfield V Preston North End which was settled by a penalty in the last minute. That goal by Mutch was replayed over and over again.

BILLY WEBB

Two of my schoolmates Nip Waters and Billy Webb lived away from the road but I spent a lot of time at both households.

Billy's father had a paddock where he kept pigs, hens, ducks, geese and a billygoat. The last two caused a certain amount of fear in me, relieved only by the knowledge that the goat was tethered to a post and I only had to work out his range of freedom to steer clear of his horns. We spent many idle hours messing round and about the paddock. Sadly Billy left the village with his family to live in nearby Sway. I well remember an unplanned expedition undertaken later by Nipper and myself to visit Billy at his home, which was all of 3 miles away. We set off walking early one morning in the summer holidays, without telling any parents and it was well into the evening when we got back to a scolding welcome from two sets of families who were more than concerned, bearing in mind that we were not yet 9, but we had seen Billy. We were sorry to hear just a couple of years later during the war that he had picked up a grenade, or something similar, which had exploded and he lost a hand.

The mention of Sway reminds me that every village served its purpose in day to day mythology and generations in our village knew about Sway Docks, although it was some 5 miles from the coast and water and there was little to attract ships! We also knew about the local treacle mines which were quite near to the docks.

DONKEYTOWN

To every village around us Pennington was known as Donkeytown. There was, in fact, a time when there were a lot of donkeys in the place but not in my day and the term was generally used in a denigrating way, when rival football teams met or as a general term of abuse, suggesting that there was something amiss with those who lived in the place.

We always had a quite a number of New Forest ponies; they obviously found the Common grazing to their liking. They were also partial to garden produce and anyone who was foolish enough to leave gates open was asking for trouble. All the ponies have owners but their only responsibility is to see that they are branded with the owners mark; this was done once a year in a general round up which includes a count and a sale of what was regarded as surplus.

HAZEL ROAD

Of a quick count of the families who lived in Hazel Road, say in 1933, I would estimate fourteen in the age range 5-12 years with my eldest brother, Bob, at the top and myself at the bottom. Our five constituted the largest family. The basic number was often augmented by children who lived round the corner or across the Common and even more during holiday times when others who were visiting Aunts or Grandparents and joined up with us. We had a long walled frontage to our house which sloped at a convenient sitting height for children. This was a favourite morning assembly point but if any child stood on the wall to look over the fence it annoyed my Mother. From here small expeditions were planned or else we would go to the Green or the slightly bigger area at Yondy Corner for rounders, if we were a mixed party or cricket if just boys. The early evening assembly point was just up the road beneath the gas lamp. In the Autumn we could stay out for a while playing such games as Creepy or we developed skills with the latest craze such as yo-yo, spinning tops or biff-bat. Then there was conkers in due season and, of course, marbles.

THE FISH AND CHIP VAN

One of the most exciting events of the week was the arrival of the local chippy at the top of the road, every Tuesday evening at 7pm. Hoards of children had their coins ready for a 'penn'th' (pennyworth) of chips. We had to wait, of course, whilst adults were served with fish and chips.

The old dark blue van belched out smoke from the coal-fired frying range. Seeing the man pulling down the lever on the huge potato slicer and then watching the fat, long chips drop into the bucket was quite fascinating for me. The novelty was all the greater because deep fried chips were not the general rule in many homes and it was well before the days of chips with everything.

Another exciting little meal, from a butcher's van, was faggots and peas.

THE KITCHEN RANGE

We had a kitchen range at home which could make or mar our food depending on which direction the wind was blowing, the quality of fuel or just according to mood when there was nothing else to blame. I have to say that my mother did in fact produce some excellent meals and good baking but there were also other occasions when it was burnt or underdone. The Sunday roast was a good testing time and sometimes we had to wait a long time for it but there are memories of roast beef and potatoes and Yorkshire pud of sheer delight, or in the summer when the new peas and carrots and potatoes were available straight from the garden to accompany the roast lamb. In those days the joint had to last the week. It appeared next day cold accompanied by a fry up (bubble and squeak) of the vegetables left over from Sunday and then again in a stew when bone as well went in and suet dumplings were the novelty of the day. Perhaps the most lasting memory is of the cakes and especially the plain madeira, the taste of which I cannot adequately describe but I have not met it since. I have a theory that the pre-war free range fresh eggs contributed to the taste and the oven produced a highly individual bake. There was one other bonus with the range which produced some excellent fires for toast. A spread of pork or beef dripping from the current joint made a tasty snack.

ROUND THE PIANO

Some of my happiest memories are of my mother sitting at the piano and entertaining us, often during the Christmas festivities when our cousins from up the road would come in. Some Sunday evenings I remember especially, when one or two friends on return from Church would drop in for hymn singing. My Mother always protested that she couldn't play much but she always enjoyed herself and was the life and soul of the party. Music played a big part in the household as my eldest brother Bob had a good voice and he was the soloist in the church choir singing, "Oh for the wings of a dove" and the anthem solos. There was a wind up gramophone and we had a collection of records. My Mother liked the Irish tenor Count John McCormack and we grew up with the sound of his voice singing the old favourites like "Danny Boy" and "Star of the County Down".

We did have a radio for one or two years before the war but I cannot remember much about it, except listening to Radio Luxemburg after school

Peter's mother

to the adventures of Marmaduke Brown. The radio came into its own during the war when it was essential listening for the whole nation and it was important for us to make sure the accumulator (wet battery) was fully charged and that the dry battery which provided the main power, did not expire when you needed it most.

THE BIG SCHOOL

Transfer from little to big school took place at age seven so by the time I got there Bob had already left to work in a grocer's shop, Kit was in her last year and Charlie and Derrick were ahead of me. The school catered for all ages to 14 when formal education ceased. Those bright enough, at 11, to pass a scholarship went to Brockenhurst Grammar School, those who were not as bright still went to Grammar School if parents could afford to pay. Our family missed out on both counts.

When I left the War had three years to run and it was to be another few years before the 11 plus and then Comprehensive Education was introduced. In general the school prepared its pupils for work in shops and offices, spelling and simple mental arithmetic were practised probably far more than to-day and neat, formal handwriting was expected. There was not much encouragement of crafts and I guess many sons followed fathers into building, farming or the local factory. For most of us our time at school was a few years of totally inadequate education terminating at age 14.

SECOND WORLD WAR

With the 50th anniversary of the outbreak of the 2nd World War now being celebrated I am reminded of those days as a 11 year old. This was the beginning of a worrying time for me which continued throughout my teenage years. My Father had always gone to sea as a steward on luxury liners and so the family didn't see much of him. I was aware from my Mother that the marriage was foundering and although there were occasional visits, separation really happened at that time. He lived well into his nineties but I did not meet my Father in over 40 years, after a brief meeting on a train to Southampton in 1948. *(Peter's father died Christmas 1993 aged 99½.)*

More traumatic was the loss of my eldest brother, Robert John Dashwood, who had volunteered for the Navy in May 1940 and was lost at sea just 3 months later. His ship, HMS Esk, sank on 1st September, 1940. Bob was 20 years old.

My two brothers were to be on very active service later and after the close of the war in Europe there was a period when all four of us, including my sister, were in the services.

The outbreak of war was significant at the village school as it attracted a number of evacuees from London, which added a little more interest.

It was natural that I should follow my brothers into the local Sea Scouts; they had enjoyed pre-war camps to the Isle of Wight but the war restricted our sea-going activities. However, our troop became very good at P.T. displays and dancing the Sailor's Hornpipe, which we showed at village socials and dances. We danced to a 78 record, on a wind-up gramophone which had to be rewound half way through.

I also followed my brothers into the church choir. Alas, it was yet another example brought home often by teachers and other elders that somehow I was not fulfilling that which was expected.

EXPANDING HORIZONS 1944-1964

FIRST JOB

I left school in July 1942, aged 14, without any real idea of what I was going to do. I had muttered something about being interested in radio to the Attendance Officer, who was meant to advise, so I ended up in a local workshop which repaired wireless sets and gramophones. I was responsible for charging accumulators and occasionally assisted the piano tuner but I was totally incapable of understanding anything about radio. My unhappiness was relieved by visits to the shop side of the business where I was involved in selling records and sheet music. It all ended about 9 months later with the "sack".

ANCIENT ORDER OF FORESTERS

I felt free now to make my own choice and I presented myself to the local district office of the Ancient Order of Foresters, which had been evacuated to my village from Southampton. There was in fact no vacancy at the time but the District Secretary decided to take me on. I had a fair grounding in general office work over the next few years, working mainly on National Health Benefits. My confidence grew too in my leisure time as I took on secretarial duties and edited the magazine of the local youth club.

Church Youth Club 1945 — Peter middle front row.

There was a happy period when my Mother and myself were alone at home, although we were anxious about my brothers, Charles in North Africa and Derrick in training for the 2nd front in Europe. It was a period of relaxation for her, probably the only time in many years she was not at the beck and call of more than one member of the family.

Signalman aged 19 — 1947

NATIONAL SERVICE

The war was over by the time I was required to do my service in the Navy, as a Signalman. Although I was only in for 18 months it was to be a most significant time for me. I was fortunate in being able to get into the Communications Branch and spent nine months training with the same chaps I had met the very first day. We were to become proficient in signalling by Semaphore, by Aldis and other bigger lamps and by running up International and Naval Flags, as well as absorbing various codes. However, the Navy provided more than signals training and over the years I have looked on that period as my 'University'.

With training over I spent 2 months braving my coldest winter ever, in 1947, whilst awaiting draft to the warmer climes of Gibralter. In fact I was only on the Rock for 8 months in the relative comfort of a Lloyds Signal Station, which was perched way up towards the Mediterranean and far away from the local barracks and its associated discipline. Our job was to report all shipping movements to Lloyds. For the Navy we were to keep track of illegal Jewish immigrant ships which sneaked through the straits, often ignoring our standard signal, 'What ship? Where bound?"

I was able to enjoy a social life based on membership of the choir of the town's Kings Chapel but it was all over too soon as demobilisation was due.

DEMOBBED

I was aware of the folk dance group in my village of Pennington just outside the New Forest in the late 30's and when I returned from the Navy in 1948 I was invited to join what by then had become an entirely ladies group. My response at that time was something like 'Not on your Nelly'.

Phyllis Sparks, who started the New Forest Division of the English Folk Dance Society and ran the Pennington Group, died, aged 92, 3 weeks before Peter and 30 years older. She learnt her dancing from Cecil Sharp, an opportunity missed!

The Navy introduced me to such classics as 'Frankie and Johnny' but it was Burl Ives who started an interest in folk song.

A CIVIL SERVANT

Back home I went back to my former employers who had returned to Southampton. Changes were due, however, and the new National Health and Insurance Schemes were to be launched, following the Beveridge report some years earlier. I was soon to be offered a post in the Ministry of Pensions and National Insurance as a Clerical Officer and so I began a career in the Civil Service which was to last for 15 years and was to take me to many parts of the country. In the first instance I was posted to a small office locally but in response to an appeal for staff elsewhere I volunteered to go North to Merseyside, which I knew a little as a result of visiting relatives in Bootle, Liverpool. It is true to say that I wanted to break away from the local environment. Those I

had grown up with were marrying within a very tiny circle which didn't appeal to me and I felt too that home was a little crowded with both brothers unlikely to leave. But really I wanted to experience another and broader world.

ST. HELENS

Despite its attractive name the approach to St. Helens by train was a cultural shock for one who had been accustomed to the woodlands of the New Forest and attractive local beaches. Here, in South Lancashire, industry, smoke and dirt were only too obvious. Yet I soon discovered that there are nice parts to every town and, more importantly, there are nice people everywhere. This was to be my home for the next five years and it proved to be a happy one.

Life in a big office was busy and I was introduced to the harsh realities of industrial diseases and horrific accidents. Pneumoconiosis and Silicosis were still rife in the coal mines and glass industry, which provided a whole range of injuries. Explaining rules and conditions of a new range of benefits to a public unsympathetic to officialdom was hazardous in itself and the department seemed to be forever on the defensive. The staff adopted attitudes to match and for me this was a far cry from work with a Friendly Society. However, we had no time to think about anything else other than to cope with flu epidemics and other pressing matters.

SOCIAL LIFE

I secured some homely 'digs' on a nearby council estate remaining there throughout my stay. There were various social activities initiated by members of staff including Table Tennis and the occasional game of Soccer. This was also the time when I was introduced to the complexities of Rugby League, as a spectator. The 'Saints' had their ground just up the road from the office and I had a lot of instruction on the rules and advice on which games to watch. I am grateful for these as I enjoy the occasional game on TV to-day. I also joined the local YMCA and amongst many other activities was introduced to basketball. My bicycle was important to me as I investigated the countryside and made regular trips to relatives near Liverpool. My first big trip on the bicycle was homewards on holiday some 240 miles away and it took me 4 days to complete the journey.

SQUARE DANCING

In retrospect I regard 1951 as a most significant turning point in my life because a change in employment and way of life arose from events which happened then, although it was to be another thirteen years before the change took place.

The young Princess Elizabeth was going about her social duties on a visit to Canada and accidentally set off a craze for Square Dancing back home. Within a few weeks of press photographs showing her dancing it seemed that the whole nation was dancing. Someone from the office organised a party to attend a local dance and we had a whale of a time. I was looking to do more and this led me to the local folk dance group. In no time at all I was hooked on country and square dances.

ENGLISH FOLK DANCE AND SONG SOCIETY

The group was full of young people, enthusiastically led by Vic Smeltzer. I paid a subscription and discovered later that I had become an associate member of the English Folk Dance and Song Society. Later I joined the embryo morris team which was practising hard under Roy Hordley's instruction. The St. Helen's Morris Team eventually made its first public appearance on a very wet Coronation Day in 1953, complete with red, white and blue baldricks in honour of the occasion. Looking back one thinks about the visits to the Stratford-on-Avon festivals, to the Lilleshall Sports Centre and to Burton Manor for a broadening of one's Folk interest. There was something special about the St. Helens Group and they received tremendous encouragement from Ethyl Anderson, the Society's industrious organiser. I speak for many who have come under her influence in paying tribute to Ethyl.

THAMES VALLEY

Although I now had a real interest in my social life I was beginning to grow restless at work and felt that a move South, within striking distance of my home, would be desirable. In 1954 I was able to fill a vacancy at The Ministry's Office in Woking. This was a much smaller office and the pace was just a little less frantic. I made friends with some of the staff which led me to the local Ramblers, this was a time to discover some of the delights of the Surrey countryside on foot and bicycle.

I was soon involved again in Country and Morris Dancing and joined The Thames Valley Morris Men, an experience I was going to enjoy for the next ten years. Although not an original member (they too had started in Coronation Year) I felt that I was part of a team which was working

Thames Valley Morris Men 1958

towards a goal. They were a close knit group sharing other social activities as well as dancing, but for me the peak was reached with the showing of the Oddington Tradition for the first time in living memory. Under the guidance of Roy Dommett, who was researching the tradition, the team worked hard and in very cramped conditions in what became quite a famous academy of learning for many Morris men, hard by the Portsmouth Road at Thames Ditton, in Jim Brooks' cellar.

One memory I like to recall is when the team visited Scotland. I had been working in Edinburgh earlier and it was left to me to arrange a dancing spot. I remember with some pride that every man Jack was on schedule ready to dance, at 3pm, on a fine Saturday afternoon at the Princes Street arena, to share the bill, in one of our greatest moments, with the band of the Scots Guards. If you had seen some of the transport involved you would have realised what an achievement this was. (The odds were 50 to 1 against John Glaister getting there at all!)

PYRFORD DANCES

I became associated with the West Surrey District of the EFDSS. Kathleen Bliss and Elsie Whiteman were the Area Representatives of the Society and led the Benacre Band, the only organised music then, as far as I know, in the whole of the South-East. The Guildford monthly dances were a feature of the local folk calendar, good calling and good music almost guaranteed.

It was about this time that Dennis Salt and I conceived the idea of a monthly dance in our village of Pyrford, which we ran. Happily it is still going today.

COLLECTING SONGS

It was a time of Skiffle and American folk songs but many more people were beginning to discover the wealth of traditional music here at home. Karl (Fred) Dallas was running weekly song sessions at his home in Walton-on-Thames and he got the idea of doing some genuine collecting. Mervyn Plunkett came up from Sussex and a party of enthusiasts set off one foggy night from Pyrford to nearby Ripley. "There will be a lot of music hall stuff", warned Mervyn, "but we might just find a bit of genuine folk." Some hours later, after much beer swilling, the party emerged from the British Legion Club triumphant, having 'collected', when all the customers had departed, an interesting version of 'The Tree in the Wood', obligingly sung by the Barman while he was clearing up.

DIGS

I had digs locally but was not settled and the idea of looking after myself persisted and eventually I found a room in a lovely old cottage in a nearby village, rented from a 90 year old lady. I was soon joined by Dennis Salt. We shared two rooms so were now able to entertain friends. It was just part of a hectic social life which found us touring a lot with the morris team and going to Country Dances and camping with a small and enthusiastic body of people belonging to The Order of Woodcraft Chivalry.

At sometime in this period Peter became engaged. Whether it was a fear of a repetition of his parent's marriage, an inability to commit himself, or another reason, I do not know, but he did not marry; nor did either of his brothers or his sister. I always had the impression that the loss of the elder brother had a devastating effect on the family. Peter was never short of girl friends, however.

TOURING AUDIT TEAM

I was conscious that promotion to Executive Officer in the Ministry would never come via this small office and so I applied for a posting to Headquarters in London. The job was with an audit team and it was attractive to a single person in that much time was spent away visiting the regions. In reality it was a boring existence checking endless columns of figures to find the occasional error of no real significance. The seeds of doubt were sown then as to the wisdom of remaining in the service but in the meantime I was relatively well off drawing subsistence much of the time.

I saw much of the country over 5 years but I was still back south most week-ends and crammed much social activity into it. Visits to Edinburgh were popular and enabled me to get around Scotland at week-ends. By now I had said farewell to my trusted BSA 250 motor bike and invested in an Austin Van. I passed the test at the 4th attempt!

The audit team visited the North-East regularly, Peter joined Monkseaton Rapper team on practise nights and became a friend of Alan Brown and many figures of the Northern Folk scene.

SOUTH AFRICA

1960 was of great significance to me in that I was to undertake the longest journey in my life to South Africa. The Afrikaaner elements in South Africa had a folk dance association, which, with government help, arranged tours of European Dance groups to many of the big towns. The invitation from the South African Government was a follow up to a similar visit by the EFDSS and other European parties 5 years earlier. I was fortunate to be included only 3 weeks before departure date. My employers co-operated and granted me special leave so that I could be away for 6 weeks. Controversy was to arise, however, before departure, on the subject of Apartheid, which was heightened by news of the Sharpeville Massacre. The Management of the English Folk Dance and Song Society decided against sending a party but the Director, Douglas Kennedy, who had also led the earlier trip, decided to form a private party, following advice from the Commonwealth Office and other participating countries, where there were no such hang-ups.

I remember not enjoying my first flight because the seating of the old DC8 was cramped and my legs were aching continually. (Rather like they do now since the onset of MND.) Parties from

Germany, Belgium, Netherlands, Sweden, Norway, Austria, Switzerland, Israel and Scotland plus ourselves from England and the home country all met and prepared for a long tour by coach. Six weeks of almost continuous travel by coach, an exhausting time of receptions and shows and entertainment were provided by our hosts. The performances were all open air, usually at sports stadiums and people travelled many miles to attend. Amidst a diet of mainly dance items England had a bonus in Pat Shaw's singing. He had a natural grasp of language and often adapted his songs according to the audience. One night, in the South, he surprised everyone as he turned towards one section of a segregated audience and to enthusiastic and heartwarming cheers he sang "Billy Boy" in Zulu.

There were so many teams performing that invariably the evening shows finished late. Talking into the night with one's hosts was another agreeable hazard and resulted in many sleepy coach trips to the next destination. The itinerary included all the main cities, Johannesburg, Durban, Cape Town, Pretoria and off duty visits to a game reserve and to Swaziland, the 'Island' within South Africa. We were also shown the Sharpeville Police Station where the massacre had taken place just a few weeks earlier.

Talking politics with our hosts was expected and as we had both English and Afrikaaner hosts we met all points of view. We tended to quote, with the customary stiff upper lip, Prime Minister Harold Macmillan's 'Wind of Change' speech. I think we could see then that there was no real future for apartheid and that many years of potential integration had been lost. Now, thirty years later, the process of dismantling is happening but unity is as far off as ever.

CHANGE

My travels at work were due to come to an end in 1962 and I was posted to another HQ department researching the rights of widows and other claimants who had written to The Queen, the Minister or to their local MP, in protest at being refused benefit. Standard letters were adapted to answer the points made by individuals. About this time word got around HQ that a lively young lady had arrived as the new Parliamentary Under Secretary. It was Margaret Thatcher at the very start of her Ministerial career. Things were happening for me too as I was at long last promoted to Executive Officer, but it marked the beginning of the end of my service.

Life at The Cottage was also due to come to an end and I needed accommodation. Some of my

Peter's houseboat

morris dancing colleagues lived in houseboats on the local canal at New Haw and the life style appealed to me. Brian Heaton scored a first by establishing the South-East Office of the English Folk Dance and Song Society on a narrow boat. I found a 25ft lifeboat which had been converted as a cabin cruiser. A carpenter friend of mine set to work to make it fit for living and eventually I moved in.

It was fun for us all, we were moored quite close to-gether and I spent two half summers and one cold winter aboard. Thankfully my life changed again before I could face another winter!

Most of us remember what we were doing when news of President Kennedy's assassination reached us. I had just stepped aboard my neighbour's boat on a social visit. You can now look down from the M25 onto the canal where our 4 or 5 boats were moored.

There was an air of success locally with Brian's music and dance days going well at Chertsey and other places but for modest callers like myself there was a new world opening up; Barn Dances, for all manner of local organisations.

Tony Foxworthy, Brian Heaton and Hugh Rippon of the EFDSS, and voluntary workers such as Peter developed Ceilidhs to include all elements from the Folk world.

1964 arrived without me knowing that this was the year of change, however, the months leading up to it were depressing. I had been posted to a department which was concerned with finances at a high level. I did not understand what I was doing and unlike life in a local office I had too much time to brood over things. I realised sometime after that I had been heading for a nervous breakdown. It was in 1964 that Brian Heaton, the South-East Area Organiser for the EFDSS, persuaded me to apply for a new post being created by the EFDSS in the South.

When Brian joined the staff of the EFDSS, on April Fool's Day 1962, Douglas Kennedy, asked if he had any private means of his own; the Society did not pay a living wage.

ENGLISH DANCE & SONG April, 1964:

Situation Vacant-South-west Area

If you have a good working knowledge of Traditional Dance (including Morris, Sword etc.), good organising ability backed by energy, drive and enthusiasm, then you may be the man to assist our South-West Area Organiser. A full-time superannuated post after 6 months trial period. Own transport, reasonable travelling expenses. Apply in first instance with details of experience and proof of organisational ability to the Administrator, (Stephen Pratt), Cecil Sharp House.

I met Bill Rutter, Western Region Officer, EFDSS, for the first time at my interview at Cecil Sharp House and I thought it was of no real significance. Meeting him and his future wife, Terry, a few days later at home in Devon, was a revelation. It was the superb lunch, we agreed later, which persuaded me, but in truth there was something about this man which made me think that the job was going to be worthwhile.

To my surprise, I was appointed over some stiff opposition, I accepted knowing that I would be living on half my current salary and was throwing away my pension rights, but I was free of bureaucracy and the next five years were to be the most exciting folk years I have ever known. For the next 20 years I was to work mainly on my own initiative. I bid farewell to the Ministry. (I don't think that Mrs Thatcher noted the departure of a very minor servant from HQ).

I danced with Thames Valley up to the moment of departure. I was on a tour somewhere near the Thames and I travelled down to the West Country with Brian Bonnett in my Morris kit. I was on my way to join the staff of the English Folk Dance and Song Society, in many Morris Men's eyes, the Enemy.

ENGLISH FOLK DANCE AND SONG SOCIETY
SOUTHERN AREA 1964-1967

On 10th July, 1964 Peter took up the post of Southern Area Representative with a salary of £700 per annum. A condition of employment for all EFDSS employees was: "All monies received in connection with the EFDSS to be passed to the Society, including Broadcasting and Television." He left a salary of £1,100, plus generous expenses and pension, with the Civil Service. His family disapproved referring to his work with the EFDSS as with 'that Folk thing'. Peter claimed that if he had NOT left the Civil Service he would have been mad, or dead, very shortly.

BILL RUTTER

The immediate attraction of working for the Society was that I was to work with Bill Rutter, South-West Area Organiser, later the Western Region Administrator. Over the years I had known some of the staff and I knew much of the background of the Society, it's work and it's attitudes. An impression from outside was of an inward looking body trying its best to get a public involved in its activities. Bill was leading the way towards expansion and I was fortunate to be involved in some of his initiatives.

It was an exciting time to be in Folk. Sidmouth Festival was on the brink of going big, Folk Camps were expanding, Halsway Manor and National Folk Week were on the horizon, all through Bill's inspiration. We take these things for granted now but for someone who has seen it grow, one can only admire the vision, the courage and the energy of Bill Rutter. I was in almost daily contact for the first year or so and I found it difficult to keep up with this human dynamo, who never tackled one thing at a time; in fact it seemed a necessity to have several things on the go at the same time.

EFDSS STAFF

At the time Peter was appointed Stephen Pratt was the Administrator; Dorothy Bessant, Financial Secretary; Peter Kennedy, Technical Representative. Hugh Rippon was London Area Organiser, Public Relations Officer and, with Tony Wales, who was in charge of Sales, Editor of Dance & Song. Thora Watkins was London Area Organiser; Ruth Noyes, Librarian; Roy Guest ran the Folk Service and organised song events; Rosemary Webb was Events Secretary. All nine worked from Cecil Sharp House. Mollie Du Cane was Eastern Area Organiser; Ken Clark, Midland Area Organiser; Sibyl Clark,

Midland Area Representative; Tony Foxworthy, North-East Area Organiser; Ethyl Anderson, North-West Area Organiser; Brian Heaton, South-East Organiser; Bill Rutter, South-West Area Organiser; Irene Harcourt and Peter working to Bill as Area Representatives. Nibs Matthews left the post of Western Area Organiser to go to America on secondment. A total of nine Field workers, plus many voluntary Honorary Representatives.

DORSET

I was based in East Dorset, in the first instance; my terms of reference were ideal in that I was to be responsible for development in Dorset and Bournemouth, a small enough area to work myself in. My first 'office' was at 'The Thatch', Worth Matravers, near Swanage, (the local inn boasted an array of country wines). Later I moved to 'The Church Hut' at Corfe Mullen and finally, to a flat in Hatter Street, Bournemouth, where I was given an old RAC telephone number. I was frequently woken in the early hours by someone whose Handbook was well out of date.

SCHOOLS

The Local Education Authorities were providing some funding so it was expected that I should be introducing folk dance to teachers; simple country dances with suggestions and practise on use of material; run children's festivals and encourage school activities. I had a circle of Secondary School Clubs devoted to Social and Morris dance. *Including Yeovil with a young Taffy Thomas.*

Then, as now, the success of such clubs depended on the enthusiasm of one valuable member of the school staff. I went in to encourage, teach, add variety and new ideas.

SONG CLUBS

Away from Education I moved in two different worlds; one a cosy, respectable and often elderly dance club scene, the other a youthful and aggressive body representing a growing interest in folk song. I began to associate myself with the problems of the Bournemouth Folk Song Club which was having difficulty in keeping a venue. Someone eventually made a breakthrough in persuading the landlord of the Pembroke Arms to host folk song (to the exclusion and anger of the local wrestling club).

In no time at all this scruffy unkempt room, which defied all health and fire regulations, was a thriving folk centre, with activities on almost every night of the week. Here was an enthusiasm to discover more about our traditions. My own interest was Morris, which led to the forming of a very successful Bourne River Morris. There was also Clog, Rapper, Country and a couple of Song nights. There was a Ceilidh night until it was discovered the floor was unsafe.

The members soon became accustomed to travelling to festivals to broaden their interests. This was a period of discovery of traditions for many young folkies throughout the country but the enthusiasm of the Bournemouth lads and lasses was boundless. Regular visits to Halsway Manor, which was in its infancy, broadened their interests and they made significant contributions to the Sidmouth Festival.

Peter's friendship with Robin and Janet Whittlestone dates from Pembroke Arms days. Robin wrote, 20+ years later:

"Peter developed a unique blend of charm and persuasion that many were to experience, finding themselves doing things they had never intended to be talked into, in order to bring folk back into the public domain. Peter's technique was to find someone with an interest and develop it. He led the rescue of the moribund Bournemouth Folk Song Club and from it grew Clog, Rapper, Sword, Social dance, at least one Band and the Bourne River Morris Men. Similar things were happening all over as Peter criss-crossed his area cajoling and encouraging his 'volunteers'. When activities began to gather momentum he withdrew into the background, on call but letting things happen. The result of this wise approach was that so much of it continued when he moved on."

ENGLISH DANCE & SONG, July / August, 1989. Citation for Gold Badge Award: Peter Dashwood 30.4.90.

CEILIDHS

Meanwhile I was also meeting a demand from a variety of organisations to call the dances for social evenings or Barn Dances.

Early on in his time in Dorset Peter worked with a group called the Yetties. They had come up through a W.I. dance display team to meet Bill Rutter's influence and started a folk club in Yeovil.

"I can remember the word going round the area that this new chap was coming to take over and none of us were too sure what this would mean. As it turned out it meant the start of a friendship that was to last until his death......I remember thinking in those days that being a member of staff was not just a job but a way of life and this was certainly the case for Peter."

ENGLISH DANCE & SONG. October, 1990. Pete Shutler.

The Yetties proved to be very versatile providing music, song, morris and dance and have fond memories of travelling to tiny Dorset villages such as Cerne Abbas and Sidling St. Nicholas, because "Peter was very keen to get people in the villages dancing." *The Yetties played and Peter* "would persuade everybody that there was nothing on earth better than folk dancing. He was good at it too, because he had an easy-going manner and very infectious enthusiasm."

After the dances the Yetties frequently had to push their car to start it in order to get home. They do not remember being paid, perhaps a few expenses, Peter promised them bigger events in the future. Although it seemed highly unlikely at the time, Peter kept his promise and involved them in events all over the country, including some of the last he organised.

SIDMOUTH INTERNATIONAL FOLK FESTIVAL

I find particular satisfaction in knowing that I helped Bill set up the Sidmouth workshop structure in the late 60's. It remains basically the same to-day and the ideas were taken up by many other festivals throughout the country.

Far less claim worthy, I'm afraid, but I also introduced Tea Dances in the Ham Marquee at Sidmouth, in 1970. Janet and I, back to work after our honeymoon, served up cream doughnuts with the cuppas.

Bill remembered Peter's first job for Sidmouth as stopping the Israelis rehearsing at 2 in the morning. In the '60s one of Peter's jobs was to produce a display team from dancers attending the Festival, practises were in the Drill Hall. He is still remembered for refusing to admit enthusiasts who were not good enough (or young enough); not a popular decision, many season ticket holders believed it was their right to dance in the team. The display team dated from the earliest days when Nibs Matthews had taken a company of 100 dancers and musicians to Sidmouth in 1955. They gave displays throughout the week, ending with a public dance on Friday and paid for the privilege.

Bill took over the Festival in the early 60s, following Tony Foxworthy, after being appointed SW Area Organiser. Peter was Assistant to the Director for several years after joining the staff, as Shows Producer, Compere and M.C.

In 1964 the Israeli University Dance Group came, in 1965 teams from Ireland and Sweden. Within a few years Sidmouth Festival was transformed with a mixture of English and International dance, song and music, including immigrant teams, such as the Karpaty Polish Dancers, whom Peter encouraged. He even found them a musician, George Skipper.

Cyril Tawney brought song into the pubs and young Yetties, who learnt from him, were the mainstay of the Festival as singers and musicians. They spread the word 'Sidmouth' through the Folk Clubs. The High Level Ranters, Rae Fisher, Packie Byrne and Tony Rose came to see, sang and were subsequently booked.

In 1967 Peter helped develop the workshops where individuals could learn the dance traditions, besides music and song. In 1968 Hugh Rippon was in charge of Morris, Paddy O'Neill of Sword, Geoff Hughes of Clog and Barbara Wood of Music.

In 1968/69 Peter was Dance Producer when there were shows in both Connaught and Blackmore Gardens and respective processions. He would set the processions off, then rush to the Gardens to compere and, if a team was late, dance a Morris jig. This tradition continued when he became Arena Producer in 1971, when he also took his own team, Eastern Folk. The Festival had outgrown Connaught and Blackmore gardens, moving to the natural open amphitheatre at Knowle, below the Council Offices. On the first Friday afternoon, when no English team had arrived for the afternoon Preview Show at the Arena, Peter danced a solo jig, Shepherd's Hey, announcing this was a rain-making dance and predicting that it would rain at 8 pm, the time of the Opening Ceremony. This was highly unlikely as there had been weeks of drought, a hosepipe ban and a disastrous summer for farmers. At 8 pm precisely, with all the local dignitaries and a huge crowd assembled, the heavens opened and a terrific storm ensued. Peter was banned from dancing again.

Sidmouth was renowned for its local storms; Peter liked to relate the time when he and Peter North went to Sidmouth for a meeting then were stranded overnight by flash floods.

There were other members of EFDSS staff at Sidmouth including Hugh Rippon, Brian Heaton and Dave Wood, Peter was included with these as the 'younger members of staff'. There were also many volunteer workers from the EFDSS membership: Dennis Manners, who founded Towersey Village Folk

Festival; Peter North assisted Peter; Ted Poole compered Song Spots; Griff Jones ran a Swappers Club where the International teams exchanged dances with the English, so much more sociable than the current 'Meet the Teams', where one doesn't. John Tether, Dick Witt, Ian Graham, Bernard Chalk, Kathie Upton, Cyril Jones, Peter Boskett, Anthony Brunt, Fred Austin, Dave Williams, all had a major input in the early years creating a Festival which was imitated and laid the ground work for future years. There will be many more names I do not know and all the volunteers, mainly from the Society, who loyally gave their holidays to steward and serve teas should not be forgotten, either. Doris Youngman, from Suffolk, is still there despite severe arthritis and hardly being able to walk. One of the regular teams of the early years were Hammersmith Morris Men, with a young John Kirkpatrick. By 1969 he was running music workshops and playing for dancing, leading bands formed from the workshops. Rivalling Hammersmith was Chingford Morris, taught by Peter Boyce and including Geoff Hughes, whom Peter asked to teach at the first clog workshops at Sidmouth. The Reading University Folk Dance Society were favourites of Peter's. Barbara and Ian Graham and Brian Jones I remember as being on the Berkshire District Committee, both men became NEC Chairmen in the future.

Peter considered applying for the job of Sidmouth Director when Bill was retiring, however he felt Bill was too hard to follow.

FOLK CAMPS

Geoff Rye had the original idea, in 1961, of a holiday where campers came together in the evenings for folk activity. Bill Rutter organised the first week's camp, for 50 people, as part of his duties as SW Area Organiser. The leaders were Bill Rutter, Geoff Rye and John Tether, musicians were Brian Heaton and Leigh Dyer of The Ranchers. The idea grew so soon there were many camps, organised by EFDSS Field Staff; Bill, Peter, Brian and Hugh.

In 1965 Folk Camps were really catching on, that was the year of the first four week long camp, set up at Kingston, near Corfe Castle in Dorset.

'Setting up' included physically shifting equipment and overseeing the erecting of the Marquee, etc. besides the organisation of finding a venue and personnel. Peter grew a beard during that month, he now looked a Folkie.

Finding a suitable site was difficult and the final high altitude choice attracted every known element in the Coast Guard's handbook, including a storm which brought most of the tents down. People still remind me of this and the dreaded "lurgie" which was with us for much of the time. Folk Camps are also infectious when it comes to the involvement of families and dancing and music making in Folk, to me the best folk invention yet. Another development took place the next year when I set up the first Spring Folk Camp at Fordingbridge and a Youth Camp with Brian Heaton, SE Area Organiser.

Peter found it very hard to lose the habit of looking for suitable camp sites, so, along with Halls, he inspected any field or site wherever we went. At one time we could have written a book on "Arts & Leisure Centres, Village Halls and Fields of England, suitability for Folk Event thereof.

Peter dancing at Corfe Castle, Dorset, Kingston Folk Camp 1965

FAITH KEMP'S MEMORIES

"I met Peter at my first Folk Camp at Kingston in 1965 when I was Caterer and Peter was in charge as Manager. Not only had I little experience of catering, but I was also fairly new to Folk. Peter was kindness itself as I muddled through. We survived that camp and went on to manage and cater together for several more.

Because he was an employee of the EFDSS, Peter was never an elected Member of the Council, but he was in at the beginning and attended most early Council meetings, acting as Assistant Secretary. He gave a great deal of his own time to the new Company and its early camping Programme.

My best memory of Peter the Morris Dancer is at Kingston where he had the job of teaching the 'Beginners' Morris Workshop. He had eight men and spent the whole week perfecting Ring O' Bells. The party on Friday night provided the most hilarious Morris I have ever seen; the eight men, clad in swimming trunks, ribbon seaweed baldrics and flippers on their feet danced Ring O' Shells directed (often fortissimo) by Peter, attired like his team.

I can also remember bumping along in Peter's Morris Traveller with a full pig bin lurching around in the boot as we took the swill to the smelliest pig farm I have ever experienced.

Folk Campers should remember and be grateful for his early pioneering work with the new Society. His style of wardening survives today. It was a privilege to have known and worked with him."

EXTENT. Autumn 1990. Published by Folk Camps.

Peter is also remembered by the family of the winner of the Morris Jig Competition at Sidmouth Festival in 1990, the year Peter died. Ian is a member of Hammersmith Morris, he attended Folk Camps as a small child and was desperate to join in the Boy's Morris but was too small to keep up. Peter spent the sessions steering the budding Morris dancer around the sets so he was not left out and discouraged from dancing.

Unfortunately not all went smoothly with Folk Camps; there were financial problems and disagreements with EFDSS NEC. UDI was declared in 1968 and a company formed. Griff Jones, Dennis Manners and Don Swaddle, all serving on the NEC, were on the original Folk Camps Council, but in their private capacity. Hugh Rippon, who had just left the EFDSS staff and Bill Rutter were also on the Council.

Donations were given to the EFDSS annually by Folk Camps. The EFDSS gave the camping equipment already purchased. Folk Camps Society, whilst independent, has to be governed by members of the EFDSS. John Tether was appointed its first chairman, he recounted much later that he had been shocked by the amount of 'dirt that was thrown at the time', he

Peter in his Morris Traveller 1967

compared it with the battle which was taking place, in the late 80s, between factions of the EFDSS over the proposed sale of Cecil Sharp House.

Bill retained his place on Folk Camp Council for 17 years, time spent developing activities all over the country. In 1978 Bill wrote:

"(Folk Camps) importance to the EFDSS is that it brings in people from outside who initially join the EFDSS to take part in the government of Folk Camps. It does not take long, however, to find them popping up on District Committees, Area Councils and other units of the EFDSS. Folk Camps have played their part in the general Folk explosion and the increase in EFDSS Membership. Something the Society should be proud that it started and continues to nurture."

Names which appear in connection with Sidmouth were also associated with Folk Camps, Halsway Manor, Hobby Horse Club, and National Folk Day, the focal point being Bill Rutter, and life-long friendships were made.

My chief memory of Folk Camps was at a camp shortly after we were married, Peter was Warden, as usual. On cook's duty we had to make oceans of chocolate pudding in washing up bowls. A few hours later we went down with an awful tummy bug and were confined to our tent for two days, too ill to move. Fellow campers did not like to disturb us, being newly-weds, not realising we were dying! We have not been able to eat chocolate pudding since.

Peter used his holidays to run Folk Camps, it was not part of his work for the EFDSS once Folk Camps went independent. When we had a family I found this too much of a bus man's holiday; Peter was still working, I was unable to dance because he was off doing something for the camp and I had a child to look after on my own, it was no holiday. We tried going as an ordinary family but Peter became upset when the Warden did not do things as he believed they should. We stopped going to Folk camps in the 70s and went camping in Scotland, on our own, instead.

HALSWAY MANOR

Halsway Manor dates, in parts, to the 13th Century and stands in 6 acres of grounds in the Quantocks, Somerset. In 1964 the Manor was offered to the 'Folk People' for £10,000 by the owner, Mrs Miller, a member of the EFDSS. Bill Rutter saw the opportunity of establishing a residential Folk centre and steamed ahead to organise it. The property was bought with a full mortgage from the owner. Several more thousands were loaned by EFDSS members secured by Debentures and a further £10,000 was borrowed in 1972.

"Halsway Manor Society Ltd. has a separate governing body from the EFDSS to protect the EFDSS financially should the 'experiment' with Halsway fail. Original Members of the Council included Dr Leonard Luckwill who was also Chairman of NEC, Geoff Rye, who succeeded him, and local members, with Bill Rutter acting in an honorary capacity with the blessing and consent of the NEC. Hugh Rippon, then the EFDSS PRO, was a member of the Council of Management, for a time. The Chairman was Gay Gayler."

NEWSFLOW 13.3.78. Bill Rutter.

Peter helped to develop the Programming Policy from Halsway's earliest days, ran some of the Courses and encouraged clubs to attend.

CHOREOGRAPHY AND FAR FROM THE MADDING CROWD

The Yetties remember Peter choreographed dancing for a television play in 1965, "Miss Julie" starring Ian Holm, with the Yeovil Folk Dancers including young Yetties. The play was filmed at Athelhampton House Dorchester, in freezing weather.

In 1966 Peter taught Julie Christie and Terence Stamp to dance Soldier's Joy for the Harvest Home Dance in John Schlesinger's film of Thomas Hardy's novel, *Far From the Madding Crowd*. Peter choreographed the Dance which was filmed in Abbotsbury Tithe Barn, near Swanage. Dave Swarbrick and Bob Common were in the band. Isla Cameron advised on songs and sang Julie Christie's 'Bushes and Briars'. Isla appears in the credits but Peter refused to allow his name to be used, he also refused to participate in the scene; he was very unhappy with the experience. He liked Alan Bates, who played Gabriel Oak, some of the minor character actors who were friendly and Peter Finch who was always polite; but I think he disagreed with the Director.

I was leaving Wimborne Grammar School to go to College, the school was asked if any of the pupils wanted to be extras; it was too far to travel so I missed an opportunity of meeting Peter! Some of my school friends are in the film.

TRAINING

The demand for Barn Dances from church and other organisations meant I was being asked to Call several times a week. Music was in short supply and callers likewise. I began to arrange training sessions with nationally known instructors and this bore fruit. Although I would be the first to say that it was the demand for Barn Dances which later inspired a wealth of music and callers in the area, it is very satisfying to know that many of those who started out in music or calling through the training sessions are still at it.

IRELAND

Bill Rutter had invented Eurotrips which involved taking parties to distant parts on the Continent. My answer to this was a more humble offering to Ireland for three successive years. We were able to show Morris, Rapper and Country and also had good music and song but we were also interested in the traditions of Ireland. One year we were based at Carraroe on Galway Bay in a hotel which with all its musical evenings was more like a folk centre. It was from here that the party set off one beautiful morning on a sailing barge carrying peat to the Isle of Arran and singing all the way.

FOLKSOUTH

It was after being involved in an old fashioned Area Gathering in South Hampshire that I had the idea of a more public orientated showcase. The result was Folksouth which was held at the City Hall, Salisbury in l967. I shall always be grateful

to that first band of workers who set the standards for an idea which I took to East Anglia as Folkeast and where it continued until quite recently. The formula altered over the years but I believe the original conception was right: part show, part concert and participation in simple dances. 800 people attended that very first event, most of them new to folk.

FOLKSOUTHERN

I needed a magazine to publicise events in the area and encourage exchange of ideas. Peter and Jo Sparks became editors. Folksouthern was later described as a 'trail-blazer'.

ISLE OF WIGHT

One of my favourite trips was to the Isle of Wight and The Sloop at Wootton for occasional Ceilidhs. With Roy Middlebrook and his newly formed Bogtrotters Band we packed a lot into an evening including a bit of morris.

During the famous Isle of Wight Pop Festival of 1969, Bob Dylan's band borrowed Roy's accordian and it wasn't seen again, leaving the Ceilidh without an accordian. I had to borrow one for him from the Mainland.

FAMILY.

Around 1968 my Mother became ill, her condition was described as senile decay. Looking back on her behaviour I would assume that it would be described to-day as Altzeimer's Disease. She lived for another 10 years and died at the age of 84.

Peter reckoned she had never fully recovered from an accident when her bicycle brakes failed as she came down Lymington High Street and she crashed through a shop's plate glass window.

NORTH-EAST ORGANISER.

In 1967 the Society needed a Organiser for the North-East. Tony Foxworthy was recalled to London to be Assistant to Nibs Matthews, who had been appointed Artistic Director in 1966. Stephen Pratt, the Administrator (a nice man, according to Peter), who succeeded Douglas Kennedy, had been dismissed in 1965. A 'triumvirate' of Kenneth Goode as General Secretary, Peter Kennedy as National Adviser on Folk Song and Nibs Matthews as National Adviser on Folk Dance lasted only a year. Management suggested that Peter be moved north to replace Tony. Peter was unwilling to leave his work in the south and his mother. Bill wrote to NEC warning them that Peter would resign if they insisted. Fortunately, for me, he stayed in the South.

THE SOUTH and JANET 1967-1969

Three years had gone by and my Area had expanded to include Hampshire, Berkshire and Wiltshire besides Dorset. I was in regular contact with volunteer workers in all four counties. It was to be another 2 years before I moved on and during that time I was to see real developments in the whole of the Southern Area which was now alive with new bands and callers. I could look back on the setting up of clubs, workshops and new events, in particular Folksouth. More importantly, I was to meet Janet who was to become my wife. Our meeting happened during my visits to the Portsmouth College of Education where I was encouraging a group of students who were interested in folk dance.

PORTSMOUTH COLLEGE OF EDUCATION — FOLK DANCE CLUB

I went to the Portsmouth College of Education in 1966 to train as a Junior teacher. For my first year I had a room close to a third year student, Rose, who was President of the College Folk Dance Club. The club met weekly, dancing to records. Rose encouraged the first years to go along; I had enjoyed country dancing in school and nothing better to do. Sometime during the winter a balding, plump, little man, called Peter Dashwood, turned up with an accordionist, Kathie Upton, and called a few dances. Half way through a dance he said, "You've done this before, haven't you?" It was probably just something to say to Peter, but he was a lovely dancer, quite a contrast to the boy with two left feet I normally danced with. I took it as a compliment. I thought, initially, that he was married to Kathie Upton, but when we all went back to Rose's room for coffee Rose and Peter flirted. I decided he wasn't married.

Our next meeting was at a dance at Portsmouth YMCA, which Peter was running. He had encouraged all sorts of groups to attend, he made the event sound as if it should not be missed. Most memorable of that evening was the very large Guide leader in full uniform, including whistle, who danced as a man; in progressive dances one invariable met this ample blue bosom. I don't think we went to any more YMCA dances.

In my second year I shared appalling 'digs' with Eileen Haynes, a friend from Hall. The landlady chain smoked, there was cigarette ash on everything, including our food, Eileen and I spent most weekends away. Eileen went to her boyfriend's flat. I had no particular boyfriend so generally went home. I had

been out with Chris Bean, a student in my group, not the most sensible choice. In the first year Chris had taken a group of inexperienced students sailing; the yacht capsized, coastguards were called out, the students were lucky to survive. When Chris took me sailing, the mast fell off! We had to wait until the tide had gone out so Chris could walk to shore, pulling the boat in. I learnt to swim after this. In March we went up to Portsdown Hill for my 20th birthday. I thought this romantic, but Chris had taken me there to tell me he had found someone else he preferred. I was most upset that he had ruined my birthday. I don't remember being very upset about losing Chris. Later he was the Treasurer at Sidmouth Festival for several years.

NEW FOREST FOLK YOUTH CAMP

In June I heard over the Student Union's tannoy about a Folk Dance weekend in the New Forest, Chris was going, was anyone interested? I decided to go as an alternative to going home. It was Midsummer, June 21st/22nd, 1968.

There were only the two of us from College. We caught the train to Cadnam, then walked 5 miles to the campsite, which was owned by the Order of Woodcraft Chivalry. Chris told me that Peter Dashwood had hired it for a Youth Folk Camp. As we wearily walked down a very long, winding path, I was not sure I had made a wise decision, I had no idea so much walking was involved. I said to Chris, for no particular reason other than being fed up with walking and not wanting to dance with Chris, who had the two left feet, "If there's no one else worth having here I'll get off with Peter Dashwood."

There were very few other people on the weekend, a couple, Colin and Veronica, and a few odd bods, generally very odd! Peter was in charge, Dave Williams came in to sing and play for dancing. We did country, sword and Morris dancing and some singing, I think we were supposed to go on walks too, but the weather was too bad, it poured most of the weekend. There wasn't anyone else worth dancing with so I danced with Peter, which was a joy. I think he was flattered by the attentions of someone half his age, Peter was 40, I was 20, and amongst the odd souls who were there we had a lot more in common with each other than anyone else. He already had a steady girl friend, Kate, who was nearer his age and had money, being a full time teacher but I felt as if I had been hit by a sledgehammer. I had had boyfriends but as far as I was concerned Peter was THE ONE. I also knew I had a fight on my hands, but was never one to give in easily, nor was I used to not getting my own way. I was also naive enough not to know better.

HAYWAIN, CADNAM

There was great interest in a new venture initiated by Dave Williams and myself in the New Forest in 1968. The Haywain at Cadnam was already established as a centre for Country and Western. An old Nissan Hut in the backyard of the pub bulged at the seams at times with young people from miles around for our regular weekly dance.

From this grew a display team which offered Country, Morris, Sword and Song. Dave Williams played and brought along Ted Duckett, an old boy from the Area who played the bones and still did step dancing. He could bring the House down. Peter took this team to the Isle of Wight for a much more sedate Festival than the Pop one.

CONVERSION TO FOLK

I volunteered to become President of the Folk Dance Club and was duly elected. I then arranged mini-buses to take us to the Haywain at Cadnam each week instead of meeting in College. I took friends from the Art course as well as dance club members, in order to make the trip viable. Peter was pleased that numbers were swollen, we all had a good time and I saw Peter. Come the summer holidays Peter was convinced I was interested in Folk and asked me to go with him to a dance. I should have beaten a retreat then and there, if I'd had any sense. What I thought was a 'date' turned out to be a dance in Dorset where he wanted me to look after the EFDSS sales at refreshment time, so he could talk to people! An essential part of his work I was to discover. I was not put off, so I was invited to the Thomas Hardy Festival in Dorchester. I really did not know what I had come to. I remember Bournemouth District members, including Ann and Francis Clayton, dressed up in costumes of Hardy's time, dancing the Triumph. Taffy Thomas was around being manic and the Yetties were playing. They seemed somewhat bemused by my being with Peter but were very kind and did talk to me, few other people did, they did not know who or what I was, Peter was old enough to be my father.

Peter then went to Ireland for 3 weeks for the group holiday he had organised; then to Cambridge Folk Festival with Kate. I went to look after my sister who had had her second baby and was very upset that he did not write.

Back at College, now in my third year, I rented a flat with 3 other girls. I continued the trips to the Haywain and Peter took me to dances around the south. (Kate was more interested in song). At one I was asked what did I do? They thought I was the singer. I also became aware of the looks of suspicion from women all over the south who also had designs on Peter.

SONG CLUBS

Peter regarded an essential part of his job was to visit ALL clubs in his area, to encourage, find key workers and be an 'EFDSS presence', these included song clubs as well as dance. On the way back from a dance or meeting we would drop in on what I regarded as less desirable places, pub rooms full of smoke and beery men, (I had led a very sheltered life). Peter was greeted with much enthusiasm by the likes of John Paddy-Browne in Southampton and encouraged to sing 'his' song, 'The Cruel Mother'. I thought this song of a mother stabbing her babies a dreadful story and Peter's singing was not in the same class as his dancing but in the sixties participation was as important as performance, if not more so.

When Bill Rutter visited song clubs he would sing 'Johnny Todd', used as the theme tune from 'Z Cars'. Later he wrote a column in English Dance & Song under the pen name of Johnny Todd. The articles make interesting reading for anyone interested in the development of the English Folk Dance & Song Society, look between early sixties to late seventies.

COUNSELLING

I could not make Peter out at all, he seemed to enjoy my company but would not give up Kate. He thought we could be friends, nothing more. I felt he would never take me seriously and went to see the College Counsellor who dealt with personal problems. I explained about the age differences and how Peter thought it was too great and would not give up his other girlfriend. Mr Ingleby advised that perhaps Peter would never see things as I did but that should not matter for one should "enjoy what one has, remember the good times for they cannot be taken away and not regret what you haven't had". It was tremendously useful advice that has stood me in good stead through many problems. At the time I wasn't impressed.

MEETING PETER'S FAMILY

In the winter Peter took me to see his mother at Lymington. I knew she wasn't well but she was a bit of a surprise. She confused Peter with his brother Bob, who had died in the war, then complained about Peter's beard. (None of the family liked his beard, maybe that's why he kept it.) She talked about soldiers marching outside her window, keeping her awake.

Peter's two brothers, Charlie and Derrick lived at home, his sister Kit in Bournemouth, (none had married) but a neighbour, Norah, was the one who looked after their mother. We saw Charlie at the garage he worked at and Derrick briefly as we passed him on the way home as he returned from work as a bus driver. I must have met Kit at Christmas, she was a personal secretary.

LAKE DISTRICT

In March Peter was to go to the Lake District on a mini-tour with the Yetties. It was the weekend of my 21st birthday and I was determined to spend it with Peter. In February Kate still did not know of my existence but the strain of seeing us both was becoming too much for Peter, especially as I was not prepared to accept only 'friendship' and nagged. Peter seriously thought of giving us both up. Shortly before my birthday he finally told Kate he had been seeing me. I went to the Lakes.

Peter hired a van to transport a huge cooker for Folk Camps to be stored in a Lakeland barn. The Yetties proved useful as the cooker had to go up a ladder into a loft, they pushed it up between them. We collected the cooker from a Course Bill Rutter was leading in Bath. This was my first meeting with Bill and I was not looking forward to it, Peter talked so much about him. Bill used to lay bets as to whether the latest girlfriend would be the one to marry Peter. I don't think he thought I was even in the running. He quite terrified me. My first impression was of someone larger than life, who bellowed down the corridors at people and snored very loudly. He was in the next room to mine.

We had a lovely time in the Lakes. It was fun to see Peter's name on a poster in Keswick. The Yetties had brought out an LP, Fifty Stones of Loveliness, which they were excited about as it had been given to Princess Margaret as a present by the EFDSS, (Princess Margaret is President of the EFDSS.) They did not believe that I was genuinely celebrating my 21st.

Peter teaching dancing in Holland, 1968 or'69

HOLLAND

In April Peter was one of the instructors at an International Dance Week in Holland for the second time. He enjoyed these weeks as the Dutch work very hard at their dance and were appreciative. He put in a lot of preparation. He wanted me to go with him but as he only received expenses, his fees going to the Society and I was on a grant we could not afford the travel. He stopped going once we were married because we still could not afford for us both to go.

EASTERN AREA

Around this time Peter was asked to move to Cambridge to take over the Eastern Area on the retirement of Mollie DuCane. He did not want to go and, in March, decided to resign rather than move. He was very dissatisfied with the Management of the Society, where the advice of members of staff was ignored. (This did not change.) He also protested about his salary. He had started with a very low salary for his trial period of six months and never recovered. No allowance was ever made for his age and experience. In November 1968 his salary was £1,030. All that summer he argued with himself whether or not to go through with his decision to resign. He was depressed at the thought of leaving the South, where he felt he had achieved some success and influence. He would no longer be working with Bill, who acted as a buffer between Peter and Management. It was a different job working to Cecil Sharp House directly.

Initially I applied for jobs in the South, as my parents lived there, but didn't get any offers. I then applied all over the country and was offered posts in Birmingham, Canvey Island and a tiny school in Dullingham, Cambridgeshire. I would be the Infant Teacher for 14 children aged 4 to 8 years. This looked the most interesting, despite my being Junior trained. I moved to Cambridgeshire in September, lodging at the Vicarage. To the surprise of us both Peter moved to Cambridge at the end of October, 1969, after Folk South. Many in the South were as sad to lose him as he was to leave so it was an emotional day. I remember Jeff Jerram standing alone in a spotlight, in his Winchester Morris kit with battered straw hat, singing 'All Around My Hat', pre-Steeleye Span. My Aunt Alice, who had sung this in school in the 1900s was in tears. I won a prize in the raffle.

EAST ANGLIA 1969-1980

MOLLIE DU CANE

Molly Du Cane, the Eastern Area Organiser, was to retire in 1969 and I was asked to succeed her. Her main sphere of influence was in Hertfordshire and the number of successful dance clubs in the county is just one indication of her work. She had also established a fine working relationship with the LEA and with many schools. The grant from the LEA was one of the highest in the country.

It was a daunting task to follow Mollie as the EFDSS representative. The affection and respect accorded to her was apparent to me, when, as a newcomer, I was invited to attend events around the area. It did seem to me, at the time, that all functions I attended were 'Mollie Farewells', and, in my bewildered state, I was being asked to take part in the demonstration of yet another newly composed dance in honour of the occasion!

EASTERN AREA ORGANISER

I moved up, reluctantly, in Autumn 1969. Janet had come up to teach and live near Newmarket and I was based in Cambridge. A trip round the Fens, on a wet and foggy Sunday afternoon in November, almost persuaded us to return South. We didn't, of course and the next ten years proved to be a very happy period.

At the Vicarage, the vicar's wife assumed responsibility for encouraging and discouraging friends. Chris Bean, who taught in Haverhill, was encouraged, given cakes and tea when he visited; Peter was not allowed through the front door. I soon found new digs in Newmarket with a Scottish teacher, who was separated from her husband. Life could be exciting here as the husband, also a Scot, would turn up very drunk and try to beat up his wife. I locked and barricaded my room!

I would catch the tiny train from Newmarket to Cambridge which stopped at Dullingham, then walk or cycle the mile to school. On occasions I only just made it when flocks of sheep barred the road. It should have been idyllic, however the Headmaster, who was also the Junior Teacher, had become paranoid that the village was against him and eventually stopped me from talking to anyone. I waited until I had passed my probationary year then resigned, without a job to go to. The Head declared that I had ruined my career. I got another post within 6 weeks, in Newmarket.

Peter did not know many people in the East, unlike the South where one couldn't move without tripping over

a girlfriend, or, at least, women who hoped to be, competition was therefore narrowed considerably. In his new Area we were accepted as a couple from the start. Most of the 'volunteer workers' were my age rather than Peter's, this also helped.

My brief was to develop East Anglia as a whole. Getting to know my patch was difficult and journeys to Essex, Hertfordshire, Norfolk and Suffolk were long in the days before road improvements, however, it was essential to get to know the local voluntary workers and to give them support. It soon became apparent to me that the local committees and clubs were very inward looking and one objective I had in mind was to encourage more travelling to interesting and prestigious events. There was an even more urgent need to find more music and callers to meet a demand for Barn Dances from local organisations, which were beginning to take off just as it had done in the South.

FOLKEAST

I had an office in Hatter Street, Cambridge and it was from there that I was preparing my first major event in the East with local helpers, mainly from the Crofters Folk Club. I had the idea of an annual event which would be held in a different town each year. The first Folkeast was held in the vast Corn Exchange at Cambridge which in size, acoustics and decoration rivalled Paddington station. This was to be a whole day of activity

Folkeast 1970- — Cambridge

including children's dances and workshops and evening of folk dance and song. It set the pattern for future editions. The location changed each year and it was necessary to book big public venues some 2 years in advance. It was essential therefore to persuade (not always easy) Districts to set up a local sub-committee years ahead. This meant that I was working with three committees, all in different stages of preparation for 3 events.

During my time Folkeast was held at Cambridge (2) Bury St Edmunds, Bishops Stortford, Norwich (2) Southend, Hemel Hempstead, Chelmsford, Stowmarket and Ipswich. Apart from Corn Exchanges, venues included a redundant Church, a converted Maltings and two modern leisure complexes. What fascinated me about Folkeast was to note the workings of a small band of volunteers over years of preparation. One person would eventually emerge to take the whole project by the scruff of the neck and make it work.

We had a variety of workshops over the years and on two occasions we had an auction of musical instruments, books, 78 rpm. folk dance records and other folk material. There was just not enough competition on both occasions and one feels that the bidders got good bargains. Craft fairs were introduced, thus giving a more public attendance during the afternoon. We take it for granted now but the idea of craft fairs with folk events was an EFDSS invention from Yorkshire. Grahame Binless, my colleague in the North, passed on news of successful ventures and we, along with many other festivals, were not slow to try them out.

The structure of the event changed over the years not always to my liking. I had set out in Salisbury to make it a public relations exercise and it worked there and in Cambridge. We then began to separate a mainly dance occasion from song and had two events where the facilities allowed. This was OK from the point of view of the enthusiast but it was not the public presentation of folk that I was looking for.

In 1978 Norman Bennett, new to Folk, was recruited to assist in running 'Eastern Area's event of the year'. He wrote about his experience:

"Month by month we meet to sit around Vera's polished table, drink her coffee and munch her biscuits. There are seven of us in all and we feel like mountaineers climbing a cruel mountain, wearily spending our time going to and fro and, apparently, getting further from the summit. Such is the fate of those whose wild ambition persuades them to sacrifice themselves to the highest ideal a man can have, to serve on the Folk East sub-committee... This must plan and carry through the finest Folk East of all time — and make a profit!

It is these two characteristics which seem always to create conflict — but that's life. The labour is performed mainly so that you will visit us in Cambridge, that you will enjoy your visit — aye and help to make us a profit! See you at the summit."

NEWSFLOW, an EFDSS newsheet edited by Bill Rutter.

Even Peter admitted that he didn't meet many who relished a second term on a Folk East committee, but if you could cope with Folk East you could cope with anything!

In the Spring issue of Dance and Song Roy Rodwell wrote a review of Folk East '77, held in Hemel Hempstead:

"Jennifer Millest persuaded Peter Dashwood to perform Fool's Jig. It was delightful to see how elegant his steps were. You don't become an EFDSS Regional Organiser without knowing all aspects of the folk business!"

It was a treasured moment; Peter had been scooting around to organise something to stop the dance teams slipping on the highly polished floor when Jennifer finished her set and called him down. Quite unrehearsed and not on the Programme Peter danced one of the most difficult morris jigs alone in the spotlight of a huge hall, to rapturous applause.

TRAINING

Music for dancing was rare in East Anglia as a whole and it was in this department that I began to think we could make some progress. The Crofters ran a very successful song club in Cambridge and were involved in the local EFDSS district committee. Two of their number, Andrew and Claire Kendon, had very kindly offered accommodation, which I gratefully accepted, so there was a natural link. The Crofters were beginning to take an interest in playing for Barn Dances and Ceilidhs. I took every opportunity of bringing known musicians, particularly Denis Smith and John Kirkpatrick, to the area to encourage local development. Demand for Barn Dances, from, it seemed, every known organisation around, was growing, and this again greatly stimulated the growth of bands.

FOLK SONG CLUBS

I had heard from Tony Foxworthy at staff meetings that he had been teaching some lads 'a bit of Rapper' at a Folk Club in Hoddesdon, Hertfordshire. Hoddesdon Crownsmen emerged later, adding a women's clog team in time.

Peter looked to Hoddesdon as a means of salvation amongst the dance clubs in Hertfordshire, which didn't need his help. They came to Peter's Festivals and Training Days and learnt. In return the club provided a superb Rapper team which Peter used on numerous occasions, District Committee members, notably Snowy, Liz Rose, Mac Jones and Dave Hislop, later to become EFDSS Chairman; Folkeast organisers and friends.

Another song club Peter encouraged was at Chelmsford. They were interested in doing some dancing so Peter went along, taking John Kirkpatrick. From this came the band Lumps of Plum Pudding with Colin Cater and Bill Delderfield as caller. It must have been there that we first heard Nic Jones sing. We were smitten and listen to his singing to this day, on tapes, but his 24 verse ballad didn't go down well with Felixstowe Festival public. Peter was always ready to extend the boundaries of Folk, but I don't think Felixstowe was ready to be extended.

FELIXSTOWE FESTIVAL

The Society had 2 or 3 residential festivals around the country and I began to think of creating one in my area. It was normal to have festivals by the sea and I chose Felixstowe, based solely on the memory of a fine Saturday evening's dancing at the sea-side some years earlier with Thames Valley Morris. It was soon quite clear, however hopeful we were, that Folk interested people were not going to travel in great numbers to what was regarded as the end of the world, especially once petrol prices had risen. The Pier Pavilion held an awful lot of people, so it was a fight for audiences from the very beginning. This paid off with a genuine public attendance at many of the events. The Craft Fair, a combination of craft stalls, selling wares, and displays by Festival teams, attracted 700 paying customers in 1978, 1,000 in 1979. The Children's Dances became popular immediately and with an ever increasing contact with schools in Suffolk, Norfolk and Essex the event acquired some status in educational circles and is still highly regarded today. Another simple idea, originally to encourage local song clubs to participate in the Festival, has stuck, The Chorus Cup. It is a lighthearted song competition, taken seriously by some, to discover the best team at singing. It is still the highlight of the week-end for many.

The group of people Peter organised/conned /charmed into running Felixstowe have proved very loyal over many years. Dr. Irvine and Gill Reid provided a 'hotel' in their enormous house for most of the staff in the early years (although they did draw the line at Brenda Wootton who needed a reinforced bed!) and countless meals for Peter at meetings ; Phil and Pat Woodgate, Ann and Graham Potter, Pip and Barbara Sadler all stalwarts who continued to run the Festival, for the EFDSS, up until 1989. The same people also ran Suffolk District, several Folkeasts and Wolsey Folk dance Group and became close friends. Later, when Peter's Area included the South-East, he could return home earlier from an evening meeting in London, or even Brighton, than from one in Felixstowe or Ipswich. I never could work out if the Suffolk lot were too polite to throw him out or they encouraged him to talk. He did not need a lot of encouragement.

EASTERN FOLK

For Felixstowe, Folkeast and other events I thought we needed a show team and so Eastern Folk was founded in 1971. We had couples mainly from Cambridge, Colchester and Ipswich. They practised frequently in a hall at Long Melford, a picturesque Suffolk town currently featured in the Lovejoy series on TV. The team went abroad to Amsterdam, on an exchange visit, and Sidmouth. They offered Country, Playford, Rapper, Longsword, Clog, Morris and Song. The Morris team which was part of the company went under the title of Men of Anglia. Considering the different backgrounds of the men this team was particularly successful. Individual members from Eastern Folk went on to found their own teams in Ipswich, Cambridge, the Fens and Somerset.

Men of Anglia — 1973

ACCOMMODATION

The digs Peter had with the Kendons, who were newly married, were supposed to be temporary. Peter was quite happy there. After 4 or 5 months Claire realised that she would have do something about finding Peter somewhere else to live, if he were not to become permanent. She found him a little bungalow to buy but it was too risky to take a mortgage on Peter's salary; however she did sew seeds of having a place of his own. At this stage Peter was still very reluctant to marry, he still claimed it was the difference in our ages but he had been engaged before and withdrawn. He was reluctant to make a permanent commitment and was quite happy with the life we had. I wanted a home and family. By Spring 1970 I decided I was on firm enough ground to give Peter an ultimatum; marriage or we finish. There were a lot of arguments at this time; I would not have been surprised if he had opted for the second and easier choice. I'm still not sure why he agreed to marry. At the time I felt he wanted children and I was young enough to have them. I could not imagine life without him.

THE BOTHY

Janet and I were engaged early in 1970 and began to make plans for marriage. We had no money but an opportunity to live cheaply and save arose. We had been offered a tiny two room genuine 'Bothy' (a residence for single farm workers) on the edge of a field which was part of a large Estate near Newmarket race course. It had a splendid address: 'The Bothy, Lower Hare Park, Six Mile Bottom, Newmarket and housed us cheaply for over 12 months enabling us to save up towards our eventual home.

Bob Common, of the Yetties, sent congratulations on our wedding signing himself 'Six Yard Bottom!! The Bothy had been unoccupied for a couple of years, an old roadworker had reputedly died there. It was literally two rooms with a chimney in the middle and an earth closet outside. There was also a lean-to shed against what had been the walled garden of the original estate. One of my pupils lived in what had been the Estate Manager's house, which is how I heard about the place. We took out the Victorian fireplace and the rook's nest above it. Rooks had obviously nested there for years and did not take kindly to interference. For months they continued to drop sticks down the chimney. We cleaned the place completely and painted it. Then installed a table and 4 chairs, an electric cooker, (which we still use), some cupboards, a homemade book shelf, a second-hand carpet, a single bed from my home which doubled as a settee, a tin bath we found on the estate and a second-hand boiler for heating water for baths; there was only a cold water supply. Heating was by electric fires. Peter moved in during the Spring while I was still in Newmarket.

MARRIAGE

We made plans for the wedding in July but resolved to keep the news just within the family, not among the Folk world. It was to be a Registry Office wedding at Poole in Dorset, where Janet's parents lived. On a Monday morning, 24th July, 1970, we were married in a simple but friendly ceremony with family and a few friends.

The reception was perhaps not as quiet as planned, as we had been placed in one corner of a restaurant and our best man, Robin Whittlestone, in proposing the toast addressed the whole assembly in the restaurant as if they were all guests. After the speeches a vicar appeared from the restaurant tables and gave us his blessing.

We trundled off in the Morris Traveller on our honeymoon and ended up for a few days near to the River Dart at Stoke Gabriel, where they had hung the vicar in a previous century. We were due to go up the coast to Sidmouth, a situation that was to become all too familiar as the years went by.

Back at The Bothy we had to fit ourselves in, create a home and prepare to spend a winter on the edge of a large field and within sight of mainly derelict and rat-ridden buildings. The rat problem was solved by Tanya, a cat we had brought from Janet's home together with her latest litter of kittens. In her determined efforts to feed her young she regularly dumped rats on the kitchen floor and night after night I had to find a new spot in the field to bury them.

The mansion, which had previously stood nearby, had been demolished years earlier but there were reminders of it's bygone luxuries such as the squash court which remained recognisably intact. Another feature was the water tower which supplied our needs although the pipes leading from the tower were forever springing leaks due to the field having been deep ploughed and plumbing skills were an acquired necessity. *ie. Peter would wedge a stick in the end of the severed pipe.* We boiled all drinking water. I don't know how we coped in The Bothy during that winter of 1970/71 but I'm sure we made a resolution that there wouldn't be another. I remember we were both ill at different times, myself with awful leg pains following an attempt to diet which was described as a calcium deficiency, although it's difficult to understand how I was deprived of calcium.

Wedding Day — 24th July 1970

Despite the smallness of the Bothy we did manage to entertain. John Kirkpatrick once slept in the kitchen on the spare bed, Peter and Angela Davis, Claire and Andrew Kendon would come to tea and walk round the estate. We were a mile from the main road so the cats could also go for walks with us. We kept one of Tanya's kittens, Bonnie; she grew so used to walks we could take her in the car and let her come with us collecting blackberries, away from traffic.

NORTHERN AREA AGAIN

Early in 1971, when we were beginning to think of buying a house, Peter applied to take over the Northern Area when Ethyl Anderson retired and Dave Wood left under a cloud. Peter had been moved from the south, the wrench had been made; we both had roots in the north, the houses were cheaper, there was a much larger population to work with, many of the activists Peter knew personally from his days in the Ministry and Peter felt very strongly that it was not fair to put a new, untrained and inexperienced member of staff into such a large area, which stretched from Sheffield to Scotland. NEC refused to consider Peter's application as he had been in the East for only a year. We were very disappointed. Peter especially felt he could have made an impact on the Folk world with such a large population to work with in comparison with the East.

WICKHAMBROOK

After a year in the Bothy, paying 25s (£1.25) per week rent, we had saved £800 but the prospects of buying a house seemed remote. However, Janet was thinking positively and we spent the summer months looking around. We were not making much progress when we thought a visit to property in Wickhambrook might be worthwhile. A row of one up, one down cottages had been converted into two family residences which were available for £5,150 each. They were called Hill Top and High View, although the original name was Cooper's Row. We were granted a viewing there and then and we fell for one of them. We gazed at the place from all angles, very conscious of the fact that this was the first day the properties were on the market. We had to act and did, making an offer the same day, reflecting on our good fortune as house prices soared during the next few months.

After the usual delays we moved in early November. Our home life then really began. Wickhambrook lies roughly about 10 miles from Newmarket, Haverhill and Bury St. Edmunds. Janet was teaching at Newmarket and my office was still in Cambridge, so I had quite a daily trip to transport us both. When we moved in we had no money to furnish the place so it was a time of creating things which would do for as long as necessary. We were anxious to get rid of the existing wallpaper so decorating was on the agenda soon.

With the arrival of the Spring we were able to look at the garden which covered almost a third of an acre. From the very beginning work in the garden was a shared experience for both of us and was regarded as recreation rather than a chore. In fact it was a good garden to work; the top soil was black and the fine tilth suggested that it had been dug and manured well over many years. The solid clay lay about 15-18 inches down and ensured that moisture was retained even in very dry times.

There were unforeseen hazards, however, which we discovered when vegetables were growing; who would have believed that pheasants and partridge had such an appetite for greens!

The job was demanding in travel but in those days Janet could come with me on some expeditions. The wife of an organiser of folk activities soon learns to avoid particular functions but there were many times during our stay in East Anglia that Janet was able to browse round the shops or galleries in such lovely places as Norwich, Colchester and Cambridge, as I went off to a committee meeting, or to London on my trips to Camden Town for staff meetings. We were also able to go to some nice dances round the area even though it was official business and we made many friends. At home we actually had time to make home-made wines and I remember taking very much to Orange.

GILES ROBERT DASHWOOD

Named after a character in a Thomas Hardy novel and Peter's brother who was killed in the war.

We can only look back now on pre-family days when we had lots of energy to do things. News that Giles was on the way came in the spring of 1972 so we had the summer to prepare before his eventual arrival on November 3rd, ten days late. I should say that the period of waiting was spent gathering beautiful big blackberries from the paddock which backed on to our garden.

Giles was on the way in the morning but by late afternoon it was realised that he was in distress and the decision was made to deliver by Caesarean. More delay while another operation was got underway but a very big Giles (9lb) arrived sometime after 8pm. Janet was OK beforehand but the anaesthetic induced nightmarish images and left a big impression. I was in a bit of a state and there wasn't any chance of my being in at the birth as planned.

The day after Giles was born Peter was booked to run a Ceilidh with the Yetties at Norwich University. He found someone else to call but by Saturday night I was too tired for visitors so Peter went anyway. He was on a real high having just had a son, people thought he was drunk. So far the Yetties had been around for one of our first dates, my 21st, our engagement, marriage (at Sidmouth) and now Giles' birth.

Giles swallowed meconium prior to his birth and developed pneumonia so was in an incubator for a week. Peter held him briefly after he was born, I did not see him for three days. These were the days of three days in bed following operations.

It was soon discovered that Giles had dislocatable hips and was put in a splint to correct. The anguish and distress caused to a child, who otherwise was a loveable and calm baby, and to parents over the next few years to put this matter right I find difficult to describe now, but the experience was to prepare us for further problems later on.

Every parent will recall the first few traumatic months with a new baby. Many sleepless nights and meeting a continuous demand for attention tests the stamina of the best, but in our case Giles was also restricted and frustrated by the splint to correct his hips. Things came to a head at Christmas when we had unwisely agreed to lead the holiday folk activities at Halsway Manor.

Peter with Giles, aged 7 months

With no more than 4 hours between feeds we were shattered.

Giles spent nearly two out of his first five years in plaster and three operations to correct his hips, retarding his physical development. However, I was concerned that, even allowing for this, he was behind his peers in things like dressing, doing jigsaws and talking besides walking. I took him to paediatricians for advice only to be told I was a "fussy mother", as a teacher I "expected too much". In his private report the doctor advised that Giles would probably need special schooling in the future. He did not tell us.

In order to help Giles I read all I could on early child development, including the Montessori methods of teaching children. I came across a book by Glenn Doman, Teach Your Baby to Read. At last Giles found something he could do. He loved reading and through it he gained some confidence.

Once he started school the Headmaster called in a psychologist to advise as to why Giles was still way behind his peers. It was 1978. The psychologist told me Giles would never learn to read or write and needed to go to a Special School at 8 years. I did not accept this assessment either, Giles had a reading age of 6+ years according to the Schools Remedial Adviser. I looked for alternatives to the conventional plans for 'Special Needs' children. The result dramatically changed our lives.

In January 1980 we were one of the first families to be assessed by the British Institute for Brain Injured Children at Knowle Hall, Bridgwater, paid for with money raised by people throughout the East and South-East Region. Giles was 7 years old. He had sustained developmental damage before his birth, possibly due to a virus I had contracted in the second month. The Programme we were given to compensate involved 10 hours per day physical work, with another 2-3 hours education and necessitated a rota of helpers from the village and school where I taught. I had taken a part-time job as the Headmaster's relief teacher when Giles started school. Peter took over Programme when he was home in the evenings and worked weekends so that I could continue teaching. We did not have holidays, trips out or visit families, who disagreed with what we were doing. The improvement in Giles' co-ordination, confidence and perception was dramatic, he returned to school a year later.

Looking back on the bleak outlook at the time it is rewarding to know that a 17 year old Giles is now undertaking a foundation course at a local college and is guiding himself towards independence.

HIGH VIEW

Janet and I were to discover that we could work together in practical ways but it soon emerged that she was the leader in most things to do with the family. We had to be economical in making a home and so there were adaptations and creative, but functional, uses of wood for home made furniture. I was the labourer and learning fast in a new do-it-yourself age with electric drills and sanders and a firm belief in the qualities of modern glues. The skills of both of us were fully extended when it came to making suitable equipment for Giles when he was in plaster for his hips.

We were both nervous of making any structural alterations to the cottage until Claire and Andrew arrived to 'help'. We started well by dismantling and burning the old privy in the garden. Then Claire got the urge to knock down a wall inside, whereas we had only been thinking about it. It must have been then that we set up our now long established rule of never finishing a big job in a hurry. The wattle and daub wall proved difficult to remove on the day but the resultant hole in the floor remained for many years and provided a good talking point for countless visitors who had to step over it.

NEWS PAPER ARTICLES

In January 1973 The Cambridge Evening News featured a profile of Peter under the headline, 'A Man who Nurtures the Idiom of the People.' by Deryck Harvey. (See Appendix). This was followed by being runner-up in the 'Husband of the Year' awards organised by the Bury St Edmunds' weekly paper. He won £15 and a free night out, which is why I had put his name forward; we were pretty poor and £15 was very useful. Peter was quite good at looking after Giles, who was in plaster for his hips, at a time when the 'New Man' had not been invented.

OFFLEY and HENGRAVE

One of the nicest events which I inherited from Molly DuCane was an annual week-end residential course for teachers at Offley Place, arranged in conjunction with the LEA PE Advisors. I continued the tradition and with Hertfordshire District Committee cultivated a good team of instructors. Interest in the course had been maintained because there were many school dance clubs around the county encouraged by the big annual Gorhambury Festival happening at St. Albans.

Weekend courses were becoming a feature elsewhere, especially with the discovery of Hengrave Hall, a beautiful Tudor mansion near Bury St Edmunds. It had been a Convent and Girl's School and the Sisters were looking to develop the place as a residential centre. Claire Kendon taught a deaf girl at the convent and told us about the place. We ran one or two training weekends a year, eventually a week long Summer School with staff including Dorothy & Trevor Beckford, Mike Wilson-Jones, Gerry Phelps, Rick Smith, Barbara Woods, Cyril Jones, the Rangers, Geoff Hughes and Bernard Chalk, over the years.

ANGLIAN BROADSHEET

I found East Anglia to be made up of isolated units, way behind the development I left in the South. I therefore set out to get folk travelling more to events. I introduced the Anglian Broadsheet, a diary of events around the region, in 1972. This also advertised the Folk shop mail order, aimed at schools, run from my office in Bury St. Edmunds. The Broadsheet inspired the setting up of local magazines such as Essex Folk News and Folk London.

> "Peter Dashwood started it, with his cherubic smile. He usually starts it, whatever it is. The District, he said, needed more coherence, so how about a newsletter? Being naive and not noticing the marked reluctance of the others to reply, I ventured an opinion. Something about insurmountable difficulties and reluctant contributers, I believe. Ah! said everyone, we have a volunteer. Peter smiled. He usually does."

Brian Martin, first editor of Essex Folk News. Editorial EFN, Summer 1973. EFN celebrated twenty-one years this year.

PAT TRACEY

When I moved to East Anglia I was aware that Pat Tracey, a traditional clog dancer, was living in the area. I was also aware that she was not being used. When I contacted her she was bringing up a young family and much later acknowledged to me that before I came along she was turning to other interests. I soon had her operational for workshops at Folkeast, Felixstowe and later at Broadstairs and before long it seemed she was all over the country.

TRAVEL

The next three years saw me travelling throughout the area preparing for big events and servicing the various committees, arranging Ceilidhs for youth (YMCA) in Norwich and universities in Norwich and Colchester, Folk Days in Ely.

In 1975 the Ely Day included the Etchingham Steam Band and Richard Digance. There were more Folk Days in Cecil Sharp House, Saffron Walden and Thaxted; Festivals at Harwich/Clacton, St Alban's, Bedford, Linton and a Holiday Camp near Lowestoft. Peter arranged teacher's courses to service the Festivals. Most of Peter's festivals had an element aimed at schools and families as he believed it was essential to give children an exciting and enjoyable introduction if Folk is to continue. He was also a leader on training courses, a caller and dancer.

CONFLICTS WITH MANAGEMENT

In 1972, when Giles was born I left teaching to care for him, we were thus living on one salary. The oil crisis and inflation hit us and we found that the mileage allowance did not cover expenses. We asked for a Company car, as we could not afford to run our car. Management refused. We threatened to use taxis. A year later, when Sibyl Clark retired, Peter was given her car.

This was followed by the 'Telephone Saga'; Peter's office was in Bury St. Edmunds, he would set out at 8.00 am and not be seen again until 8 or 9 pm. because he had to phone people when they were home in the evening. I had no idea when he might arrive for dinner as we couldn't afford a phone. We asked the EFDSS to provide one so Peter could make and receive calls from home. It was refused by NEC on two grounds: the Dashwoods might use it for personal calls and it would disrupt our personal life!! We eventually got round the phone problem by insisting we ran the office from home, although not without a fight. Our income increased as we were paid a small rent and at least we saw Peter, if only at mealtimes.

It was probably around this time that I actively discouraged Peter from calling dances. This was a great shame because he was a good caller, particularly for beginners and he enjoyed it. However, according to his contract all fees must go to EFDSS; Peter was scrupulously honest and they did. He reclaimed allowable expenses which generally didn't cover his costs. It did not make sense to go out in the evening when he had already worked 10-12 hours in the office or travelled miles to meetings, including weekends, for no financial reward.

REGIONAL DEVELOPMENT OFFICER — EASTERN AREA

In 1975 further responsibilities came my way when I was asked to oversee the South-East and London as well as East Anglia. It was a very interesting period with 5 new London Districts coming into being and soon the opportunity for me to develop another festival at Broadstairs and assist with establishing Eastbourne Festival with Peter Mayes and events at Michelham Priory. I was now travelling over an area from Chichester to The Wash before the days of useful motorways and working with over 20 committees.

Work in London included the London Folk Music Festival, St. George's Festival (with many arguments with Chris Turner) and Folk London magazine.

OFFICIAL JOB DESCRIPTION

Implement policy; Advise youth, schools etc.; Encourage development skills; Hold sales Training for members/non-members; Provide information; Assist in collection and research; Maintain standards; Spread interest to General Public; Develop P.R.; Submit LEA reports for grants; Apply for new grants; Ensure Society active in all parts Generate income.

PETER'S INTERPRETATION

General encouragement to local volunteers on District Committees and working parties; Working together on major events; Putting forward national and other view points; Passing on information; Accepting complaints.

BROADSTAIRS

The Broadstairs Folk Show held during August had been going for some years. Jack Hamilton, the founder and Director, invited me to develop a festival to support the show. In 1975 this was a very humble public dance in a church hall with Peter and Angela Davis.

Four adults and three small children processed through the streets to drum up custom, Peter called, the Davises played, I took the money on the door, served refreshments then I took the kids back to the public park where we were camped with the Folk Show and baby sat.

The next year the accommodation improved for the Director and family to the floor of the Church Hall office! That year Dorothy Beckford and I fed umpteen Irish dancers and Belgian Flagwavers from the same Church Hall. The bread pudding is still talked of in the recesses of Kent. I think Dorothy was booked (not paid) to teach clog and call dances; one had to be adaptable at Dashwood's Festivals. Dorothy's memories include sewing up the split britches of a Flagwaver, with the

Belgian still in them. I think we must have served beans for dinner for the memory is less than savoury!

Recently I found a photo of one of our most enthusiastic supporters. He came from Japan encrusted with cameras and bowed, most politely, at any opportunity, saying "Ah, so." He was a delight, although not to everyone. At the workshops he danced with an English lady whose husband did not dance. At the end of the week the Japanese gent gave out presents as if it were Christmas, calculators, watches and trinkets. The husband, who had done nothing all week, received an expensive watch, his wife, who had danced all week, a trinket. She was most put out.

The next few years saw quite big developments as Broadstairs blossomed into a normal festival where folk stayed for a week of workshops, dances, ceilidhs and concerts. Making this one happen was difficult because I was living approximately 150 miles from Broadstairs. The Folk Show formula of presenting a rehearsed show every afternoon and evening did not help as it was difficult to get any interchange of performers. I spent ages looking for camping and workshop facilities, the Education Authority eventually providing a school. Pam Porritt was a staunch supporter and helper and to this day runs the festival.

Jack Hamilton held very strong views on keeping the Show exclusively English and was upset when Peter brought teams from Ireland and Sweden to the Festival. There was a long period when we didn't open letters which might have come from Jack until after breakfast, one needed a strong constitution to cope with the language. I had told Peter he shouldn't touch Broadstairs with a barge pole, back in the days we were camping in the public park, but Peter was never one to buck a challenge where Folk was concerned!

Other attempts at innovation were also met with stiff opposition. There was an outcry when Peter booked The New Victory Band for a public Ceilidh. They were one of a new wave of Ceilidh bands and played superb dance music but the 'dancers' objected. It is one of the few times I have heard Peter swear at the punters in public. He said something like, 'If you can't dance to this music you're not bloody dancers!' We loved dancing to them, it was exciting, not sedate EFDSS or American based, both of which Peter objected to. Peter must have been about 50 then, so hardly a young upstart.

I came to look forward to Broadstairs, the weather was usually good, there is a lovely beach, we had a good team helping to run the Festival, (Dorothy & George Beckford, Bev & Ray Langton, David Jex, Dave Williams, Bernie Chalk, The Cottagers band, Barry

Skinner and many others), some super events in the Grand Ballroom, including one year a spectacular team from Sweden (a contradiction if ever there was one!), annual Music Halls and big names in Folk. The last one we ran was in 1980.

Broadstairs led to other things in Kent. We had a training week-end for callers and musicians, week-ends for teachers and I was invited by the Education Authority to fill an impossible void left by the late Pat Shaw at their annual summer school which included folk music and dance.

EXPO

Back in East Anglia I was to start a project which I'm still involved in to-day. I was invited to put on a Folk Show at Expo, a big charity event at the East of England Showground, Peterborough.

Strangely Peter never regarded Expo as Work. Perhaps it was because we had been going to the event before being involved, as a rare day out away from Folk; more likely because it was relatively easy to run. Peter was given a set budget by the Show Management, with little argument, to spend on teams etc. as he wished. He had only to ask for facilities such as stage, lighting, camping and they would be provided by the showground staff.

The audience was ready made as the public came in thousands to the main event and on site there were further hundreds of steam enthusiasts, firemen and stall holders. One memorable year there were hundreds of the Sealed Knot who stage battles of the Civil War. They came to the dances in spurs! We had to ask a General if they could be removed as they were dangerous but, as part of the uniform, could not be removed without permission.

Teams, initially not keen to dance on Bank Holidays, found the event ideal for families who were not Folkies. Over the years we built up a regular team of loyal workers: Ivor Maycock, who introduced us to Expo, and his Squarecrows Band, John Tether as Compere/MC, the Yetties to sing and play, Peter and Angela Davis as producer and treasurer, Rhona Baldrey's Irish Dancers, Peterborough Morris and many others. This meant that in 1988 and 1989, when Peter was having increasing difficulties through Motor Neurone Disease, the show ran just as smoothly.

Even this event was not without controversy. Peter chose to stage his show in the Foxhound Arena, an open barn with buildings around for changing and song sessions. It was well away from all the main public attractions on site. The pessimists said we wouldn't attract an audience, we should be near the main attractions. Peter stood his ground and the attractions came to us; in a few years we were surrounded by stalls and a 'Village Scene', pub, hog roast, demonstration crafts and market. The audience came in thousands, frequently with standing room only so the fire-engine enthusiasts brought their ancient machines to sit on. We had some magic moments when the arena was packed and Bonnie (Yettie) would sing Linden Lea or Pete played the bowed psaltery or a tiny Irish dancer brought rapturous applause. Our audience came year after year, most having no other contact with Folk.

NATIONAL DEVELOPMENT OFFICER

In 1980 the Society advertised for a National Development Officer. Peter felt the Festivals and work he had initiated in the Region were well established and that he would welcome a fresh challenge. He was the most senior member of the Field Staff with an understanding of the Society's structure, staff and members, many of whom Peter knew personally, with experience and personal contacts throughout the Folk and, increasingly, Educational, Sports and Arts worlds. One of Peter's aims was to: "create a more cohesive unit amongst my colleagues in order to promote successful ideas for adoption nationally."

He received a duplicated note informing all applicants who were not be considered, after the interviews had taken place.

CARAVAN

At the end of 1979 we had some savings, Giles' Programme was mainly paid for by donations and we did not have time to spend much. The village held a charity auction with a new caravan, worth £1,250, as the final item. The bids went to £800 and stopped, we looked at each other, the days of camping in a cold tent could be over. Peter bid £850, it was the most money we had ever spent on the spur of the moment, we were shaking. No-one else bid, we owned a caravan. A year later it was worth £1,000 in exchange for a super new caravan.

VILLAGE

After we had finished Programme with Giles we missed the friends we had made who came regularly once, or several times, a week to Pattern Giles. We also wanted to thank them for all the help they gave so freely so we ran a Ceilidh for all those associated with the programme in the Village Hall. It was a great success and ran several more by popular demand before we left.

THE NORTH 1981-1986

ANOTHER EFDSS CRISIS

The regular EFDSS crisis appeared again in 1981. The Society was undertaking a review of what it was and what it should be doing, but this was overtaken by financial matters.

Sadly, this was the end for two of my colleagues, Grahame Binless and Barry Lewis, when the Regional Development Officer's posts were abolished. I was invited to become the Society's National Training Officer based in the North, just one of two staff in the Field.

Although the Society could no longer afford RDOs, Peter was retained on the strength of support from his Area Representative on the National Executive Council. However, there was no option about moving North. Eastern Area wrote to NEC of their deep regret at losing Peter.

Tom Brown, who had replaced Bill Rutter in Western Region when Bill retired in 1979, was the other Field Worker. He was National Organiser in charge of events with particular emphasis on song.

Most noted was his 'Everlasting Circle', 1982, a brave attempt to produce a show for theatres based on Folk traditions, dance and song. Peter went to one or two rehearsals. It was not in his brief but either Tom asked him or he went out of his own interest. He came back very concerned. He felt, based on his own experience, that there was not enough sponsorship for the venture to be viable and that the theatres which were booked were too large for the size of audience the show was likely to attract. Peter passed on his fears to Management but was told it was all under control and none of his business. Everlasting Circle lost at least £15,000. Tom Brown lost his job. We felt this was not fair. He was relatively inexperienced and few people in Management took any interest until it was too late.

Brian Willcocks was appointed "Senior Executive: Development and Marketing, charged with improving the Society's images and with developing additional sources of income, including sponsorship." He resigned after a year when it became apparent he could not generate enough income to cover the costs of his post.

There was discussion on whether Nibs Matthews, Director, should take early retirement, he had 4 or 5 years to go. NEC decided they could not afford to finance the enhancement of his pension. Peter told the Chairman that this was a fatal mistake for the Society but the NEC, as others before and since, went for compromise, missing an opportunity to revitalise the Society. Nibs became Artistic Director with responsibility for teaching.

Colin Maynard was appointed Company Secretary/Accountant. Jeane Howard became Sales and Liaison Officer, with special responsibility for Cecil Sharp House. This was not to last. Colin took over much of Jeane's responsibilities with the backing of NEC. Jeane took a post in charge of Voluntary Services in London. I'm sure it was more remunerative and less of a hassle than working for the EFDSS.

John Dowell remained as Sidmouth Festival Director and was given the additional responsibility of Magazine Marketing. Malcolm Taylor was still Librarian and Dave Arthur freelance Editor of Dance & Song.

Peter was instructed to go North on the strength of three letters from members objecting that there was no Northern presence. We made the best of it, we had been considering moving to a town with facilities for Giles anyway. We bought a smaller house, without a mortgage, in the heart of a good motorway network; nevertheless there were the inevitable problems with H.Q. Peter had been promised '£3,000 removal expenses', "We don't want you to be out of pocket." and two salary increments, by the Chairman, Dave Hislop. Despite four letters to the Company Secretary, Colin Maynard, asking for written confirmation we received no reply. After we moved, with a new NEC Chairman, we received £1,266 of very basic expenses and one increment, despite having to buy a house with room for the Society's office. Never work for a Charity if you want fair play.

We had happy times in Suffolk and established many friendships. We had worked hard to improve the cottage and the garden which had provided us with many hours of relaxation. It was from here too that we had set out for some enjoyable camping holidays in Scotland, despite the fact that most of them were wet.

1, GALLOW TREE ROAD, ROTHERHAM

We had a big choice of area to live in, we went for Rotherham because of its educational system and access to two motorways. We left our country cottage for an ordinary semi-detached house on a big housing estate. We didn't know until all arrangements had been made that another child was on the way.

William was born 13th June 1982 and one got the impression immediately on arrival that he knew where he was going in this world. After 7 years I've no reason to think otherwise. The move also co-incided with an operation for co-arctation of the aorta for Giles which took place at Guy's Hospital in January.

For the second time in my life I was to live in the North but this time on the other side of the Pennines. For Janet it was a return to her county of birth and for both of us it was to be a totally new experience. I was to undertake longer but fewer journeys in the course of my work and the family were going to enjoy some beautiful countryside within easy striking distance. As with our last abode we spent many hours re-organising the garden. In the beginning we didn't expect to spend much time or money on the house. How wrong we were.

Once again we moved in November; it was blowing a gale and raining as we towed our caravan northwards. It was quite a wrench leaving our cottage and many friends in both the village and East Anglia. We had viewed our new house in summer when the garden was surrounded by a hedge of flowering roses. In the winter this no longer provided privacy and there was a steady stream of people walking by. I was used to fields on three sides of our garden; apart from ploughing and harvesting times, we saw no-one. One of the first things we had to do was erect a fence or I would have to move.

The garden, tiny in comparison with the one we left, was completely renovated over the years; enormous rocks moved, paths and lawns dug up and the front garden, against all northern convention, made into a vegetable garden. We grow super peas and have no trouble with pheasants.

We chose a house with an extension sun room in order to leave the front room free for the office. When William was born we had to block up the doorway between the front room and dining room to try to insulate Peter from William's crying. A year later, during gales, we discovered the plate glass windows of the sun lounge were bowing under the pressure. We replaced much of the glass with walls and installed patio doors.

GUY'S HOSPITAL

In January 1982 we returned south for Giles' operation to correct a narrowing of the aorta, the main blood vessel to the lower body. Giles was 8 years old when this congenital defect was discovered, if it is treated before 4 years of age there is less likelihood of complications, Giles was now 9. The operation involved taking a piece of artery from his arm to repair the aorta, thus Giles does not have a pulse in his left arm. We were told the prospects were good, a 50/50 chance of survival. This was good?!! After a few days on the Children's Heart Ward at Guy's I realised they were: two babies died; the doctors could not stop a 7 year old from bleeding; a 3 year old who had been running up and down the corridors was still on life support machines when we left two weeks later, after a repair to a hole in her heart.

Giles' operation was a success but afterwards he suffered from very high blood pressure. He was put on drugs which changed his personality from a calm and quiet child to being hypersensitive and emotional. He lost all confidence in himself, many of the physical skills gained through the sheer hard work of Programme were lost. It was heart breaking. Giles was accepted in a school for physically handicapped children, the most suitable establishment in the area to meet his needs. Later, Peter was to serve as a parent manager at the school.

HANDSWORTH TRADITIONAL SWORD DANCERS

Peter's responsibilities in the new post were national and mainly administrative he therefore made a decision not to get involved in local folk activities. He decided to join a local dance team as an ordinary person, not

Handsworth Traditional Sword Dancers — 1983

as staff of the EFDSS. He chose Handsworth Traditional Longsword Dancers, the nearest to us. With the demands of the job and unsocial hours Peter did not often dance out with the team, but we usually went on Boxing Day, when the Mummers Play was also performed, outside Handsworth Church. We also went with Handsworth to Felixstowe and Whitby Festivals and Peter was part of the team at the Morris Ring's 50th Anniversary Meeting in Birmingham and the team proved good friends in tough times.

WILLIAM JOHN DASHWOOD
(Named after Bill Rutter and my father.)

One good thing of the trip to Guy's Hospital was that I was offered a scan to see if there was anything wrong with the new baby. I was only four months pregnant yet the technician could detect any heart defect. There were none discernible. We could also see, quite clearly, that the baby was a boy. This was disappointing as we all wanted a girl, but it did give us time to get used to the idea. We were only just getting used to the idea of another baby!

William was something of a surprise. We had deliberately chosen not to have another child until Giles' problems were sorted out which didn't seem to happen. It took five years to correct his hips, then we were confronted with 'brain dysfunction' and undertook the Programme, then they found the co-arctation of the aorta. Giles needed me to be with him, I had seen families torn between the needs of their children in hospital and those at home and did not want to have to face the choice.

As time went on we decided we could not deliberately bring another child into the world which might have to suffer as Giles as done, however Fate had other ideas. I had stopped taking the contraceptive pill for about three years and we did not get on very well with other forms of contraceptive. We were lulled into a false sense of security. Then the village was shocked by several families breaking up, it became almost an epidemic, one setting off another so we wondered who would be next? The separations had the opposite affect on some of us, grateful for what we had. William was not the only unplanned new arrival.

Peter was 54. My doctor was almost as surprised as we were. He offered me a amniocentesis to see if the baby was alright. We refused because there is a risk attached and if something was wrong we would not have had an abortion. We had not chosen to have this baby, it had chosen us, we could not kill it. Mind you, after he was born there were times when we could happily have given him back! William proved to be a very demanding baby, only sleeping when he was near me, yelling if he wasn't. I do not remember a great deal of the first year in the north as most of the time was spent looking after Giles then William. We regretted not being near friends who might have shared caring. My mother came up to help and walked miles with the pram to keep William quiet.

I joined the National Childbirth Trust, in order to meet people. We held coffee mornings in each other's homes so the children mixed. When William was about 2 years I had about 15 children and their mums in the house and garden, it was a riot, I decided there had to be something better.

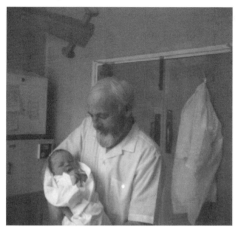

William, aged 30 minutes.

PLAYGROUP

We were definitely not having any more children, Peter had a vasectomy to be certain, but William was in danger of being spoiled as Giles was 9 years older and we all gave in to William's demands on occasions. I decided to start a Playgroup in the house with a friend from NCT so William had to learn to share. Peter agreed. We converted the extension and dining area into a play area, Peter constructed a climbing frame/Wendy House. We were duly registered with Social Services for ten children, opening in 1985 for two sessions a week. William was 2½ years old.

We moved the EFDSS Office upstairs into the smallest bedroom, so playgroup did not disturb Peter. The house was a hive of activity some days with Peter's secretary, Barbara Wood, typing upstairs, Peter meeting some one to do with work in the front room, converted back to a sitting room and Playgroup parents arriving to collect their children from the living area.

Sessions gradually increased and when William was 3 I started an older group where I taught the children to write and the beginnings of reading and number. I thoroughly enjoyed this, all the work I had done with Giles was benefitting other children. Life was really not bad, without a mortgage we had surplus money for the first time in our married life. We spent it on the house, we had some lovely holidays in the caravan, Scotland is much nearer to Rotherham than Wickhambrook, as are the Peak District, Yorkshire Dales, North York Moors and Wales and we saw more of Peter as he wasn't out every night. It was all too good to last.

NATIONAL TRAINING OFFICER

I didn't like the title but it suited the needs of the Sports Council and other Authorities when it came to funding projects. I knew that the atmosphere within the folk world was not right for what had gone before in the way of training. The festival scene provided a far more informal workshop structure. Local initiatives to encourage callers and musicians were likely to be more effective than something organised centrally by someone who may be seen as a bureaucrat. However, from my earlier experiences in London, I had some faith in courses spread over several weeks. It gave one time to get down to essentials. It was hard going in that it was difficult to raise much enthusiasm around the country, nevertheless, I set up courses in Leicester, Darlington, Sheffield, Bromsgrove, Luton, Preston, Stockport, Birmingham and London with some success. Later I turned towards the organisation of big youth events with far more success.

OTHER RESPONSIBILITIES OF N.T.O., EFDSS

Convener and secretary to new POLICY & DEVELOPMENT COMMITTEE, chaired by Bill Rutter, now NEC member, advising on long term planning, artistic training and publications.

Compiled NATIONAL TRAINING REGISTER.

Editor of the annual FOLK DIRECTORY 1983 and 1984. Contributed to the 1985 edition. The Directory lists details of folk dance and song clubs, festivals, archives and kindred organisations.

M.1 FOLK DAY, Luton.

Sought GRANT AID from Arts and Sports Associations, LEAs and Private Companies. Proved that monies are available to support projects such as:

FOLK MUSIC FAIR in Stockport, 1985;
YOUNG TRADITIONS in Derby, 1985 & 1986 including Photographic Exhibition.
SCHOOLS' TOUR of East Midlands and Humberside as introduction to Young Tradition.
Organised annual EXPO at Peterborough.
Attended SIDMOUTH FESTIVALS.
Arranged and M.C. at NIBS MATTHEW'S RETIREMENT PARTY.
Organised Folk input at YOUTH DANCE FESTIVALS in Hexham and Wakefield, 1985 & 1986
M.25 FOLK DAY, Bedford.
Edited the national FOLK DIARY, 1986, for English Dance & Song.
Convener of CERTIFICATION WORKING PARTY.
Liaised with Sports Council, Music Officers, Leeds Dance Centre and Arts Officers, including Peter Stark, of Northern Arts.
Liaised with local dance animateurs. (I am one)
Reliant entirely on local workers, *Brenda Godrich, Mary Meeks, Milly Chadband, Mo Bradshaw, Liza Austin plus others.*
On my own in the Field.
"The basis of my work has been to involve volunteers in the running of committees, events and other development projects. My task was to initiate and run events and festivals until the volunteer workers were ready to take over."
PED. 1983.
The battles with NEC did not change, although individuals within NEC did. At one stage Peter asked for a photocopier so he would not have to go three miles, to the Library, every time he needed something copied. Management suggested he shared a copier with Malcolm Storey who was editing the Directory and running Whitby Festival. He lived in Hull! We thought the Library was more convenient. After a battle Peter did get a copier of his own.

NEW DIRECTOR

Nibs Matthews was to retire in 1985. The NEC decided to appoint a Director Designate to work concurrently with Nibs for nine months. Peter suggested that no appointment be made before the Society had a defined Artistic and Development Policy; he knew debate was essential in a membership based Society and agreement gained if one is to carry out major reform without serious opposition. He believed that the NEC was hoping for the salvation of the Society through, "The next passing GOD who happens to drop in".

By not appointing a replacement Director immediately the Society would save salary and

expenses thus be in a better financial situation to undertake development in the future. Peter even suggested that, as the most senior member of staff, he was willing to act as temporary 'Senior Officer', to give time for a concensus to be taken both inside and out of the Society. Peter was in a unique position knowing most of the membership and leading activists in the Folk World. He made the offer not for personal glory but for the good of the Society, despite the certainty of being rejected by the voluntary officers who run the Society. He was told, very firmly, that the Society could not manage without a Director.

John Dowell and Peter were invited to meet the candidates for Director at their interview. John and Peter had no say in the appointment but Peter felt that the committee made a 'safe choice', in Jim Lloyd, presenter of Folk on 2, BBC Radio 2. He was not the one Peter would have recommended.

THE YOUNG TRADITION

Peter found difficulty in writing about his last few years with the Society. The years in the South and East had direction, following Bill Rutter's lead, then developing his own ideas. For the first few years in the North Peter struggled with what was an impossible task of raising enthusiasm and money for training projects. Then he hit upon the idea of The Young Tradition, "a multi-cultural day of workshops and concerts for young people". *He was fired with his old enthusiasm and felt this was a way forward for the Society.*

The first Young Tradition happened in 1985, after two years of preparation and was repeated in 1986, in Derby's Assembly Rooms. The dance traditions at the second Y.T. included Asian, African, English, Irish and Ukrainian. A wide range of music was performed by: a Steel Band, a Gaelic Choir and a Folk Group from Cheethams School of Music, Manchester. There was also a session on Derbyshire Folk Songs with Mick Peat and a very popular activity for many children was to take part in a Mummers Play. The Y.T. also provided the opportunity to launch a photographic exhibition by Brian Shuel of British Customs, which was to tour the country.

Jim Lloyd, as Director, attended the second Young Tradition. He reported:

"I attended and enjoyed this event in Derby. I was particularly taken with the enthusiasm of the volunteers who were initiating children in the Folk Arts. Obviously an area for development here. The Photographic Exhibition too was most impressive. A powerful new weapon in our promotional armoury."

Kate Badrick wrote in a report for the Teaching Fellowship Scheme of the Essex Institute of Higher Education:

"This event provided an excellent opportunity for young people to mix with their peers and experience different folk activities. There was co-operation between many official bodies and some support from the public. Most of the children I spoke to were thoroughly enjoying themselves.... It would be good to see more events of this nature organised about the country."
FOLK DANCING & THE SCHOOL CURRICULUM. Kate Badrick. 1986.

John Shaw and Phil Heaton, organisers of Dancing England: "

Where's the next generation (in Folk) interest? Worry no longer. There is enthusiasm, life, interest, youth, etc. just waiting to be tapped. It was all there at the YOUNG TRADITION in the Derby Assembly Rooms......In a bold and imaginative venture the EFDSS (Peter Dashwood) approached the schoolchildren of the area and offered them a school trip to a centre of multicultural traditional dance, and hundreds came!.....The success of the day gave us some very broad hints as to where the future lies — I hope they can be picked up.......If there is to be a thriving, enthusiastic, lively folk scene for us to watch from our wheelchairs and walking sticks there is some groundwork to be done...and very enjoyable work it is."
ENGLISH DANCE & SONG, Summer 1986

Unfortunately it was not to be. The Young Tradition could have been an insurance for the Society in encouraging youth. It brought together children from different cultures, involving them in their respective traditions.

I viewed the Young Tradition as a potential national movement and plans were well under way for similar events in Bristol, Bolton and Newcastle. Just at the time that I was getting the development programme off the ground yet another financial crisis hit the Society and at the end of 1986 I was made redundant.

Longsword Workshop at the Young Tradition, Derby Assembly Rooms, 1986

REDUNDANT

We have had many difficulties to face in our lives with finances, family, Giles, and finally Motor Neurone Disease, yet none compare with the awfulness of the redundancy. Generally, we retained some control and choice in our reaction to situations, in redundancy we were in the hands of others and felt helpless and useless. Peter did not write about redundancy and I am writing this four years after the actual events. I have written in some detail because few knew how much it affected us and because our experience of redundancy and our reaction to it influenced the way we coped with future problems.

In the summer of 1986 there were the usual mutterings of financial problems in the EFDSS. Peter spent Sidmouth week assisting the Director, Jim Lloyd, along with Brenda Godrich, in drumming up members and answering queries in a caravan on the Ham. Things didn't look TOO bad for the EFDSS.

Jim Lloyd spent some of his time at Sidmouth composing his "Wayahead" for the EFDSS, based on the meetings he had had on his tour of the country in '85/'86.

We went to Whitby Festival for a day and Peter jokingly told friends that he might be out of a job soon, but he didn't believe it. We assumed that taking into account his age, 58, his experience, the job he was doing and the reaction of the Membership, Management would not have the nerve. How wrong we were.

EARLY RETIREMENT CONSULTATION

On Thursday September 4th, 1986 Peter went to CSH for a meeting about the EFDSS magazine, Jim Lloyd spoke of his vision for the future; he needed around £1,000,000 to fulfil it. After the meeting Peter asked the Director if he could find out the position of his (Peter's) pension prospects if he took early retirement. We were looking to approximately 1 or 2 years hence to implement our long-term plan of my being the bread winner, once William, then 4 years old, was settled in school. Peter hoped that the Young Tradition would be established as a Movement which he might be able to direct on a part-time basis. Peter was suffering from Irritable Bowel Syndrome, a stress related illness which caused him some pain; he wanted to be able to spend less time travelling and more time doing what he enjoyed, if we had enough to live on. In fact it took us a further 6 months to have the pension figures. As we would have had less than £2,000 pa. pension, with no other secure form of income, early retirement would not have been feasible.

General Purposes and Finance Committee

On that Thursday Peter had no inkling of the impending doom. In the evening General Purposes and Finance Committee, consisting of Jim Lloyd, Director EFDSS; Colin Maynard, General Secretary EFDSS; Roger Marriott, Chairman GPFC; Brian Jones, Chairman EFDSS; Roger Barnes, Treasurer; Derek Schofield, Ted Holt, Dai Jefferies, Sue Burnett, Malcolm Storey and Janet Wood, met in Cecil Sharp House. Although Peter was in the building he had no right to attend the meeting nor would it have been considered appropriate or necessary to consult him, despite decisions being taken which had an immense effect on his future and that of the Society for which he had worked for 22 years. The decisions taken were ratified by the NEC meeting on Saturday, September 6th.

That weekend Peter started a week's work at the National Youth Dance Festival being held at Wakefield. Peter had arranged for other instructors, besides himself, to teach Folk Traditions to young dancers from all over the country. These could be the Dance Animateurs of the future and were a valuable contact for the Society.

On Monday 8th. September I was on my own, hanging out the washing on a lovely day, listening to Nic Jones singing 'The Warlike Men of Russia' when the phone rang. Grahame Binless, ex-EFDSS staff and current NEC member, said, "My advice is that Peter had better start looking for another job. I think NEC decided he had to go on Saturday." I had to wait all day before I could tell Peter.

Two options had been put to NEC to either close Cecil Sharp House completely, or to allow 'minimal use' of CSH, for the immediate future, both with a view to selling Cecil Sharp House. Both options included closing the Rotherham office. Grahame asked if that meant Peter Dashwood was out of a job? The answer was, from Malcolm Storey, that Peter wasn't well and was looking to leave. This was not true, and, although Peter had asked about the prospects of early retirement, he had also assumed the enquiry was in confidence. There was relief all round. NEC agreed that a full-time Director was necessary. Derek Schofield objected to the loss of the Assistant Librarian. There was no support for the National Training Officer.

Grahame should not have told us all this but he had suffered redundancy 5 years before from the EFDSS, the handling of this had been appalling so his loyalty was more with Peter than EFDSS, however we had to pretend we didn't know.

WAYAHEAD

At the same meeting the NEC accepted the Director's 'Wayahead' in which he proposed that:

"The Society's name be changed to 'The Folk Trust of England';

The membership be: Member, Friend and Member Emeritus;

Districts and Areas be abolished to allow direct access between the membership and central administration;

The composition of the NEC be broadened to take account of the wider interest in folk and the need for business expertise;

The number and quality of professional staff should be sufficient to undertake the expansion of the Society."

The proposals in the Wayahead became entangled in the proposals over the House. Jim received a lot of 'hate mail'. How much the selling of the House, which it was hoped would raise £1,000,000 and Jim's proposals, requiring funding of £1,000,000, were coincidence or necessity, I am not in a position to judge.

On Tuesday, while I was running Playgroup, Jim Lloyd rang to speak to Peter, who was in Wakefield. If I had had more courage I would have said something, but the moment passed. Peter returned the call in the evening. Jim wanted Peter to meet him at the Garden Festival at Stoke-on-Trent, where Jim was organising the Folk section. (He had asked Peter to do this earlier in the year, until he found out there was a considerable budget so he did it himself. This amused us, one knew where one stood with people like that and good luck to them.)

Peter refused to travel to Stoke, 2-3 hrs drive, when he was engaged at the Dance Festival, so he was given the news 'officially' on 15th September, a week later, at the House. We presumed that there would be some explanation and some figures. I had done some research in the Library. Peter's legal entitlement, on his salary of £8,875 pa was £4,650 redundancy pay. This could be increased to £25,000 tax free, at the generosity of the Company.

When Peter met the Director and Company Secretary they had no figures on redundancy or retirement but put to Peter; 'Did he want his leaving the EFDSS to be expressed as either early retirement or redundancy?' There was no option of staying employed. If we had chosen retirement Peter would have lost his right to redundancy pay, we had no figures on the pension. There was no advantage to Peter for it to be expressed as early retirement, although it would have sounded better to the EFDSS members from the Management viewpoint.

Peter returned from London very upset. He'd spent a whole day out and learnt nothing except that he would be out of a job on 31st December. He wrote to the Director on September 18th: "The label is quite clear. If one has no choice about going then it's Redundancy. The Society's part is in the realisation of their moral obligation to secure the best terms possible for one who has served 22 years and is within 7 years of normal retirement."

Since when did the Society have any 'moral obligation' to Staff?! To the Library? Yes. To the Journal? Yes. The Magazine? Yes. Cecil Sharp House? Yes, by some. Staff? No. Ask anyone who has worked for the EFDSS.

ISOLATED

This was an horrific time. The silent phone was deafening. We were certain some one from NEC would phone to say they were at least sorry, many of them Peter counted as friends. However NEC had been told to say nothing until Peter was informed and Jim waited until a mailing was due, a week after Peter had been told 'officially', to tell NEC that Peter knew he was out of a job. All, except Grahame Binless, kept to this injunction, so we were in limbo and shock for 2 weeks before the silence was broken by Janet Wood.

Those two weeks seemed endless. For years holidays, gardening, reading bed-time stories, meals etc. had been interrupted by the telephone ringing with some Folk enquiry, to my annoyance. I would have given anything for that phone to ring from someone who was sympathetic to our situation, but Peter was a very minor casualty in the Great EFDSS Crisis, NEC had swept him under the carpet and could now forget about him and get on with much more important matters. Janet and Grahame were the ONLY members of that NEC, 24 in all, who contacted us voluntarily. Many did not speak to or contact Peter again.

Brian Jones, Chairman, was composing the announcement of the decisions for the EFDSS magazine. These included closure and sale of Cecil Sharp House and redundancy of the Cashier, Receptionist and Assistant Librarian. Peter's loss was to be expressed thus: "As a further measure the National Training Officer and his Secretary will become redundant". None of the Staff had names! Peter was furious. The lack of consideration was making him ill so I persuaded him to ring Brian, who then added a regret at the loss of "Peter Dashwood. It is hoped that he will continue with some projects for us on a freelance basis." The rest of the staff still did not warrant being named.

FRIENDS OF CECIL SHARP HOUSE

When the news became public there was an outcry about the closure of Cecil Sharp House, which started a long and bitter battle within the Society. Brenda Godrich led the revolt, founding the Friends of Cecil Sharp House to run the House while the EFDSS sorted itself out. This was not surprising as she was about to take up a post offered by Jim Lloyd, on the EFDSS staff, to develop activities at Cecil Sharp House and in London. She had been working on a voluntary basis to Peter as a Project Officer, organising training sessions, beginner classes etc. and, against all odds, a permanent Bar in Cecil Sharp House. Peter did not entirely approve of her appointment, he felt it was a bad career move for Brenda and that she did not have the vision and experience necessary for the job she was to undertake. However, partly because of the way Peter was treated she refused the job although it was still on offer in September and October. I believe it was to be separately funded.

Brenda's original aim was to raise money to keep the House open on a short term basis to give time for debate on the future of the Society and, long term, to save the House from being sold, if the Membership decided that was desirable.

Obviously Peter remained friends with Brenda, they had been friends for years. He did not feel strongly about either keeping or selling the House, although he had been part of the Policy and Development Committee which had examined the costs of running Cecil Sharp House in 1983. The conclusion then was that it was not economic to move due to the restrictions imposed by charitable status. Peter did object to the way GPFC were steam rolling their decisions, without consultation or proper consideration of the consequences.

One of Peter's trips to London coincided with a meeting of the Friends of Cecil Sharp House, in the House, in their very early days. Peter went out of interest. At the meeting someone (Colin Hume?) jokingly declared that: "The Friends will save the House, then (turning to Peter) we can see to your job, Peter!" Peter was not amused, this remark hurt him deeply, a building meant more than all that he had striven to achieve, which was being thrown away. We did not join the Friends.

The Friends' meeting coincided with a meeting of GPFC being held upstairs in CSH. The Friends' asked to meet with GPFC, which they did. Peter went upstairs with Brenda and others as an interested member of staff. Brian Jones saw him at the door and said that Peter may as well come in too. Peter went in as a member of staff and observer, hoping he might act as a go-between. The meeting was not amiable. Janet

Wood stated in the minutes of that GPFC meeting that Peter attended as a member of the Friends. This was not true.

We subsequently heard that Janet and others stated that we were members of the 'Friends' publicly. In view of the strong feelings aroused by the battle between GPFC and the Friends, this false assumption made about us had an unfair effect on our future with, or, as it became, without, the Society. There were many accusations of lying by both sides, I do know that Janet Wood did not write the truth about Peter. The minutes still stand. When I asked Janet to alter them she replied that I should have to take the matter to Court. We did not have the finances or energy to consider this and the damage was done.

The belief that Peter was opposing the NEC, combined with his association with Brenda Godrich as friend and working colleague, may have accounted for the attitude taken towards Peter by GPFC, he was treated as a spy and part of the ENEMY from October onwards. Peter knew personnel on both sides of what became a great divide, he had worked with them and encouraged many. He volunteered to visit Districts to explain the current proposals, but his offer was rejected. It appears that others, including Jennifer Millest, who could also have helped the situation were rebuffed, so we were not entirely paranoic.

Dave Arthur, editor of Dance and Song, phoned Peter to find out what was happening. Peter was "the only one I can trust". Unfortunately, Peter was not trusted by those in power and knew little of what was going on. Dave Jones, organiser of Bromyard Folk Festival, phoned with support and offered Peter free tickets for a nominal job at the Festival. We were still devastated by what was happening to us and could not face people knowing that Peter was to be sacked. I have wondered since whether our attending the Festival might have drawn support for Peter rather than the House. But Peter was not one to seek support for himself, only for Folk, and we did not go.

FINANCIAL SETTLEMENT

Three weeks after hearing that we had no future within the Society we still had no news on a financial settlement and the worry was telling on both of us. Our job prospects, in an area with 24% unemployment, one of the highest in the country, were very grim, we rarely slept beyond 5 am. I would get up and write long letters which were not posted. The best we had got by September 24th was from the Chairman, in response to a letter I did post, of a "promise that we will be as fair and generous as possible." I also asked for the official reason for Peter's dismissal. Brian replied that it was necessary "to cut back on on all areas of net expenditure." This did not make sense to us. When the Society was suffering from a cash flow problem it had to find extra in redundancy payments. Peter's initial request was to consider retirement in 18 months time. They could have paid his salary for a year, instead of redundancy and retained Peter's experience. The saving of Peter's salary (£8,875 pa) and his part-time secretary, would not have made a highly significant difference to the overall finances of the EFDSS for a year, especially as we had understood that Peter's salary was paid for out of the Sports' Council Grant of £36,000.

The Sports Council was changing its criteria for funding, wanting grants to be given for projects and 'feet on floors'. We argued that the Young Tradition, which had attracted 600+ young people and was on target for becoming a series throughout the country and the Training Days, fulfilled these criteria, but we were told it was not enough. It was quite clear that from Management viewpoint Peter was not doing a good enough job and that his 'image' did not fulfil the needs of the new Director. He had to go. We felt that the financial situation was, in part, a good excuse to get rid of Peter with which the Membership could not argue.

SUPPORT

As news of Peter's redundancy spread we received some welcome letters of support from Members. Two were very precious as they gave back to Peter some feeling of self worth. The first came from Pat Tracey, the clog dancer whom Peter had encouraged to start clogging again. He used her at countless shows, workshops and Festivals and she contributed considerably to the explosion of interest in clog dancing which took place in the '70s. In October 1986 she wrote;

"So it really is true that you have been made redundant. I find it incomprehensible. I should have thought that any programme aimed at putting the Society back on its feet would have needed your services and experience as National Training Officer at its core. . .
Of course, it was you who gave me the incentive to get back into the clog world again. .... I thought it unlikely that I would clog dance again when, out of the blue, came your letter inviting me to put on my clogs and get dancing! Since then the clogs have hardly left my feet and it's been fantastic. Thank you, Peter."

Peter gained great satisfaction that one small act, such as encouraging Pat, could have an enormous

influence. This is where his real talent lay, but it was not tangible.

The second letter came later, in December, from Douglas Kennedy, ex-Director EFDSS, then in his nineties:

"It has been borne in on me that amid all the sound and fury over the future of Cecil Sharp House — you are an innocent victim of the campaign and have been jettisoned cavalierly by the current governing body.
The effect of this on you and your family causes me deep concern and if there is anything I can do to help please let me know. It's twenty-five years since my retirement, the present generation in power hardly know me and I am almost without influence in the Folk world, but I can give you a reference if I were guided in its application to your needs. I will not dwell on the feelings I have over this whole chapter in EFDSS history but some of it is thankfulness that most of the pioneering spirits who were involved are now dead and spared the grief and anger that would fill their breasts if they were here today. The world has changed to such a degree in the last two decades that I have no regrets for myself in being out of things, but I mourn for those left in the melee that dislike everything that goes on now which has no place in the aims of the pioneers."

A fortnight later we had a further letter from Douglas in response to the NEC request for donations to a leaving present for Peter:

"I feel angry as ever more evidence of the misplaced optimism is revealed in the Society's direction over the recent years, but the damage is much worse than the 1940 'Bomb' caused and a damage much more difficult to repair." A bomb fell on CSH in the war. "I am glad to see that the NEC are seeking sources of compensation for your own treatment but I prefer to have my own little private gesture than do anything which the NEC might take as approval of their policies. So please accept the enclosed as a Christmas present not only from us both but colleagues (like Elsie Whiteman) who fortunately are spared the knowledge of the present plight of the EFDSS."

Douglas spent many years and much effort seeking a site and the finances to build Cecil Sharp House as a memorial; to house Sharp's library and as a

Headquarters for the English Folk Dance and Song Society. He died 7th January, 1988, aged 94.

There were other letters and phone calls of support, including friends on Suffolk District, but generally I think members did not believe that Peter was leaving involuntarily.

By November Peter had been told, verbally, that GPFC was considering a lump sum equivalent to a year's take home pay in settlement. This would have been around £6,000 and did not take into account the 'perks' of office rent, £500 pa, Company car and telephone. The sum could have gone towards the pension instead, at best giving a pension of £3,200 pa in 18 months time. As this would not provide for a young family, was only guaranteed for 5 years and would be taxed if either of us were lucky enough to find work, we still rejected the pension idea. Peter wrote to protest that he did not regard the offer of £6,000 as either 'fair' or 'generous'.

ANNUAL GENERAL MEETING EFDSS

At the Annual General Meeting in November we finally talked with the Treasurer, Roger Barnes. The 'meeting' was held in a corner of the cafe during the evening dance because I asked to speak to Roger.

The AGM was particularly trying. The Society was in disarray over the House. Few people seemed to remember Peter was a casualty of the crisis, Griff Jones was the exception, he intended to raise Peter's position at the meeting. The normal business went through. Hugh Rippon, an ex-member of staff, received the Gold Badge for his contribution to Folk. Bill Rutter, who had died in June, was remembered by the Director, Jim Lloyd. Volunteers and NEC were commended by Brian Jones, Chairman. Peter Dashwood sat throughout, after 22 years on the staff, working all hours for meagre pay, knowing that the future held the dole and the end of his career and he did not even merit a mention by anyone. The meeting became a battle ground. Griff didn't get a chance.

Peter was VERY VERY upset. When an NEC member told him to hold a begging bowl to collect for the Society from fleeing members at the end of the meeting, she was lucky he was only rude! Peter had expected there to be thanks as a matter of courtesy, and had composed a short speech for reply. As he did not have the chance to give it, I include it here:

PETER DASHWOOD'S UNDELIVERED SPEECH TO AGM, 1986

"It is a far cry from 1964 when there were 12 staff in the Field and several more artistic staff here in this building (CSH). Today's Gold Medallist, Hugh, was, like myself, described as one of the 'younger' members of staff. Another of the younger set, and friend, was Brian Heaton, who had been responsible for pushing me in the direction of applying for a vacancy in the South. Both Brian and I had been inspired in our earlier days in St. Helens by the hard working and highly respected Ethyl Anderson. At the time I was appointed Nibs was just leaving for America.

One of the saddest things for many of us this year was the death of Bill Rutter and one of my proudest claims is that I was appointed by Bill and worked to him for 5 years at the time when he was developing his own ideas and was for me, and many others, a very exciting period. His many achievements have been catalogued but I shall remember him for his happy knack of involving and identifying the people who were doing the work at grass roots. He always claimed that it was other people who motivated him and in my own simple way I have found this to be true.

The flack is considerable, the pay is low, so many of you must want to know why on earth anyone actually wants to work for an organisation such as this! The rewards in this job come from a quiet satisfaction which only you yourself know about. If I hadn't done this — that would not have happened; what a good thing I encouraged so and so because he or she has gone on to make a significant contribution to the Folk scene. Usually one keeps this knowledge to oneself but it so happens that I have received a letter which confirms one of these personal secrets. When I moved to East Anglia to succeed Molly Du Cane, I was aware, through Albert Hall performances, that there was a talented lady living in the area but somehow had been forgotten. Her letter to me recently tells all:

Here he quotes the letter from Pat Tracey, mentioned earlier.

The Folk world is full of nice people and Janet and I have good reason to be thankful for the friendships enjoyed and for the kindnesses shown at a time in the East when it was most needed, in support of our elder boy, Giles." PED November 1986.

At the evening Gathering, Members actually asked if we would now move house and what would we do in retirement, as if everything was O.K. — it was unbelievable. They had no idea that we had no security, or hope of it. The South had very different unemployment figures and many members have good jobs and pensions. They were in a different world from us.

LEGACIES

By December substantial legacies had been willed to the EFDSS, which saved it from bankruptcy. Jim Lloyd took up his option of withdrawing from the Director's job as the fighting over the House became more entrenched. Colin Maynard, Company Secretary, was made redundant under a cloud of mismanagement. Peter suggested that perhaps it would make sense for him to stay until May 1987, to see the Bristol Young Tradition through; they were paying him redundancy money, a few months could not have made a difference to finance but would have been an enormous difference to the Young Tradition events and to Peter's self-esteem. We heard nothing from Management. The Bristol people told Peter that GPFC were not willing to back the Bristol YT financially, so it was cancelled. All the development work Peter had put in was lost. It was heart breaking. We decided that there was only one thing worse than being made redundant — to remain EMPLOYED by the Society.

SETTLEMENT

In December we actually had in writing the offer of £4,650 + £4,500 ex gratia plus the car, an A registered Ford Orion. Peter asked for a further £2,500 in line with the amount needed to enhance his pension to a reasonable amount, if we had taken that road. It was refused "in consideration of other members of staff who have also suffered redundancy in the recent past." There was no concession to Peter's age or length of service. Of those made redundant with Peter, the Cashier, Receptionist and Assistant Librarian, were all re-employed by the Society, the Assistant Librarian with money from the Folk Music Fund. Only Peter and his secretary remained unemployed. The 'Friends' had succeeded in keeping the House open temporarily, staff was needed to run it.

Peter's secretary, Barbara Wood, worked part-time so did not qualify for redundancy pay. She (and I) received a bunch of flowers on 31st December 1986, that was all. Four years later she still hasn't found another job.

OFFICE

After December 31st 1986 Peter was no longer employed by the EFDSS. This was emphasised when Janet Wood, on instruction from NEC, came on the last day of 1986 to collect the office equipment and files for return to HQ. We couldn't understand what they would do with the files but they were NOT to stay here.

We were allowed to keep the typewriter and dictation machine and a photocopier, which was on hire from a Leeds firm, until it was returned. However, GPFC were not content to stab Peter in the back, they had to twist it as well. Up until the last day we really didn't fully believe, along with many members, that Peter would go. We couldn't envisage life without the Society, despite the bumpy relationship, so Peter asked to stay on the Certification Committee as a volunteer. He asked Janet Wood when they were next meeting. The reply was that Roger Marriott did not want Peter to attend future meetings. Peter received no other notification of what happened on or to the Committee or an explanation.

At this stage we were still under the delusion that the promise of projects would be honoured and felt that the office equipment would also benefit the Society, however Peter's suggestions did not receive replies and the Library was desperate for a photocopier. It was arranged that Ian Russell, Editor of the Folk Music Journal and local Headmaster, should collect this. Unfortunately he rang to collect it during a playgroup session. With 10 small children in our charge we could not leave them and asked Ian to call at a more convenient time. This was translated as a refusal to hand over equipment by Derek Schofield of the Library committee and Peter was accused of 'non co-operation'. It was all too much, not only useless and a spy but also a thief.

ACTING DIRECTOR

The final straw came when the phone rang, by now a novel event, Janet Wood told Peter that Jim Lloyd's resignation had taken effect, he also left December 1986, and Nibs Matthews, the retired Director, had been asked and agreed to take over as Acting Director. I don't remember that Peter could think of anything repeatable to say in reply. We were both stunned and could not believe that any sensible people could take such a retrograde step, yet here was Janet very pleased with what she had to report. I don't know why she felt she should tell Peter, the man she had just thrown out of a job, that the person who 'led' the Society, by default, into the mess it is still in today was now re-employed by the same Society. It spelt the end of the Society, as far as we were concerned. After this we turned away from the Society for our own survival. We did not attend Society Festivals, including Sidmouth and avoided most contact with anything EFDSS. It was all very traumatic.

Four years on I am still angry that PEOPLE could do this to Peter. People who by the constitution of the EFDSS were voluntary; Folk was their hobby, not their livelihood. The new Director, Jim Lloyd was paid but did not have voting rights; no-one else who made long-term decisions on the future of the Society and its staff were supposed to have a monetary interest. In all the time I knew Peter staff were rarely consulted or asked for advice; if it were offered, in the face of blatant stupidity or ignorance, they were firmly told to mind their own business, which they had been doing!

Peter was honest, hard-working and loyal, with considerably more vision than most people gave him credit for, including ourselves. Redundancy brought not only financial insecurity but loss of status, self-esteem, confidence, direction, friends and health. In Peter's words; "Our world fell apart." There followed a year of illness and disillusionment. It was such a waste of knowledge, experience, contacts, enthusiasm, good will. All that work for nothing, not an apology or a thank you.

UNCIVILISED CIVIL WAR

1987 saw open warfare within the Society. The two largest Society Festivals, Sidmouth and Whitby, became independent and no longer have any connection with the EFDSS. Thousands of pounds given in legacies were used up in legal wrangling. A minute proportion would have supported the Young Tradition, but no one was thinking about development work. The only concern was either to sell the House, or

keep it, depending upon which side one was on. There was no course open to the vast majority of members, including ourselves, who wished to see a time of consideration as to the future of the Society. It is a sad story!

Recently I have contacted two people who were part of the GPFC which made the decisions in an attempt to understand their thinking about Peter. Both, independently, went into long explanations about why they thought that selling Cecil Sharp House was correct. Consideration of Peter or his work does not feature in the assessment of that time.

POST SCRIPT

There was a promise that an "Appreciation of Peter Dashwood's Work" would appear in the magazine. Derek Schofield took pictures for it. We wondered who would be asked to do it. To make things easier and to give himself something to do, Peter started writing notes. He sent a draft to the Editor of Dance & Song; Fate struck again; money ran out; the magazine was cancelled. There was no "Appreciation of Peter Dashwood" in the magazine until he was dead. I'm sorry he could not read some of the things written about his work after he died. It would have cheered him up when he most needed it.

*Peter on the day he was made redundant,
15th September 1986 © Derek Schofield*

FINDING A FUTURE, WITH A LIMP 1987-1988

From Grahame's phone call in September the obvious choice for providing an income was that I would return to teaching. We were not happy about this as William was only 4 and needed me. He is a determined child whom Peter found difficult to control, our life was in turmoil, my going out to work would add to this; nevertheless, we had to eat. We were entitled to £48.80 pw Unemployment Benefit, the £9,650 redundancy money was for emergencies.

In the following two years I applied for around 50 teaching posts from Nursery age to top Juniors. I was granted three interviews but no job. We were living in an area of high unemployment, the steel works were decimated, pits were closing, the town was still recovering from the Miner's Strike, our position was not unusual. I had not taught in this area and found it impossible to get a permanent post.

PLAYGROUP

After Peter was redundant, with no obvious job prospects for either of us, we decided to continue running Playgroup together, to give ourselves time to sort out our future. Peter registered as a Playgroup Supervisor, working for me on a voluntary basis. This was not an easy position for him, he had to be second fiddle and he didn't particularly like small children. However, he spent a lot of time in the garden teaching 4 year olds to ride bikes and play football and after a few weeks he saw that what he did had an influence on the children's development and gained pleasure from that.

MORE BAD NEWS

We had hopes that 1987 would prove a better year than 1986 but it didn't start well. Two weeks into January there was a terrible cold spell; my Father went into his loft to thaw the frozen pipes, suffered a heart attack and died in the loft.

My parents lived in Dorset, the roads were blocked with snow and railway points frozen. I couldn't get down for three days. That wasn't all, in the confusion no one remembered the reason Dad had gone into the loft so the water was not turned off. Mother went to my brother's for the evening, when they came back the pipe had burst and the house was flooded, making the electricity unsafe. When I eventually got to my mother's there was not only all the paperwork and clearing up associated with the death of someone who hadn't thrown a bill away in 20 years, but also the house to make habitable, without electricity. It was awful.

Peter stayed at home to look after the boys. He was already depressed by the redundancy, leaving him on his own with two children who were more used to seeing him only at mealtimes, was not a Good Thing. The Irritable Bowel symptoms returned with the extra stress. I returned in a state of physical and mental exhaustion to find Peter expected me to take over as if nothing had happened.

The whole episode was further training for what was in store. It particularly brought home to us our mortality, especially as a friend and key worker for Peter, Mac Jones, had also died of a heart attack, on Boxing Day, 1986. He was 50. It came as a deep shock to many in the Folk world besides ourselves. It was a very depressing time. On the day of Mac's funeral I was travelling south to sort out my Father's.

ADAPTING

From January, Peter decided he would get himself fit and took himself off swimming every morning before breakfast. One day in February he returned complaining of pain in his calf muscles. Within a short time he was confined to bed by a vicious virus. He was in considerable pain with very severe flu-type symptoms and was in bed for weeks. He had never been so ill.

In April he was still too ill to make the adjourned AGM. In response to my protests over Peter's treatment at the AGM in November there was to be official thanks and the presentation of a collection (£500). We were glad of the excuse not to go. The thanks were hollow if they had to be requested and we were beginning to think a little more constructively, the meeting would have re-opened barely healing wounds.

Over Easter, when Peter was recovering from the virus, we planned our first family holiday abroad, using the leaving present. In May we camped in France and Switzerland with Eurocamp for three very happy weeks. We could have gone on for ever. It was idyllic. The illnesses disappeared, the boys rarely argued, the sun shone, perhaps life wasn't too bad! We decided to come again for longer next time.

EFDSS FOLK DIRECTORY

The Society was still in disarray, fighting over Cecil Sharp House, 'Projects' did not appear to be on the agenda; however there was a suggestion from Ted Holt, then Chairman, that Peter tender for the Folk Directory. Peter had edited this in 1984 and 1985, now he offered to overhaul it, giving it a new image and format, if he could have the go ahead by May/June. He put in a tender in line with this. I can't say we were keen; we had too many memories of sitting up to 1 am poring over the wretched thing in the past but we needed money. Peter asked that whoever was deciding the future of the Directory should come back to him to discuss it. They never did.

On the initial approach we understood this was to be a 'Project', it turned out that Peter was one of several approached. We didn't know this until much later when we had tried contacting the Society several times as to the position. It wasn't until the end of October, when no-one could have got the Directory out on time, even in its current format, that Peter phoned John Seabourn, EFDSS Manager, to be told the Directory was being done by someone else. Peter had spent a lot of time and some money in research, the Society did not even have the courtesy to tell him he was not successful in his bid.

OTHER JOBS

There were a few other prospects during the year. He applied for the Lincolnshire Folk Animateur post, which went to Rosie Cross. It was similar to the job he had done in Dorset 20 years before but he wasn't granted an interview.

By Autumn, when we finally realised that the Society was not interested in what Peter had to offer and I hadn't found a job, he applied for a few jobs created by the Community Programme Agency, specifically for the un-employed. This hurt his pride but he persevered, with encouragement. In January 1988 he was actually offered a job with the Scouts under this scheme. This also turned out to be a non-starter as one only qualified if one was receiving Unemployment Benefit, Peter's year ran out a few days too soon!

MONEY

I went to a local financial advisor, to see how best to invest the redundancy money and for advice on the pension. We had decided not to take the pension until we knew our position. If we did get jobs we would have to pay tax on the pension, also, the pension was only guaranteed for 5 years, if Peter died after 5 years of having taken the pension I would get nothing. The difference in our ages meant the Company would not extend the pension to include me. I did not think this a very good deal! We decided to transfer the pension to another Company, in the hope that the return would be greater thus a more reasonable pension in the future, although the conditions would be the same. Again we hit problems. Philip Bloy, once Treasurer for the Society, was the broker, we asked for transfer figures.

These eventually came and we wrote back, but a dishonest postman stole our mail and vital letters went missing, without our being aware. We thought that Philip was being deliberately slow. Because of the delays the pension was not finally transferred until October, and then at a lower figure than had originally been quoted. We were assured this was correct but did not understand the reasoning behind it. The whole episode further soured our relationship with the EFDSS.

I found that because I was working, running Playgroup, I was entitled to Family Income Supplement. This was a life saver and lack of money did not appear to be quite the problem I feared. I had plenty of opportunity to practice frugality as an EFDSS wife but I surprised even myself by having a surplus at the end of 1987, out of an income of, at most, £6,000 pa, for a family of four.

SMILIES' PLAYGROUP

After a year of 'coping' we began to sort ourselves out and plan the future. William was settled in school by Christmas 1987; Playgroup was a nuisance in our home once William had outgrown it; Unemployment Benefit ceased in January and under the new rules on capital we did not qualify for any other benefits; we could either move Playgroup and charge a lot more to pay me properly or set it up with a parent committee while I did supply teaching to keep us.

Many parents were not keen to pay more, although there was support for me. After a lot of heart searching, meetings and looking at various premises, we compromised by moving to a nearby church hall, in April 1988, with my equipment and a voluntary committee with myself as Chairman, Jane MacBride as Secretary and Elaine Brittain as Treasurer, with the new name of "Smilies". We found Supervisors to run it if I should get supply work. We envisaged that it would only run long enough to see those children attending through to school and that I would only have a few days supply. Instead I was offered 3 weeks supply before Playgroup even opened. I was in no position to turn this down, although the committee was upset that I wasn't there for the opening. The 3 weeks extended to 6 and Playgroup found they could cope without me.

WORKING IN FOLK AGAIN

Meanwhile Peter had decided to go self-employed. We had spent a year avoiding most Folk, especially the Society. He was now thinking positively and had various ideas for Family Folk Holidays; Dance Assemblies; working with the local Dance Animateur; Resource lists; Educational Directory; Festival Guide; Folk in the Community Guide; Performers tours;

Yetties in schools; perhaps embarking on a Young Tradition. He had his contacts and some of his old enthusiasm. He was still running the Folk Show at Expo, Peterborough, which was a basis and he was awarded the Enterprise Allowance of £40 pw. With income from supply teaching things weren't too bad. We weren't secure but could live. We even planned another holiday abroad. There was only one problem. In August 1987, at Expo, Peter had started limping.

THE LIMP

Peter didn't know why he was limping but said his shins hurt. He went to the doctor beginning a long association with Dr. Proctor who thought there was a trapped nerve but prescribed no treatment in the hope that it would go away. By Christmas the limp was so marked that we bought a walking stick. The doctor prescribed physiotherapy. Peter went to the hospital twice a week in January, 1988, where he was put on traction for half an hour at a time. Peter felt better afterwards but there was still no real idea as to what was causing the limp, so we carried on under the presumption that it would get better, booking the holiday, moving Playgroup, Peter going self-employed.

By April 1988 things were a lot worse. Peter was having trouble driving as he could not pull his foot away from the clutch pedal. We cancelled the holiday, assuming we would go later. I did not drive at this time. When we had the money to take lessons I didn't have time, and vice versa. After redundancy Peter was depressed enough, if I had taken over another aspect of his life it would have undermined even more of his shattered self-confidence.

In the belief that the problem was orthopaedic Peter paid an osteopath. He went twice but was in such a bad state and pain when he came home I persuaded him not to go again.

In April 1988 Peter went into Rotherham hospital for tests. It was finally confirmed that the limp was not caused by either a slipped disc or trapped nerve. He seemed to come out in a worse physical state, things did not look good. The 'limp' was beginning to affect our lives and we were worried but no-one seemed willing to give us a diagnosis or any suggestions as to what it might be. The next route was neurological investigation. We were now anxious to establish what was causing the problems so we agreed to pay for a private consultation, however I determined to find out what I could while we were waiting. From my experience with Giles I had learnt that doctors are inclined to only tell you what they want, not what you want to know, especially if the condition is regarded as untreatable. There had been no suggestion of anything

serious, Peter did ask about various possibilities that I had read about but was told there was no point in speculating. In view of the final prognosis there was every reason to speculate. It was Peter's life which was slipping away and WE did not even know that it was a possibility. It was OUR life, not the doctors'. I very strongly disagree with the theory that patients should not be given even a hint of bad news until there is no doubt, it may be too late.

During May I spent hours after school in the Library searching through all the medical books I could find. I don't think Peter altogether approved of this so I didn't always tell him where I'd been. He had an old fashioned belief that one doesn't necessarily question the experts. There must also have been the thought that my search might find something nasty. It did. By a process of elimination it seemed as if the 'limp' might be caused by Motor Neurone Disease. I don't think we'd even heard of it, like many other people.

"MND affects the motor neurones (nerve cells controlling muscles in the brain and spinal cord). A progressive breakdown of these cells results in gradual loss of muscle function. Weakness gradually affects all muscles including those that control breathing and swallowing."

"Prognosis: MND is inexorably progressive and invariably fatal. Death usually results from pneumonia and respiratory failure. The final state resulting in anarthia (difficulty swallowing), asphagia (inability to speak) and widespread limb weakness in a patient fully aware of his state, is unbearably distressing for the patient and his family."

I did not tell Peter what I had found at this stage and I never showed him the final paragraph. The phrase tends to haunt one.

HOLIDAYS WITH A LIMP

As Peter's driving was affected we couldn't go abroad, we decided to go to Chester Folk Festival for Spring Bank Holiday as it was all on one site. By now Peter could not walk far and couldn't lift heavy things. He used the walking stick most of the time. Giles and I packed the caravan and, with our two cats, we set off. When we reached the festival site we saw nothing but caravans. Not the place for cats we thought, but we found a spot. Someone helped me with the awning. We had a lovely weekend. The most memorable part was hearing Artisan, an unaccompanied harmony group, for the first time. William, a confirmed non-Folkie at 5 was impressed, "How do they make that noise?!" The 'noise' was wonderful, the presentation smart and professional; they cheered us up. Here was something new and refreshing on the Folk scene. Seeing them helped to inspire Peter to think positively about getting back into Folk. He had spent a lot of his time finding venues and events to encourage the likes of Artisan, a valuable friendship developed.

From Chester we camped on the Wirral visiting a canal museum and other places. Peter could not go on walks, but we had a good time and I tried not to think about what I had discovered in the Library. I could be wrong.

GOLD BADGE

We returned home to find Griff Jones had been trying to contact me. He wanted to propose to NEC that Peter be offered the Gold Badge (presented to people who have made a unique and valuable contribution to Folk) and wished to know if Peter would accept it. I was very glad of the opportunity to tell someone about the seriousness of my suspicions, Gold Badges did not figure very high in importance to me in view of the prognosis of MND, so said they could try asking. It could not make amends for the way he had been treated but at least he figured in someone's thoughts and it may help to bring him back into the Folk world he very much missed before it was too late. I knew it was not an easy suggestion for Griff to make to NEC as those who had sacked Peter were still in power. In the meantime I was sworn to secrecy as we set off for a week in the Lake District, although Peter was somewhat hurt that Griff wanted to speak to me rather than him.

JUNE 1988

We had lovely weather in the Lakes. I missed Peter walking with us but he decided to try sketching. William often joined him while Giles and I walked. At Brockhole, a National Trust house and grounds by Lake Windermere, we borrowed a wheelchair so that Peter could see round the gardens. I had my first experience of how difficult they are to push, especially down hill on a camber. Despite the problems this was a good holiday. It was the last time we went away with Peter without me being shattered.

After we returned home in June Peter had a private consultation with the neurologist. He confirmed that the problem was neurological but would not commit himself to a diagnosis without a special test. There was a long waiting list for the machine which was used. I went back to the Library. I combed through all the books but couldn't find anything other than MND which fitted Peter's symptoms. Multiple Sclerosis was a possibility but the symptoms included sensory loss and problems with sphincter control. It didn't fit Peter's symptoms. This time I photocopied the relevant pages and showed Peter. I didn't think I had the right to keep this knowledge to myself, it would make a big difference as to how we planned our future. Peter reacted to the suggestion of MND by denial. He just could not have anything so awful. He clung to his theory that it was something to do with the virus he suffered from 15 months before. He took up swimming again, every day. He also went to an acupuncturist. He was willing to try anything. This man told Peter that there was nothing wrong with him that was not caused by stress, (this fitted nicely because of the enormous stress caused by the redundancy), and that acupuncture would cure all. Peter believed him. He would not entertain the possibility of MND, this man said it wasn't and the Doctors had not indicated there was anything serious. I found this quite hurtful, he preferred to take anyone's opinion other than mine, while Peter probably thought I was wishing his life away. He was convinced he would get better so we didn't discuss the situation.

I also told Peter about the proposal to present him with the Gold Badge. He was very angry; with NEC, "They cannot buy me off like that!" and with me, "You should know that I don't approve of EFDSS staff getting them, there are too many deserving volunteers." Bill Rutter was one exception Peter allowed. Peter admired Ethyl Anderson, NW Area Organiser, who was also badly treated by EFDSS who refused the Gold Badge; Peter did the same. I was sorry because I saw the 'retirement party', he'd never had, receding. I couldn't see how we could afford to put one on ourselves.

During July physical deterioration seemed to have slowed a little. Peter took this as meaning the acupuncture was working. I tended to think it was more due to the swimming. Ironically Peter was feeling very well, fitter than he'd done for ages both physically and mentally. He began to work out his programme for self-employment. He even tried the Society again with the Young Tradition, as John Seabourn, the Manager, had asked for projects to fulfil the Sports Council criteria. As usual there was no reply.

Also in July the EFDSS sent out the financial figures for the years 1986/87. In it the Administration costs, including redundancy payments, were put at £25,000. This appeared to confirm to the members that Peter had been treated well. Peter was upset by the figures as an unfair representation. He would not let me write to the magazine so I contented myself by writing to prominent members of GPFC: Janet Wood, Chairman, George Deacon, Gordon Ashman and Vic Gammon. To our great surprise we actually received one reply to this letter, from Gordon Ashman, whom we did not know. He wrote positively about reintroducing the Young Tradition. At last Peter was not totally ignored!

SIDMOUTH 1988

In August we went to Sidmouth Festival with the caravan. I was rather unsure about this as Peter was having trouble walking on rough ground and with stairs. There are also terrible parking problems entailing miles of walking between venues. Peter had trouble walking 100 yards.

We arrived early to get a reasonable camping spot and took a tent for Giles so I didn't have to struggle with the awning. It still fell on me to do much of the fetching and carrying and I was quite surprised that we actually enjoyed the Festival. New venues had been taken up in the theatre and Church, both within the walking capabilities of Peter. We solved parking by getting early into the Manor Theatre car park, there was a playgroup for William next door and meals for sale.

Peter spent most of the week at the theatre but did go to a few sessions elsewhere, discussing the future of the Society. He saw little chance of contributing and certainly wasn't called upon, but there were friends around which boosted his confidence. Several asked about his health and to one or two I told my fears. Peter shrugged the problem off saying we were still waiting for tests.

One problem he found he couldn't ignore. I would leave Peter at the Manor Theatre while taking the boys to whatever they wanted to see or to go shopping, there were stairs between the halls or a ramped access outside. Peter relied heavily on his stick, I told him not to attempt the steps without someone to help; one day he did and fell. This frightened him and could have been serious. I think he began to realise then that it was something more than his theory of a virus and things were getting worse. He told Giles not to tell me he had fallen.

Whilst we were at the meetings on the Society we made a useful contact. I took the opportunity to approach Gordon Ashman, from our discussions I was encouraged that there could be a useful partnership of benefit to both the Society and ourselves. We were looking to using Sports and Arts Council grants to support an event based on the Young Tradition. We promised to send ideas and costings after Sidmouth.

HALLAMSHIRE HOSPITAL

We came home to good weather, planning that we would do some gardening before setting off again on holiday. In a couple of days we had a phone call from the Hallamshire Hospital, Sheffield; someone had cancelled their appointment, "Could Mr Dashwood come in on Tuesday?" This was the GREAT TEST. There was no reason why he couldn't go. This is what we had been waiting for. I wish we'd been somewhere else. On the night before Peter went into hospital I knew life could never be the same for us. Peter remained, as ever, optimistic.

He took himself in for a few days of tests on Tuesday. He was there at 9 am. The test was done by 9.30. For the next three days —- nothing! I cleared out the shed, the garage, washed the kitchen floor, yelled at the kids. The waiting was HELL. It was much worse for Peter who was amongst strangers, with serious conditions, with nothing to do and no one who would tell him what was happening.

On Thursday I was asked to go into the hospital on Friday so we could hear the results of the test together. This was the first indication to Peter by anyone other than me, that his condition was serious. Do they think that calling a spouse in doesn't spell out DISASTER!? I did not sleep; I should have been with Peter. This was intense cruelty and I don't think they have any idea that they inflict it. Why couldn't Peter have come home after the test?

DIAGNOSIS

I left William with a friend, Giles on his own and caught the buses to the hospital. We were seen by a Registrar. "The tests show that Peter has Motor Neurone Disease. Do you know what Motor Neurone Disease is and what it entails?" I was well read by now so said I did. He drew a little diagram of how nerve cells affect muscles, advised us to go on a world cruise and bid us good day. "Contact the hospital if you have any questions".

Peter really did not take it in. The idea was too new to him. One of the patients on the ward had said to him the previous day, not knowing why Peter was in, "Pray that you never get Motor Neurone Disease, that is the worst thing possible." It wasn't a good start.

We went back to the ward. What do we do now? They sent for a physiotherapist to talk to us. She gave a little advice on keeping joints moving. We could have stayed to see the Consultant when he did his rounds but that was some time off and there didn't seem any point. We just wanted to get home and try to make sense of it all. Our world had fallen apart again but I was determined we would make the best of it. Time was not on our side this time.

LIFE AFTER DIAGNOSIS

We arrived home calm, at last we knew what was wrong with Peter, but in a state of shock. It felt as if we had been abandoned in a strange place and told to find our way home without a map or signposts or anyone to ask. We were entering a different world — of the disabled.

The hospital, although they did say to phone if we had any questions, had given no indication that there was anyone to help, if there was we would have to contact them ourselves. We were not in a fit state to make any sort of sensible assessment of our needs, there should be contact from the hospital within a few days. The problem with people new to disability is that they do not know what questions to ask, therefore are not given the answers. It is Catch 22.

Today, 15.1.92, I have heard of an MND patient diagnosed 15 months ago, who is confined to bed, upstairs, until two neighbours assist getting him to the toilet. His elderly wife washes, dresses, feeds and toilets him with no other help. He has no equipment, no statuary help, no Attendance or Mobility Allowance. When the doctor was called in by a volunteer his defence for his ignoring these people was that they did not ask. They did not know they could ask!

We were eventually to find ourselves in a system of doctors, nurses, therapists, social workers and assessors who had little more idea about MND than ourselves. Motor Neurone Disease is not well known, despite there being as many people contracting it per year as Multiple Sclerosis, MND sufferers don't live long enough to have an impact on the community. Although 5 years is given as the average life expectancy, 2 to 3 years is more likely and many patients spend that time housebound.

HOME

Peter was doing his best to come to terms with the diagnosis. He told Giles that the hospital had found that it was VERY serious. I wasn't sure that this was the right time to say anything to the children, I wanted things clearer in my own mind. However Giles was 16 and knew two children at school who had died from Muscular Dystrophy. I think he realised what Peter meant. We told William, 6 years old, that Daddy wouldn't get any better. This was accepted. There wasn't anything one could say.

In the afternoon, by one of the strange quirks of fate, Brenda Godrich phoned us from Cecil Sharp House to ask if Peter was interested in some development work for the Society. Brenda was an elected member of NEC by now and on the Activities Committee. It was the first definite offer of work from the EFDSS in 2 years and it came on the day that we'd been told he would soon not be alive, never mind work! It gave Peter something positive to think about. When he looked at the proposed event he thought it had all the hall marks of another EFDSS disaster and wrote to advise Brenda of his fears. So far as I know, the event was cancelled. At the same time he wrote out his proposals for an event which he sent to Gordon Ashman, with a copy to Brenda. It is difficult to remember that we started in such a positive mood but we heard nothing from Gordon. I was surprised at this as he had given the impression that he was courteous, even if he disagreed with what you were doing and he had seemed to be keen on Peter's ideas. I was disappointed that nothing came of it, especially as Peter needed something positive in his life but we were accustomed to the lack of response from the EFDSS so did nothing more.

TELLING FRIENDS

Within the next few days I went into my usual mode after bad news and wrote to close friends to tell them the latest. I hoped that by talking to people we might get things a bit clearer. Eileen, my College friend and her husband took the day off work to come to see us a few days after diagnosis. We hadn't seen them for a long time, we enjoyed their company and they were usually very helpful in the garden. We both looked forward to their visit. It turned out to be a mistake. I badly needed the chance to talk to someone and, without thinking of what it was doing to Peter, worked out in the garden, cutting the hedge, which needed doing, leaving Peter on his own, reinforcing his disabilities. Part of our friendship with this couple, as well as our marriage, was based upon doing things like the garden together, yet Peter was now excluded. At mealtimes I found we were talking as if Peter was not there. Later Peter said that Eileen would not look him directly in the eyes. It was a very bad start to beginning an acceptance of the future and I did not help.

ORGANISING LIFE — AGAIN

There were various decisions to make, most urgent was Peter's self-employment, the Registrar had suggested working as long as possible but the work Peter hoped to do entailed travel, dancing, seeing people, all this had to be built up. We had no idea what time scale we were working to. I rang the hospital.

"What type of MND does Peter have?" (There are different types with different prognosis.) Peter had the 'progressive' type. This, I thought, was slightly better news, "Progressive Muscular Atrophy", according to my book, "runs the most prolonged course; death usually occurs in 8 to 10 years from the onset." It was wrong.

"How long had Peter had it?" Probably 18 months to 2 years, ie from the time of redundancy.

"What is the likely course?" One cannot predict.

There must have been lots of other things I should have asked but I couldn't think what. This news did appear to give us SOME time. We were thinking along the lines of 3-5 years. Even so the work that Peter had planned seemed a non starter. If he had been established in a job it would have been different but we were entering new territory without knowing if Peter could literally stand up. If we did not continue with self employment we lost the £40 pw Enterprise Grant and any earnings. I still had no permanent job and it was becoming obvious Peter would be needing a lot of care. Would we be able to afford nursing care?

I went to the Citizen's Advise Bureau to discover our rights and came back with a load of pamphlets which one needed a degree to understand. I ploughed through them, just as I'd done over redundancy. It did not look good. If Peter went 'sick' he would qualify for just £30 pw sickness benefit for 6 months until he could go onto Invalidity Benefit, which was slightly more generous. We did not qualify for Income Support because we had more than £6,000 capital. This all needed careful consideration. With our lives in turmoil, our financial future, as well as everything else, looked extremely bleak.

SMILIES PLAYGROUP

My thoughts turned to the Playgroup I had set up in the Church Hall, which had been running for one term. I was still Chairman, some parents were keen that I should return as supervisor, I needed moral support from the friendships I had made through the group. A combination of earnings from Playgroup and Benefits would give us enough to live on and enable me to care for Peter and there would be back-up for emergencies when I may be unable to work.

I consulted the Officers, Jane McBride and Elaine Brittain, who were also friends. They thought that it was an idea worth putting to the Committee in order to have me back teaching their children. I worked out a scheme whereby I would take over from the committee all the administrative work and run up to 4 sessions per week for a salary of at least £2,600 pa. (approximately 2/3rds of supply rates.) This involved putting up the fees from £1.80 to £2.30 per session and my payment being more than the other supervisors for the extra work, for use of my equipment and my name, and because it was our only income. I put it to the

Committee, which included current Supervisors, that if they could not pay me I had no alternative but to return to supply teaching and cease all involvement in Playgroup.

There was a lot of soul searching and meetings, it was not the ideal solution I had naively considered. The supervisors who had coped in my absence, while I was teaching, were somewhat aggrieved that I should suddenly decide I wanted to take over. I admit this had not occurred to me. Only one, Anne Wood, with whom I had run my original Playgroup, was willing to give up her sessions. This put us all in a quandry, so I withdrew my offer for so many sessions and offered to do the administration taking over as supervisors left. The Committee decided they could continue doing the administration on a voluntary basis in order to save increasing the fees. In other words, they could manage without me.

The officers did feel guilty about this and offered the playgroup back to me to run as a private business. If our life had not been in such turmoil I may have considered this more seriously but the rent for the hall took a substantial part of the income as a private business I would be unable to fund raise or qualify for grants, thus fees would have to be higher than £2.30, which was already regarded as too high. Two of the supervisors had indicated they would leave if I took over their jobs, which would have left me without enough back-up. I did not feel in a position to take up this offer and withdrew the whole proposal for the sake of the Playgroup. Thus the scheme was not put to the AGM which met in September. I returned to supply teaching.

To say that I was upset is an understatement. It was the redundancy all over again, on a much reduced scale, by people who were aware of Peter's condition and prognosis. I resigned as Chairman before the AGM in order to give time to find a replacement. Playgroup had taken the decision it could not afford me, I was not willing to give my services free. I also decided not to attend the AGM. Playgroup had to take its own course without me. This upset the committee. I gathered some of the new comers thought that as they were working voluntarily so should I, but they had a vested interest as their own children attended. My main interest was to provide my family with income. I also asked for payment for some of the equipment and the return of the rest as they replaced it. From this time the relationship with Playgroup friends deteriorated, the support I had hoped for was not there when life became really tough. Only one visited Peter during his illness. In this life I have learnt that one is basically on one's own. Support comes from unexpected sources, which one generally has to seek.

LEARNING TO DRIVE

In August we had more problems. One of the most pressing was that Peter was our only driver. We had no idea how long he could continue driving; I must learn to drive. We started by Peter showing me how to start and stop in Asda car park. I was very nervous and not at all keen. I started lessons. The instructor took me to Herringthorpe Valley Road, with lorries racing by. I was terrified. I found another instructor.

DEPRESSION

A combination of the diagnosis, our friends' reaction and my learning to drive had a disastrous effect on Peter. The Irritable Bowel symptoms returned with vengeance, Peter took to his bed. He had pains all over, he felt as if his head was about to burst, he could not breathe; classic stress symptoms. I told him this but he thought I was just being unsympathetic; he was really ill and I didn't understand. He did not realise I had the same whenever Giles went in for an operation or when my Father died, but I had not been able to go sick, I was needed. Peter felt he wasn't, worse, he was to be a burden. Peter stopped driving, would not go out. Learning to drive became more important but when I went out for lessons Peter got into a terrible state. I felt this was blackmail to stop me driving and for the sake of the family was not willing to stop.

MEDICAL HELP

We tried contacting people who might help. Dr. Proctor was the obvious start. His reaction was that this was 'something we had to go through'. I was to go along with whatever Peter wanted. I did not find this very helpful and resented the assumption that I and the boys were not suffering also. I did persuade him that Peter needed crutches and that he should order a wheelchair; in his present state Peter was not safe walking with only a stick. The doctor was unsure about either as Peter had not asked for them. I maintained that it was unlikely that he would request equipment, as that meant giving in. I also was aware that it could take some time for equipment to arrive. I felt that it was better to have things waiting than to be struggling. Dr. Proctor must have agreed for I collected crutches in August, the first of a whole array of equipment from Nursing Aids at Doncaster Gate Hospital.

We were given medication for the bowel symptoms but it did no good, the cause was not physical. At one point Peter was in such a state of pain he did not know what to do with himself; he phoned the surgery late at night getting the doctor on call. He was very short in his answer, "Take an aspirin." The medical profession could not help us.

MNDA BRANCH

We tried the local branch of the Motor Neurone Disease Association. This is run by volunteers. The person Peter rang was very sympathetic and he talked to him for a long time; this seemed helpful. However, when Peter phoned again the recipient was less sympathetic to spending hours on the phone, so that trail proved a cul de sac.

YOGA

We tried yoga. The girl was very good and felt she could do something for Peter but it proved difficult for him to manage her steps and one day he fell. She offered to come to the house and lent him a tape. I felt that if he wanted her to come that was fine but HE had to arrange it. I had full responsibility for the house, garden, children, cooking, cleaning, finances, etc. he could sort himself out. He did not contact her to come. This was a VERY unhappy time for us.

CONFLICTS

He was still swimming daily at the Leisure Centre, he managed to drive himself the short distance and it was very beneficial as he relaxed in the water; he treated it as a lifeline. Although he could drive to the pool and the Doctor's he could not drive the family anywhere, so I did shopping using the bus and for August we went nowhere. This was very hard on the boys, it was difficult to understand why we could go to Sidmouth and nowhere else when there was no great change physically in their Dad. I was beginning to be torn between children and husband.

CRISIS

A crisis was looming as August Bank Holiday approached, the time for Expo. The boys wanted to go, desperately. I wanted to go to have some semblance of normality and to see friends; this was no fun. Peter did not want to go. He was convinced no-one would speak to him. There was some justification for this after our friend's reaction and the attitude of many following redundancy. This would not have been the case at Expo and I was sure it would be good for him to go. About a week before Expo we went to see Dr. Proctor as an emergency, Peter was in such pain with the Irritable Bowel. This time Dr P. said that it was "about time I drove, what was I hanging about for?" I felt this was very unfair considering the traumas I was going through with Peter. I'd like to see a man do what I did! Dr. Proctor's psychology at that time was all wrong for me. If people say, I don't know how you cope, aren't you marvellous? I'll continue with renewed vigour. If they say I ought to be doing this, even if I am, I resent it. To be fair Dr. Proctor did not know me at the time and later was very understanding, but initially I was not impressed. I was hoping for some support from him for going to Expo, as I believed it would help Peter to get back to some sort of normality, but he repeated that we should only do what Peter wanted. Blow that! it was time the boys and I came into the reckoning. We had tried this treading softly for 3 weeks, (was it only three weeks?! it still feels like a lifetime) and it was getting worse. I decided we were going to Expo.

Peter did his best and agreed to go. Just in case of problems I arranged with Peter and Angela Davis that Giles could go on his own. Peter said he would drive. We packed the van and set off on Saturday. We got as far as Firbeck, a few miles down the road. Peter was then in great stress and could not drive at all. The boys were distraught with disappointment. I called at a house to phone the RAC to get us home. The residents were more than kind and drove us and caravan back.

Peter went to bed. 'I did not understand and the doctor had said he needn't go.' I phoned the Davises who volunteered to fetch us and put us up for the weekend. Angela sped up the motorway; Giles and I reorganised our luggage; Angela arrived expecting a quick meal and a return journey but Peter was having real problems; he couldn't walk, eat, breathe. We got him to walk round and talked to him but could not get him in the car. He wanted me to stay with him and let the boys go. I had had enough. I could see no future in carrying on as we were, I had to get away to break the cycle. If I stayed I would deeply resent it, I hoped that if I did go he might follow, but was not convinced. It was AWFUL.

I asked my sister to come over from Grimsby to look after Peter, he could not be left on his own. My brother-in-law came, rather overwhelmed by the situation, no-one had realised how bad it was but he coped extremely well. He agreed to take Peter swimming to help him relax and to bring him part way down the motorway the next day. The boys and I left with Angela in the evening. I felt as if I was betraying Peter. It was horrible but I had to do it. Peter interpreted us going as meaning we didn't give a damn about him. Geoff hid the sleeping pills which had been prescribed at some point.

EXPO '88

It was a great relief to be away from the atmosphere in the house. We arrived at Expo as the evening show was finishing. Everyone was so warm and welcoming, I had to get Peter there the next day. I phoned when we got to

Angela's to say we were safe and that he would be O.K. if he came. He agreed to come down after Geoff had taken him swimming. We arranged a meeting place. Somewhat to my surprise they arrived, late, because Peter could not cope with speed, but he was there. He was still having very stressful symptoms but we got him to Expo. It was quite an achievement.

Peter was welcomed with open arms. He talked to everyone about anything, he was the centre of attention. The event he had organised was its usual great success, even without him being there at the start, which was a credit to his organisation. He enjoyed himself. There were plenty of people able to take over responsibility for Peter, so the weekend was not too bad for me and I could give some time to the boys.

Most useful was talking to John Tether (Retired Headmaster, organiser of School's Radio Country Dancing and had a major input in Sidmouth, Folk Camps and Halsway Manor). He was an old friend, although not particularly close, had come to Expo as compere for many years. We had noted a deterioration in his health and I suggested to Peter he should not give John so much to do, but Peter said John would say if it was too much. I think he was too proud for that.

I'd had reason to be grateful to John in 1987 when he listened at great length, with patience and understanding, as Peter told of his bitterness over his treatment when made redundant. It was the only time Peter really talked about the redundancy to anyone other than me. In 1988 John proved even more useful. Sixteen years previously he had undergone by-pass surgery for his heart at a time when the techniques were new and few patients survived. He reckoned he'd had 16 extra years. We assumed that his ill-health was associated with this but not so. He told me that he had been diagnosed as having cancer 6 years ago, when he was given 2 years to live. We'd had no idea. I told Peter. This had a dramatic effect. Here was someone in a similar position to himself who gave all the appearance of enjoying life. Not only that, it did not fit the image we had of John of being fairly egotistical, here he was thinking of others. This revelation and the subsequent talks with John changed Peter's attitude to the future completely. I shall always be grateful to him.

John Tether died ten days after Peter of heart failure.

Peter Davis drove us home in a much better state than we left. The Davis's gave us a lot more support in the following months. Fortunately they still survive!

MOTOR NEURONE DISEASE, EQUIPMENT and FOLK
SEPTEMBER 1988

The boys returned to school. Our summer had gone, precious time had been lost which we could not have again. It still saddens me. If one is to receive awful news avoid the summer. It transpired that there were professionals who might have helped but they were on holiday. I still feel that counselling would have helped us. We were not able to give each other the support that was needed and set off on different tracks. An outsider may have been able to guide us at least on parallel courses. Peter said about counselling the following year, "It would be to confirm that Janet was doing the right things and to confirm to ME that she was doing the right things; getting the right equipment and about the family. It was me against the family. That was how it was."

To those who have to pass on bad news, have something to give out as a reference, a booklet with contacts and advice would have been a start. Sympathy and being told you just have to learn to cope is NOT good enough when it should have been obvious from the symptoms Peter was experiencing, we were not coping. Advise to go on a world cruise is frivolous. It may help the doctor who has to give the bad news but serves no purpose to people who have no money.

MOTOR NEURONE DISEASE ASSOCIATION

We did get the patient's pack from the Motor Neurone Disease Association, but it was not particularly helpful. It should have included more illustrations and had a better layout. There was too much small print in a small space. The information that was given was very generalised and for the later stages of the disease. It would have been useful to have manufacturer's adverts, to show what is available. I spent hours searching for this information. Most people have no idea of the vast world of the disabled, thus miss out making their lives even more difficult. Time is at a premium with MND. One needs all the help one can get immediately, if not before.

On September 8th we had our first meeting with Jane Connell, Regional Advisor for the MNDA. She was very useful as she had first hand knowledge of MND and we both found it a relief to talk to someone who knew our problems. However her Area was very large so we were unlikely to see her often. We received minutes of the South Yorkshire Branch MNDA. We were not keen to attend meetings for fear of seeing sufferers in later stages, we did not want to see what was in store for us, in fact the only times I did attend

meetings there were no MND patients present. The minutes were not encouraging, they consisted mainly of fund raising, as was the National Newsletter; this was very worthwhile, but not the information we needed.

BENEFIT FUND/GOLD BADGE

When the diagnosis was known the Folk world went into another gear. Griff Jones suggested to the September NEC meeting of the EFDSS, that they start a Benefit Fund for Peter and re-offer the Gold Badge. Janet Wood, Chairman, thought it unlikely that Peter would accept the Gold Badge, but Roger Wilkins asked her to advise Peter that NEC would like him to reconsider his refusal. This was agreed. They also passed round a hat which I believe collected £250 from NEC members.

Our attitudes differed again over the Gold Badge. I felt nothing had changed and that Peter should still reject it as he had done before. He thought it would be discourteous if he accepted the Benefit Fund, "One had to go along with the system," so agreed but reserved the right to choose where the Gold Badge would be presented. If the EFDSS redundancy settlement had been higher, or the promise of 'projects' been kept, the need for charity might have been avoided but we knew we could not afford the equipment and care we would need in the future so were grateful for the offer of the Fund.

From this time we also differed in the way we saw the redundancy and MND. Peter separated the two, redundancy had taken his way of life, MND would take his life. He came to terms with redundancy because he had to cope with MND; from then on he did not feel anything like the bitterness and anger which he had done and I still do. I believe the redundancy and MND are linked, Peter did not; that would have been too much for him.

A BREAK

By September we had come to initial terms with the inevitable future of MND and we decided it wasn't going to ruin our present life. With Peter in better health, we decided to have a few days away. Not the world cruise, we still had no money, but we did need a break. We now needed more specialised accommodation as Peter was having increasing difficulties walking. I visited DIAL, (Disablement Information & Advise Lines) in the Library; they loaned me RADAR'S Holiday Guide for the Disabled.

It proved useful so I bought a copy from W.H. Smiths. This was a very GOOD BUY, not only did it have lists of suitable accommodation by geographical areas, it also had adverts for all sorts of equipment and organisations. It opened up a completely new world.

We decided to take a short break at Centre Parc, in Nottinghamshire. It was not too far to drive, there was plenty for the boys to do and swimming for Peter. There were drawbacks; there was a lot of walking involved getting from the chalets to the pool areas and being self catering was not a break for me from cooking, however we got a reduced booking, at short notice and went for a long weekend on September 9th.

We borrowed a wheelchair from Centre Parc. This enabled us to get Peter around, cars are not allowed, but it was exhausting to push. The swimming pool sections were a Wonderland, however the main pool was only 84F, not around 90F which Peter needed. There were warmer areas but only reached by numerous steps. Peter was on crutches, the floors wet, it was a terrible effort to get up them. Nevertheless, it was a successful break, the boys were happy and we were all able to relax, at least some of the time. Peter wrote about our visit:

"Shortly after diagnosis we took ourselves off to a semi-tropical paradise, near Mansfield, (of all places). We were enjoying the atmosphere around the swimming pool and I limped into a nearby jacuzzi. Shoulder to shoulder with the other occupants;

jacuzzis are very matey places and, by way of opening up a conversation, the woman next to me said, "I believe you can get Legionnaires Disease from these things." As one coming to terms with a terminal illness I was inclined to say, 'Who cares?!' It did make us think that Life would get us one way or another!"

The Society paid for our visit from the Staff Benevolent Fund. If we had known how much would be raised for Peter's Benefit Fund we might have been more ambitious.

GILES — NEWMAN LODGE

At the beginning of the term Giles' school suggested that he would benefit from going to stay in the Residential Lodge, attached to School, they felt it would develop his independence. I was not at all keen. I didn't think I was possessive but I found it very hard that while we were coming to terms with the problems presented with MND a vital member of the family was missing. In times of stress one tends to gather family together.

Giles had always preferred that his Father or I do things, because we could do them better. We had many stand up battles with Giles to get him to do simple jobs around the house. Now Peter was unable to do many things as he deteriorated physically, I could have done with Giles to help me. However Giles was keen to try the Lodge, I would not stand in his way. He stayed from Monday to Friday from September to the following April. They did take him to a Youth Club and on trips but we did not notice a great difference in his independence.

OUT-PATIENTS

On September 22nd we had an appointment to attend the Hallamshire Hospital. We expected to be told if the disease was speeding up, or what we might expect in the progression, how we should prepare for the next stage; some sort of information. It was quite an effort to get in on crutches, we sat for ages in dismal and depressing surroundings, then saw the same Registrar, (Peter only saw the consultant when he paid). He asked if the disease had progressed and how was Peter, without any real interest. We asked about what we should expect for the future. The answer was that no-one can predict and he was not going to speculate. Then we were dismissed with: "Come back and see us sometime." WHY?!!!

On the plus side the Hallamshire provides a physiotherapist, Jane Petty, to visit all MND patients diagnosed at the hospital. This is a very useful service. She only did physiotherapy if asked but had a great fund

Peter with William at Centreparc, September 1988

of knowledge on the problems we might encounter. She was on holiday when Peter was diagnosed, so also visited us for the first time in September. She ordered an electric, elevating and reclining chair from the MNDA, to assist Peter in standing. William loved it

WHEELCHAIR

Soon after we returned from Center Parc the DHSS wheelchair arrived. It had taken around 6 weeks from ordering, an average time. To those who may need a DHSS chair, order early. At Center Parc we had used a chair which Peter could propel by pushing the back wheels. This gave a little independence and was a great help to me, as chief pusher, especially on hills. The doctor had ordered a chair with small back wheels, which could only be moved by an attendant, in the knowledge that Peter's arm muscles would deteriorate and he would THEN be unable to push a chair. However, at that moment in time, which was the only one that really mattered to us, Peter could manoeuvre a chair on his own, so this chair was taking away MORE of Peter's independence than was necessary and mine! I was annoyed that anyone had made decisions without consulting us. I had assumed, in my ignorance, that the doctor knew what he was doing. NEVER make this mistake. Question, seek out information for yourself, check every order. If it is possible for there to be a mistake there will be.

I moaned to Jane Petty. She ordered a self-propelling chair. We retained this manual chair as Peter kept the use of his arms for a long time. It did prove useful if we wanted to go any distance from the car as I could push Peter then he get out and walk in the building, or where ever, without becoming exhausted. The same cannot be said for me. The chair was very heavy, we had a Ford Orion, this has a high sill to the boot. I dreaded getting the chair in and out. If you are to be disabled, marry an Amazon, not a 5' 2" weakling, and don't buy a Ford Orion.

ORANGE BADGE

At Center Parc we could have used the car if Peter had been registered disabled. After reading the Radar Holiday Guide, I persuaded Peter we should apply for the Orange Disabled Badge for the car from Social Services. He didn't think he was bad enough to qualify but I could see that we would be split as a family because Peter could not walk far and neither of us liked the chair. Life could be easier as we would be able to park more conveniently. To his surprise we were granted one.

This contact also opened up new avenues. Peter's file with Social Services had him down as a Playgroup Supervisor. This surprised the Social worker after seeing him limp into the building from a wheelchair, but there was nothing else on his file. It was now seven weeks since diagnosis, an age in the life of MND. We had assumed that Social Services were informed about new cases by either the hospital or GP, obviously not so. She made out a referral form for the Occupational Therapist, an invaluable contact in the future.

OCCUPATIONAL THERAPIST

Diane Peake came to assess our needs on September 30th, she returned the next day and it was as if Christmas had arrived early. She brought: — legs to raise a chair in height, to make it easier for Peter to stand; — a bath board and seat, to help get in and out of the bath; — a raised toilet seat; — long-handled tap turners, to fit on the taps Peter used; — 'ultra-lite' cutlery, rocker knife and a tea-pot tipper as his grip was affected. All, except the last item, proved useful for some time. We couldn't hit the cups when pouring with the tea-pot tipper!

Like ourselves, Diane did not appreciate the rapidity of the 'progress' of the disease. There should be more liason between professionals, the hospital should contact sources of help for patients automatically and give information to the professionals, even if they feel the patients aren't able to cope with it. I'm sure Doctors did know the likely progress yet we all seemed to be working in the dark, at the time. Also, the MNDA Professionals' Booklet could be better publicised, although, incredibly, there wasn't one for Occupational Therapists at the time! Equipment is ESSENTIAL to coping with the disabilities caused by MND.

We were beginning the phase of being on the books of several professionals but with no one person in charge. If we had lived in Sheffield the first professional to have contact with a patient, whether they be Physiotherapist, Speech Therapist, Social worker, Occupational Therapist etc. would have been our Contact person. This would be very useful. We found that much work was duplicated, partly because I would contact anyone who might help in the hope that one would respond, but also because there was no one person responsible for us. Sometimes they all responded, sometimes none. One has to shout loud, long and frequently in order to achieve action.

STAIRLIFT AND RAMP

Structural alterations to a house, including anything attached to a wall, come under the Department of Environmental Health. In October Technical Advisors came to recommend adaptations to the house. We had two major problems, getting up stairs and in and out of the house, as we had steps to all exits. Peter reported after their visit that we could not have a ramp to the patio doors at the back, the most convenient exit for him, as there was not enough room for the correct gradient, 1 in 20. I found this hard to believe as we have a fair sized garden, but presumed they knew what they were doing. I had not learnt at this stage that this is a basic mistake.

Peter had put some thought into his future needs and suggested that he would require a stairlift that will take a wheelchair, for when he reached the stage of being unable to stand. I was proud of him for this, it could not have been easy to think into the future, when he was still walking independently with crutches and going upstairs with me supporting him. The type of lift he required is expensive, around £5,000. Nothing seems to have been decided at this stage.

BENEFITS

In the Autumn of 1988 we were living on sickness benefit of £31.30 per week and supply teaching earnings. We had opted to go onto sick pay at the end of August. Peter was not officially employed again. This was bad for his morale but it was obvious my days of being able to work were also numbered; we needed to start on the six months qualifying period for invalidity pension as soon as possible. Once I stopped earning our income would be very low at a time we needed more not less. I looked at other benefits to which Peter should be entitled; however, our success with the Disabled Badge was not to be repeated with the applications for Mobility and Attendance Allowances.

In 1988 there was a qualifying time of six months for these benefits. When one has only £31 secure income per week six months seems like six years. No concessions were made to the type of illness one was suffering from. It appeared to us that the State hoped that one would die in the qualifying time then they would be saved from having to pay. This rule has changed.

We did not realise the difficulties ahead, the emotional upsets in store or the traps that are set. We innocently put in our claims in the belief that because Peter could hardly walk and that I was now spending much of my life caring for him we were entitled to both Mobility and Attendance Allowances.

On September 26th 1988 we attended the DHSS Assessment Centre in Sheffield, for Mobility Allowance. We parked as close as possible. I helped Peter out of the car, as he could not stand up on his own from so low down and organised the crutches. He managed to get into the building, after being helped up a steep step. Fortunately there was a lift.

The doctor examined him, noting aloud that there was some wasting of muscles. He asked Peter to walk up and down a corridor and some stairs. Peter could manage the corridor with crutches, it was uneven ground and cambers that defeated him but these did not count in the test. The steps petrified me; at home Peter did not attempt steps without me going up behind him in case he fell. I told this to the Doctors. He obviously thought I was either neurotic or lying and insisted Peter try. It was a tremendous effort but he did it. He felt he'd really achieved something. We were not awarded the Mobility Allowance. The tests do not take into account that human nature will strive to do the best even when they are penalised for doing so. It would have hurt Peter more to have failed to climb those bloody stairs.

With Jane Petty's advice and support we appealed. I had also bought RADAR'S DISABILITY YEAR BOOK giving advice about all benefits associated with disability, from DIAL's office. This book proved invaluable in dealing with Authorities. If you know anyone even mildly disabled BUY IT.

The doctor who assessed for Attendance came to the house, in order to see the circumstances and equipment available. The initial claim was also inevitably rejected.

GOLDEN OLDIES

In October Peter had to decide where the presentation of the Gold Badge would take place. Traditionally this is during the Annual General Meeting of the EFDSS. In 1988 the AGM was to be held in Bristol, a long way for us to go and the meeting was likely to be argumentative. Peter did not wish to be party to any unpleasantness, especially as he found all the feuding very upsetting. The current Chairman was Janet Wood, she was one of those who had made decisions which were detrimental to Peter. The Chairman usually presents the badge, we were not having that. Also, Ursula Vaughan-Williams, widow of Ralph, was being awarded a Gold Badge, she is a Vice-President of the Society . Her presentation would take place at the AGM, Peter did not wish to be associated with this.

By October, we discovered that our letter to Gordon Ashman, Vice-chairman EFDSS, proposing development work for the EFDSS, had been stolen by another dishonest postman and were once again in communication with him. I put to Gordon our idea of running our own event based on people and teams with whom Peter had been associated. He was encouraging so we started the organisation.

At first Peter thought we should run it at Cecil Sharp House, in London, as it was relatively accessible from all over the country and free. However, holding it at the House would probably stop many people from attending, feelings were very high and it would NOT be accessible for Peter. There is a huge flight of steps to get in and more inside.

We went to Bedworth Festival, stayed with Griff Jones and looked for a hall. We decided on the Benn Hall in Rugby. It was central, lots of parking, lovely hall and had disabled facilities. Peter was not the only one who might need them, the membership is ageing. Now Peter had a role and he set about organising his event which he called 'Golden Oldies'.

The Amstrad 9512 word processor, purchased when Peter first went self-employed, now came into its own. Letters could be written and duplicated with relative ease. It was a very good buy as it kept Peter 'working'. He wrote to many of the teams and individuals he had worked with and we circulated many people who might not hear about the event through the EFDSS, some had resigned or let their membership lapse. It was good to be in contact with folk again.

HODDESDON CROWNSMEN'S FEAST

In October we were invited as Guests of Honour at Hoddesdon Crownsmen Feast, in Hertfordshire, in recognition of all the assistance Peter had given them in the past. This really pleased Peter, here was recognition from the ordinary people he worked with. I persuaded my sister to have the boys for the weekend. We stayed with Brenda and Geoff Collins because they had a downstairs bedroom and toilet. I hardly knew them before their invitation to stay, afterwards they kept in touch fairly regularly. Some of Hoddesdon were not sure what to say to Peter but he was his usual jovial self in public and the ice was soon broken.

PETER'S SPEECH:

"I have had the pleasure of booking The Crownsmen for many events but especially the Folkeasts, the Felixstowes, the Expos and the Instructional Days at Cecil Sharp House and elsewhere. Its true to say I've missed you when you haven't been there. I've been especially proud, too, when I've seen you 'abroad' at Sidmouth or at The Albert Hall or at those very serious competitions at Derby. You have been very supportive to the EFDSS and to myself. On District Committees (I just have to mention Dave Hislop and Mac Jones here, fellow sufferers with me in early Hertfordshire days). Taking on Hertford Folkeast organisation, Mac, Snowy, Linda and others. You have been friendly, kind and generous to myself and family. Thank you for all manner of things and, on behalf of all your guests, Thank you for having us."

There was still a lot of support for us in East Anglia, from friends in Wickhambrook and Folk. The following

months may have been easier if we had still lived there but we didn't and it was current life we had to cope with.

EQUIPMENT: STAIRLIFT Part 2

In November the Technical Advisor, Ray Sanderson, came again to discuss the stairlift. He tried to persuade us to have a lift through the floor of our bedroom from the front room. It was a ridiculous idea, there isn't room without removing all our bedroom furniture including the bed! He was not pleased that we did not agree, even though the cost of the stairlift we required was much the same as a through the floor lift, with a lot less disruption.

The outside ramp had to go through on the same grant application, although we did not appreciate this, along with any adaptations recommended by the Fire Service. There was debate on whether we should have a base for a porch to store equipment which we would pay for ourselves. No-one came for some time: we had inadvertently delayed matters by suggesting the porch.

The application for the grant for the lift did not go in until December, 3 months after we had decided we needed one urgently and we still had to wait for the grant to be processed before it could be ordered, we were warned that this could take up to a year! Fortunately we had a downstairs toilet as the effort of getting Peter up and down stairs was most traumatic.

Diane Peake, Ray Sanderson, and ourselves had eventually agreed on a stairlift that would take a wheelchair upstairs, a ramp at the front and various fire precautions but there was no way we could wait 3 months, never mind a year. We had to find our own solutions while waiting.

BENEFIT FUND

At the end of November the Appeal set up for Peter by the Society had amounted to £3,000+. Many people sent money directly to us, rather than the EFDSS. One of the first was from Brian Limbrick, of Hertfordshire, who delivered his cheque in person, which was very cheering.

More money came from Claygate Dance Group, Sussex, which Peter had helped 30 years before; from Yvonne Ransome, Hampshire District Secretary, who put out a sweet bottle for loose change and sent £150 in November (there were lots more 'sweets' over the years). There was a collection made at a Folk holiday on the Isle of Wight, organised by Jeane Howard ex-staff EFDSS. Dave Williams, friend from Southampton, donated his earnings from lectures to W.I.s., every so often we would receive cheques from some part of the New Forest. Other stalwarts included

Thames Valley Morris Men, whose only goal for some time seemed to be to raise money for Peter, they sent, in total, over £3,000. Suffolk District, in their different guises, also sent substantial amounts. Arriving at different times the cheques invariably cheered us up, showing that somewhere, someone was thinking of us; an enormous help in combating the feelings of isolation which go with such a disabling disease as MND.

In January 1989 £1,000 arrived from John Heydon's New Year Ceilidh at Haddenham, which was a wonderful surprise when our finances looked pretty grim. There were also numerous smaller donations from teams, clubs, Districts and individuals which made life quite exciting.

A year later, in February 1990 two cheques arrived on the same day. One from Bill Delderfield of Lumps of Plum Pudding, who had organised a Ceilidh, the other from Ewell St. Mary's Morris' collection. The cheques amounted to £560. At this stage Peter spent a lot of time resting in bed. I spent the money on a remote controlled stereo system so he could choose to listen to tapes, radio, CDs or even records, if I set them up first. It was invaluable in whiling away what could have been boring hours and gave some independence. Money did seem to arrive just when we needed it, by then Peter was on borrowed time, he could have caught an infection and died in days; the hi-fi improved his quality of life. Time and money have a different dimension when death is close.

The Benefit Fund totalled £14,079.94 by June 1990, an incredible amount for which we shall always be grateful. We used it to buy an electric bed, powered wheelchair, portable phone, a van and its conversion, hi-fi, holidays, nursing care and numerous smaller comforts.

THE BED

Receiving £3,000 in the first two months, gave us the confidence to look at equipment. We asked Jane Petty to advise; she recommended an electrical bed which has motors to raise the bed's head and foot separately through a hand-held switch, for those who cannot sit up or move unaided. We decided to go ahead with this purchase and site it in the front room, so Peter would not have to go upstairs every night, in view of the expected wait for the stairlift.

Purchasing a bed was not such an easy decision and turned out to be typical of acquiring equipment for the disabled. I wrote to various addresses advertised in the RADAR Holiday Book and we visited the Handicapped Living Centre at The Wicker, Sheffield. They had a water bed on special offer, which would have helped prevent bed sores. Peter was quite keen on

it, but it would not be any help in sitting or standing him up or elevating his legs, all of which were essential.

The beds which moved up and down weren't very comfortable in the shop so we had to wait for salesmen to come with their beds for home demonstrations. This was very time-consuming and we felt under a lot of pressure to purchase. We also had to wait 6 weeks from ordering while they made it. We saw three at home and refused to commit ourselves to any purchase on the salesman's initial visit, this would not be easy for someone on their own. At no time did we feel under pressure at the HLC shop, they were invariably courteous and helpful and do home demonstrations with a variety of makes of equipment. Manufacturers of specialised equipment tend to be small companies clutching their design to themselves. Many do not use retailers so home demonstrations of one item of equipment at a time is virtually the only way the disabled can see what is available.

We asked nursing friends for advice on beds as of the ones we saw only one offered the facility of the whole bed rising to nursing height, in addition to the usual independent rising of head and foot by separate motors and 'massaging' as the mattress is vibrated, but cost an extra £300. The advice was that the extra height could help save strain on my back when Peter needed turning in bed thus we decided on this, the most expensive bed, with all the facilities. This proved to be extremely useful in a way we had not anticipated. When Peter could no longer stand unaided he would sit on the edge of the bed and raise himself independently to standing as the whole bed raised. The manufacturers of other beds claim that one can use the foot raising facility to aid standing; this may be alright while one can move down the bed into the correct position unfortunately wriggling down the bed was quite beyond Peter later. It showed how essential it is to have the correct advice. We came to the right decision for a different reason.

The bed proved a very sound investment. We do not know how other patients manage to be comfortable without one. It made a terrific difference to many aspects of managing the disease.

We bought the Theralift Contour bed from Theraposture. 10/12, Fore St. Trowbridge, Wilts. BA14 SUB. Tel: 02214 69506. It was delivered in January, 1989 and cost £1,650

MOBILITY 2000

One of the other pieces of equipment we had demonstrated at this time was the Mobility 2000 electronic wheelchair. We had seen this advertised, in the RADAR book, as going up stairs. It also would go over most terrain and the seat raised and lowered to reach various heights. It looked impressive. We hoped it might solve the problem of getting in and out of the house and upstairs, on a temporary basis, and have long term use as a wheelchair in its own right.

The man who demonstrated it was the designer. He brought the machine in the back of a hatchback. William was keen to try it. The chair looked good and went up the kerb with ease. Unfortunately getting into our house defeated it. One door was too narrow, another hadn't the turning space, another the steps were too steep. We also saw that it took a lot of programming to manoeuvre; it had a computer control which looked very complicated. These problems, along with the price of £3,000, made us turn it down, regretfully. Apparently they were bought by Manpower Services, to keep people in employment. The designer was kindness itself and put no pressure on us, although his time was wasted.

SWIMMING

During Autumn Peter continued his almost daily trips to the Leisure Centre. The water helped him to relax and to walk unaided as it supported him, giving him confidence and valuable exercise. No one had given any suggestions as to how to keep fit, Peter had decided on swimming himself. I am sure it contributed to keeping his shoulder muscles and breathing for as long as he did. The Leisure Centre was not adapted for disabled and we saw very few others in public sessions. There is time set aside on a Sunday evenings for disabled swimmers but it was not convenient and we did not think Peter should be segregated just because he had developed MND.

Towards Christmas he was having increasing difficulty dressing, particularly socks and buttons. I sewed velcro onto his shirts and he often came home with his socks in his pocket. Whenever possible he took the boys with him, usually William as Giles was in the Lodge. William was very good at doing the buttons, but he found the socks defeating. I had the same problem the following year. Just try putting on someone else's socks, it is unreasonably difficult.

It was a happy time as in the pool Peter was almost like any other Dad. Out of it William was protective and took care of Peter, finding assistants, helping to dry and dress him. He was 6½. Then Peter had several bad falls while changing. Once down he could not get up, the pool attendants were very helpful but the days of going on his own were numbered.

NATIVITY PLAY

Christmas 1988, William was now a top infant. He auditioned for a part in the school Nativity Play and because he had a clear singing voice he was given the role of a King, bringing gold and had to sing a solo. He threw himself into the role with great seriousness, making a dignified and proud entrance. Peter managed to get into school by my parking near and taking the wheelchair. It was a memorable event. The school was kindness itself to us.

MORE EQUIPMENT

In November Diane brought: — a new type of tap turner, 'Handi', which gripped the taps; — jar openers to grip jam jars etc; — an 'Easi-reach', long-handled grabber, to pick things up that were out of reach; — handi-plugs, a handle which fits on electric plugs to make them easier to pull out; — and key extensions.

At this stage Diane decided she had done all she could for us and crossed us off her books. She still knew very little about MND. I later found that if I did the research into equipment suitable for our needs, Diane would make great efforts to acquire it. Later still she went on a course on the care and management of MND, although Peter was her only client with the disease. There is something about MND that brings out the best in people, perhaps because it has such a devastating effect on the body of a patient, while not touching the mind. Whatever, Diane, like many of the professionals involved with us, was very supportive of the whole family, beyond the normal call of duty.

We bought Peter a cordless telephone for Christmas because he could no longer get to the phone. This was useful until his hands became too weak to dial and hold it.

The muscles at the extremities of Peter's body were lost first so he had difficulty holding things, balancing, standing and walking. The disease does not seem to have a steady 'progression', to us it was rather like rolling slowly downhill until we came to a cliff edge and suddenly dropped over. It appeared that there has been a rapid deterioration but it is not necessarily so; muscles compensate for the loss of others, when the last ones die in a particular group a function, one has been struggling to hang on to, is lost for ever.

The sudden 'drops' involve not only loss of physical functions but of a way of life, in much the same way that redundancy affected us. Before diagnosis we were unaware of the finality of some of these losses. In October 1987 we left Handsworth's Anniversary Dance early, partly because it was noisy, the dances were simple and too similar but also because Peter was tired. Only recently did I realise it was the last time we danced together. By Christmas long walks and in June normal family holidays were in the past, followed by gardening. Things which we took for granted and gave us pleasure were gone and, as with the job, it was a struggle to replace them, to build a new way of life.

A NEW YEAR, 1989

DRIVING

When we started 1989 I had stopped supply teaching to care for Peter full time. I asked Dr. Proctor about Peter's driving and whether we should buy an automatic car. He indicated that we ought to be planning for the time when it would take at least two strong men to get Peter in and out of a car. This was a very upsetting idea but very useful as it set off quite a different train of thought.

I persevered with driving lessons in our own car as I would be taking over the full-time driving, in December we had no idea it would be so soon; Christmas marked the edge of another precipice we were about to fall over. Before Christmas Peter was taking himself swimming to the Leisure Centre, getting dressed on his own, or with William's help and managing to climb small steps, with crutches. Not long after Christmas I had to go with him to lift him in and out of the car, undress, help him in and out of the pool, dry and dress him. The Leisure Centre staff were very good, putting the First Aid room at our disposal for changing and they helped Peter into the pool, but it marked the end of Peter's independent life. From this time on he could not manage without assistance.

On January 10th we went to Leeds DVLC to be assessed as to whether Peter was fit to drive. We did not have much hope that he would 'pass', deterioration had been so rapid. William came with us, taking charge of the scooter Lichfield Folk Dance Club had donated; we were trying this out to see if it gave Peter more independence. In fact the scooter could not manage even small kerbs with Peter on, so he walked slowly on crutches while William whizzed round on the scooter.

The assessor at the Centre was kindly and considerate, a contrast to our previous experiences with 'officials'. He did not seem to know much about MND but noticed some wasting in Peter's hands. We told him about my learning to drive and he was aware that we had a young family with William around.

He advised that Peter could keep his driving licence and be reassessed in a few years (he mustn't know about MND!). However Peter needed to inform his insurance company of his disabilities, they would ask for a doctor's certificate and it would be unlikely that Peter would be covered by insurance, effectively stopping him from driving.

We both felt that the assessor was being very kind; by allowing Peter to keep his licence I could drive with Peter until I passed the test. This had disadvantages for both of us; Peter had to accompany me shopping, then sit outside because he could not walk round the store, was too proud to use the scooter and hated

shopping anyway. He also went with me while I practised reversing and turning in the road when he would have preferred to be at his word processor. I had to take Peter swimming. After getting him dressed in the morning, with difficulty, I had to do it all again at the swimming pool. It was a difficult time for both of us adjusting to our dependence on each other.

We made an appointment with Dr. Proctor for an assessment to satisfy the insurance company. In retrospect we should not have bothered, both Peter and I knew he was no longer fit to drive so I took over. Dr. Proctor said it would be useful to examine Peter to see how he was, only afterwards did he tell us he had to charge for filling in the insurance form. We had to pay for the privilege of being told that Peter would not drive again. It made me cross, we should not have gone but kept to our own decision and retained some control. It was a very negative experience, another nail in the coffin.

MANGAR BOOSTER

At home the simple bath seat and board became obsolete when Peter's muscles could not push him to stand, so Diane brought a wonderful seat, to put in the bath, attached to an electric motor which produced compressed air. At the press of a lever the seat would raise on an air cushion to the height of the bath, Peter could manoeuvre round and be sat down, I would lift his legs over the bath side, then he could lower the seat by letting the air out of the cushion. It saved a tremendous amount of effort. There were disadvantages: it had a solid back, so Peter could not lie in the bath and, being raised, needed a lot of water to cover him. Also it had to be lifted out of the bath when the family wanted baths and it was heavy. Nevertheless, it was a very useful piece of equipment.

As Peter could no longer sit himself up and we were waiting for the bed to be manufactured, Diane also brought a backrest for the bed and a 'bed ladder', a sort of rope ladder which is tied to the bottom of the bed; the occupant pulls himself up hand over hand on the rungs. Unfortunately Peter did not have the strength in his hands to do this and the ladder was usually out of reach so I had to rescue it; it was as easy for me to sit him up. When the bed was delivered this problem was solved, Peter pressed a switch and the top of the bed would rise to whatever height required, so Peter was effortlessly put into the sitting position he wanted.

HYDROTHERAPY

As the muscles in Peter's calves, hands and arms wasted it became increasingly difficult to get him out of the swimming pool, even with help. We solved it for a time by pushing him into the water on a shower chair on casters, but there wasn't a ramp and the effort of it all, combined with fluctuations in the temperature of the water so it was often too cold, meant we had to admit defeat and give up the swimming pool. Later we wrote to the Authorities to suggest the installation of a hoist, which would have been more dignified and secure than being man-handled in by strangers. The reply was that there was plenty of staff to help. A hoist is not exhorbitant considering the independence it would give to individuals.

Jane Petty suggested we try Firbeck Rehabilitation Hospital. This was in a huge house, in lovely grounds, originally converted by the Miner's Union to be used for recuperation after mining accidents, later taken over by the NHS. It had a Physiotherapy Department and a hydrotherapy pool. Jane referred us and we had to go to be assessed. To our surprise we were accepted. Peter was not the usual patient, there were accident victims and people suffering from arthritis or strokes. All had the potential for improvement, unlike Peter.

He was supposed to join a physiotherapy class before going in the pool but he quickly found this exhausted him, so we kept to pool only. We went twice a week for a year, a round trip of 20+ miles. Sometimes it was lovely, walking round the grounds which had a lake, ducks and multitudes of wild flowers, occasionally we took a picnic. During school holidays the boys were allowed in the pool too, so there were some happy family days.

FINANCE

After six months of £31.30 per week sick pay Peter went onto Invalidity Benefit of £99.50 per week for the whole family, a positive fortune! We had not been granted Mobility and Attendance Allowances, my only income was Child Benefit; we were thus very grateful for the Benefit Fund money which came in as it was obvious that we would need a substantial amount to combat the effects of MND. However, the Benefit Fund was a one off, not for living on, I had to find some other means of income to supplement benefits and, looking into the distant future, a means of supplying financial support and employment for when the inevitable happened.

When we moved the Playgroup out of the house, one of my supporters, Lynda Elvin, suggested setting up in a portacabin. I did not think it was worth the investment, at the time, but the idea resurrected itself with the more urgent current needs. There were many advantages to siting a temporary building where our double garage stood, at the bottom of the garden: I would be able to see to Peter and the boys; all the mess

would be away from the house, yet the children would still have access to the garden; I could run it on my own, with emergency cover; I would be my own boss. There were disadvantages: neighbours might object; setting up costs would be very high; it would involve a lot of work on top of what I was already doing; fees would have to be very high.

I spent a lot of time working out the costings and potential income and it appeared feasible. Peter was unsure, it involved a large capital investment and a lot more work for me. I went ahead because the Nursery was something I enjoyed, it did not involve MND and would give me an existence of my own besides badly needed income.

In January I applied for planning permission. The Planning Department advised that if I kept numbers to 6 or less children I was less likely to run into trouble, on the basis that one could have 6 children of one's own under 5 years! I put in appropriate plans for a portacabin and wrote to neighbours to explain what I was doing and why, not all knew about the MND. There were mutterings about cars parking but no outright objections.

I investigated portacabins and ordered one 10' x 20', to my own design, large enough to take 8 children under Social Services rules of 25 sq. ft. floor space per child. The vendor was very keen to make a sale and offered to buy the garage so that the portacabin could be delivered. Giles and I found ourselves spending more time moving furniture and equipment around, this three years of essential rubbish accumulated in a double garage. Most of it resided on the lawn for the next few months. Men came and dismantled the garage and we removed part of a very solid garden wall to give more room. It was Easter 1989, the weather was atrocious, Giles and I were out in the snow and a gale knocking down the wall. At that time I was not sure I had made the right decision!

On Good Friday the portacabin arrived at 8 o'clock in the morning, on a huge transporter with accompanying lorry. We had been assured that delivery was easy; a lorry would back up our drive, drop the cabin onto its hydraulic supports and drive out. Not so. This one came with a crane and had to be lifted into place, over next door's telephone wires and dropped next to our caravan. One man stood on top of the cabin as it swung in the air, moving the chains holding it between the wires. How it missed hitting the caravan or severing the wires I do not know.

EVER MORE EQUIPMENT

Now I was a full-time Carer I took on organising equipment and seeking help for Peter where I could. We had a demonstration of the MANGAR BOOSTER

CHAIR, made by the same company that produced the bath lift. This also rose on bellows with air from an electric pump. It could be put onto a caster base, so was then movable or the seat section could be used in the bath to raise or lower, or on the floor if Peter fell, whereas the bath lift was too heavy to move around. Peter was still using crutches around the house but would find that his legs gave way, without warning. I found it difficult to get him up, despite being shown how to use cushions and books to raise him, as he could give very little assistance, I usually had to call in a neighbour. No one told us that one can call the ambulance service to lift people. I never tried it, so do not know if this is feasible. The Mangar chair proved too expensive for us at over £1,000 but we were impressed.

We also had a demonstration of the SQUIRREL wheelchair, designed partly by Lord Snowdon. It was a sensible design having motors to all four wheels making it very manoeuvrable inside and out, including over rough ground, unlike conventional chairs which are rear wheel driven. It was extremely stable and not exhorbitantly priced but the joystick proved to be somewhat erratic and we felt it needed more work before we were ready to commit ourselves. We suggested that the Squirrel and Mangar manufacturers got together to create a wheelchair with a seat that could rise, which would have given more independence; this was feasible but too expensive.

STAIRLIFT SAGA CONTINUED

By February 1989 we were becoming desperate for the stairlift. Peter was using a zimmer frame for stability so stairs were very difficult. I phoned Environmental Health, Occupational Therapists and suppliers daily, sometimes three times a day; they were not going to forget us. They would recognise my voice instantly. I must have been a nuisance but it worked; by agreeing to forego the front ramp for the present we were to have the lift fitted in March. This was very quick. I felt as if I'd had to move heaven and earth to get this far but it would be worth it if Peter could get upstairs to bed, have a bath, have the freedom of the house again.

The fitters came from Clarkes, they took most of the day to fit the rails. It wasn't until they had nearly finished, with a chair attached that I realised they had fitted the wrong one. I just could not believe it. It had not occurred to me to check the order, we had all agreed on the type which could take a wheelchair, this did not. I was distraught after all my efforts. I phoned the man who dealt with the grants. we were quite friendly by now as he had come out with all the grant applications and was a lot more useful than the Technical Advisor. He did not know what had happened but assured me it would be sorted out.

I phoned Clarkes. They had fitted what was ordered. I contacted Diane; it turned out that the Technical Adviser, had ordered the wrong one. We asked them to change it; Diane advised that if we did the Council would not be happy at the extra expense so may not look kindly on future applications, should we need them and we would have to go through the whole process again. Reluctantly we agreed to keeping the lift. The Department did try to improve it by fitting a swivel chair, as the original left Peter suspended over the stairs. We also felt that the track should have been higher so that the chair stopped on the landing, but this proved too expensive. Ray, who had caused the problem, had the nerve to suggest that if we had taken his advice and had a lift through the floor we would not have had this problem!

So we acquired a stairlift, several weeks after it became an absolute necessity which was obsolete in 6 months. From the first we were not happy using it as there was danger of Peter falling backwards down the stairs during transfers. Eventually it involved six transfers and two people in order that Peter could take a shower. It was not worth the trauma and effort to all involved.

RAMPS

We still had the problem of getting in and out of the house. We used the patio doors, where the steps were small. After Christmas someone had to be with Peter in case he fell. There was no hope of the Council's ramp being built for months. In fact it was eventually constructed in summer, six months too late and was rarely used.

Our solution was to pay for our own ramps to be built from the patio doors to drive giving easy access. In January we asked a friend to build it who needed the money. This was a mistake as he would not charge us a reasonable fee so we did not feel we could insist he complete the work. He did a little at a time and it caused us considerable inconvenience waiting for the next bit to be completed. However, early in 1989 we had spent much of the Benefit Fund on the bed and driving lessons and were looking at means of transport, we did not like to commit ourselves to too much outlay. We kept hoping Kevin would turn up 'this week' to finish it.

By March, I had to push Peter out in the wheelchair, on the bit of ramp which was done, until we reached the 'drop'; put the brakes on the chair, position the zimmer frame on the lower path, manoeuvre Peter out of the chair so he slid into a standing position on the frame, take off brakes, lift the chair onto the path, put on brakes, help Peter to sit by lowering him onto chair, take off brakes, hitch frame to chair, push chair to car, put on brakes, take frame off chair and position, lift Peter out of chair, lower Peter into car and lift in his legs, take off brakes, push chair to boot, open boot, fold up chair, lift it into boot, close boot, stow frame in back of car, fasten Peter's safety belt. Then we could set off!

On the return we would have to all this in reverse. Getting Peter onto the chair which was on the higher path could be hilarious or dangerous, depending on our moods. We did this for several weeks, at least twice a week. The ramp was eventually functional by Easter, but we did wish we lived in a flat location.

THAMES VALLEY MORRIS MEN'S BENEFIT

On February 10th we were invited to a Ceilidh organised by Thames Valley Morris Men for Peter's Benefit Fund at Claygate, Surrey. It took some organisation but Peter had the chance to meet some old friends. We stayed at Eileen and Brian's in Letchworth. I drove down the A1, then Brian Limbrick collected us and took us the rest of the way. All sorts of Peter's past acquaintances turned up, including colleagues from the Civil Service. A happy evening.

Eileen had brought a bed settee downstairs for us. In the morning I could not lift Peter from sitting to get him dressed, the bed was lower than ours. Our days of being away from home were over unless something could be done.

When we got home I contacted Diane and suggested that the Mangar Booster Bug, which we had seen demonstrated, would solve many of our current problems and as it was portable we could take it with us when we went away. Fortunately Social Services had just been granted more money so Diane ordered one, in the meantime swapping the bath lift for a Booster cushion only. This turned out to be the Japanese version, made for export, which goes higher than the normal cushion; why the Japanese need a taller version, I do not know! This proved a boon as the cushion went so high it took very little effort to stand Peter. When the caster base arrived we kept the Japanese cushion.

THE DRIVING TEST

In February I was taking at least two driving lessons per week and practising turning and reversing every day. I went all out for passing the test first time as life was becoming very difficult just getting Peter in and out of the car. If I could drive alone it would give us both some independence. It was not easy learning but once Peter stopped driving our attitudes changed; I was no longer taking something away from him. In a way I felt as if Peter was driving as I took over his role. He felt the same, he was driving through me and rarely commented or complained if I did something wrong. I took the test on March 17th, the day after my 41st

birthday. To my immense surprise and relief I passed. Everyone was overjoyed. Peter was very proud.

MOBILITY ALLOWANCE continued

We went to the DHSS Centre again on March 23rd to appeal. Peter now used the wheelchair when outside. I lifted the chair out of the boot, erected it with great difficulty as we were parked on a steep hill, man-handled Peter into the chair, locked up the car and managed to get him to the entrance of the Centre. I then had to go inside to find someone who could get the wheelchair up the step. Once inside we called the lift but the lift was too small to fit a wheelchair and attendant in, so I lifted Peter out and onto a stool in the lift, folded the chair and squeezed into the lift myself. I reassembled the chair and got him out at the top and pushed him round to the office. By now I felt I needed to get Mobility Allowance! We realised afterwards that if one could get into the Assessment Centre you were almost certainly disqualified from Mobility Allowance! Ask the assessor to come to you.

The Nurse in charge asked to weigh Peter. We explained he could not stand on the scales, she looked disgruntled. The Doctor noted a bit more wasting of muscles. Peter refused to attempt the stairs, on my strict orders (we badly needed this income and he would never attempt them normally) but he could manage the corridor using the zimmer frame; I did not have a lot of hope of us being granted the Allowance. However, Jane Petty had asked the Consultant to write a covering letter and this may have helped. We were awarded £24.40 per week in June 1989, ten months after we first applied, back dated 6 months to January.

ATTENDANCE ALLOWANCE was also granted on appeal in June 1989. This was given at the higher rate of £34.90 per week for both day and night time care, back-dated to April 1989.

AMINO-ACIDS

In March I read in the newsletter of the MND Association of research in America where MND patients were given amino-acids with apparently beneficial results in slowing the progression of the disease; the advice was to consult our doctor. This I did; Dr Proctor was cautious and said he would look into it.

Amino-acids are the 'building blocks' of the body's protein, including nerve cell and muscle protein. Limited research indicated an imbalance of amino-acids may have an effect on MND patients; by taking a compound the imbalance may be partially corrected. I felt that anything was worth trying, we didn't have a lot to lose, but Dr Proctor wanted to be sure they could not do any harm, especially as they were expensive and could not, at that time, be given on prescription. We had to be patient although MND was rampant, Peter's physical condition was deteriorating visibly, almost daily.

After several weeks Dr Proctor came back to us with the news that he could find nothing against taking amino-acids although there was no guarantee that they would have any beneficial effect. He knew we were very keen to try them and I think he thought it would be good for our morale, so long as we did not rely upon it as a miracle cure and were willing to pay approximately £20 per week, as they were still not on the recognised list of drugs. This was a lot of money but worth paying.

I contacted MNDA for a supplier and was given the number of a laboratory in Newcastle. Not only could they supply what we wanted they told me that the amino-acids had just been put onto the drugs list, so our GP could prescribe them; we would not have to pay. Peter started them on 21st April 1989. I had to put a scoop of the white crystalline powder into fruit juice and shake it to try to mix it, three times a day, half-an-hour before meals. Terribly inconvenient and they didn't taste very good either, however we felt we were doing SOMETHING to combat this awful disease.

TRANSPORT

In February I started to look for alternative means of transport for Peter as lifting the wheelchair and Peter into the car was too much for me. There was very little information easily available, I had to write to each firm individually. We joined the Disabled Driver's Motor Club, (Cottingham Way, Thrapston, Northants. NN14 4PL.) This gave useful addresses. I also discovered the Spastic Society's Newsletter, DISABILITY NOW, through a friend. This proved to have lots of information for all disabled people, I wished I'd been told about it earlier, it would have saved a lot of time. Note: none of the professionals involved told us of any of these contacts, nor DIAL, I had to search.

I discovered that a new vehicle converted for a disabled person was not liable for car tax and VAT. The most interesting conversion of a car, for us, was on the Nissan Prairie. The roof was raised and the back able to take a passenger in a wheelchair, up a ramp. However, even allowing for car tax and VAT to be deducted it was extremely costly. There was not a lot of difference between the conversion and a motor caravan, so we did the rounds of dealers and wrote to manufacturers. Peter was busy with his Golden Oldies event and took very little interest but had to go with me until I passed the Test.

It turned out that to have a motorcaravan converted would entail removing furniture and equipment to make room for the wheelchair; this seemed a waste of money; also, we could not find any one motor caravan ideal. In the end, I decided to have a new van converted to my specifications. In view of the time, energy and frustrations this subsequently involved, it was a mistake; MND does not give time to sort out niceties; we could have had a motor caravan in a fortnight. We were promised this by the converters but it actually took them over 6 weeks after a lot of threats and hassle. With hindsight I would go to a firm which fits ramps and clamping systems and have a local joiner make cupboards, sink and bed seats; nevertheless, the van gave us essential mobility and is still very useful today.

After a lot of research I chose the Renault Trafic T1000, short-wheel base, low-top version. This, and the Volkswagen, has the lowest loading height, allowing us to fit ramps at £300, any other would need a lift at £1,500+. As we wanted ramps fitted at the back door the Volkswagen was ruled out with its rear engine.

I studied lots of interiors of motorcaravans to decide on our specifications, carried out by K.C. Mobility of Batley, Nr. Leeds. The dealer who sold us the van had to arrange the conversion in order that we qualify for deduction of tax and VAT. We could not take delivery until the conversion had been passed by Customs & Excise.

Starting with the basic van they fitted lining to panels, doors and roof; 3 fixed windows in side door and rear sections (opening windows would take 8 weeks to order); a sun roof; a cupboard, behind the driver's seat, containing a hob and sink and portapotti; seats to make into bed above wheelarches, leaving space in between for the wheelchair when travelling; table to fit across space to make into bed; an extractor fan above cooker; rear telescopic ramps, rails and clamps along centre of floor; 3 interior lights and carpet. I supplied much of the equipment from a camping shop to ensure we had what we wanted. Later we had to have rear seat belts, curtain rails, insulation and a cigar lighter fitted, which K.C. omitted.

Other problems we found were that we had not allowed enough turning space between the back seats for the front casters on the wheelchair, necessitating moving them manually so that Peter could reverse out of the van; they were very heavy. Also, I had asked for the seats to be made the height of the wheelchair, the joiner did not allow for the cushions to be on top, thus they are too high. Carfour fitted a cassette radio + 4 speakers, essential for travelling with the two boys. The seating at the front remained; the Trafic has a fixed driver's seat and a double passenger seat which will tip forward, as in an estate, or the back goes down making a seat if one wants to face into the back. This proved very useful when we had meals in the van with a table by the side door.

We took delivery of the Renault at the end of May. It cost us approximately £10,000, less the exchange on the Orion, several thousand £s less than a motorcaravan and a lot of hard work.

POWERED WHEELCHAIRS

By this time I had also researched electric chairs. We started with scooters but soon realised that they would be unsafe as the disease progressed. Our ideal chair would be manoeuvrable inside and out, have an elevating seat to aid standing or reaching things, a reclining seat for comfort, to ease pressure and for sleeping, a headrest for comfort and the time when Peter could no longer support his head. I found the very chair 6 months after he died, the Ortopedia Series 935, new on the market at a mere £3,500.

In Spring of 1989 we test drove various chairs at the Handicapped Living Centre and at home. Peter was very keen on the Meyra, German make, front-wheel drive, would go over very rough ground and up kerbs, but it had a fixed seat, little support, would be difficult to manoeuvre inside and was £3,000. After weeks of indecision we went to Birmingham to a sale of second-hand chairs and found a Poirier for £700, marked down from £900. It was a large and imposing chair which gave good support, including a head rest, it reclined by the carer pulling levers, into various angles, it would go outside but not up kerbs, inside it was difficult to steer because room had to be allowed for the front casters to swing round, it was rear-wheel drive, it did not have an elevating seat and we found the footrests uncomfortable. It was a compromise, but was good value at the price and it served it's purpose most of the time. Importantly, it did not look like an ordinary wheelchair, it was quite imposing and this helped to give Peter confidence. He caused considerable comment in Rotherham Physiotherapy Department, everyone came out to see this majestic chair.

GILES

By April it became essential that I had more help so Giles stopped at home instead of at the Lodge. Both Peter and I noticed a difference from the time when he took on responsibilities, we are both very proud of Giles. He began to do things he would never have attempted before Peter had MND simply because there wasn't anyone else to do them. We both felt that if any good had come out of MND it was to give Giles a role and self-confidence. Giles took over household chores in order that I could give more time to caring for Peter.

William and Peter on electric chair — February 1990

THE BEST AND THE WORST OF THE SOCIETY

GOLDEN OLDIES FOLK DAY

While I organised equipment, portacabins and life for the family, Peter was working on his Golden Oldies, for April 30th. 1989, when he would receive the Society's Gold badge. The word processor worked overtime. I had to fill envelopes and stick stamps as Peter's hands were badly effected but Peter was back at work and enjoying himself.

The event was of necessity nostalgic, with performers and friends from Peter's past, however he also planned it as a family day out in its own right. We *hear that friends' children still talk about it, which would please Peter. We had told many friends about the day in our Christmas mailing and advertised in local and national Folk magazines. In all 400 people turned up from all over the country, including Scotland, although only a few from the NEC of the EFDSS, who were presenting the award. This did not matter as Peter valued the recognition of fellow workers, not NEC, but it was rather discourteous. Many people had not met for 20 years.*

Gold Badge Presentation, 30th April 1989 — Peter, Janet, Giles & William

PETER'S SPEECH

"I started my Folk dancing round the maypole at school, that is if I wasn't one of the lucky boys who rushed to hold the maypole. Further more, I actually danced the Sailor's Hornpipe with the local Sea Scout Group; so, that's where it all began. I remember today that wind up gramophone which had to be wound up half way through the recording.

No-one but myself and Janet can recognise all the groups who have come from all parts today. I could go all round the room but we'd be here all night, so perhaps I can just say Thank You to those people; those whom we've worked with over the years; they are the people who make things happen. I've relied upon ordinary people, like myself, to undertake the various projects and so I would like to think that I am accepting this Badge on behalf of all those people, many of whom are here today.

Now, you will have realised that Janet and I, and the family, have had our troubles and they are continuing; we have been touched by the kindness and generosity of the Folk world. There is something special about Folk and the fact that you have come today proves that. I'm just extremely grateful for having met you all."

We persuaded Dorothy Beckford to write about the Golden Oldies Folk Day for a Newsletter Peter planned, unfortunately he did not have time to produce it.

DOROTHY BECKFORD'S REVIEW:

"A packed Benn Hall in Rugby, on Sunday 30th April, witnessed a positive demonstration of the affection and respect in which Peter Dashwood is held. Seven hours of song and dance, not to mention varied activities for the junior members, provided a most enjoyable and satisfactory occasion to meet old friends and provided the opportunity for Pat Tracey to present Peter with the Gold Badge of the English Folk Dance & Song Society and to acknowledge Janet's support of Peter's work throughout. We were all kept fully occupied, nevertheless we managed to chat about old times and the fun we had dancing to-gether. Indeed, many who attended are still deeply involved in folk activities initiated by Peter during his time with the Society, including Folk Camps, Felixstowe, Expo and Broadstairs.

The Highlight for me, now regrettably a non-dancer, was the concert. I especially enjoyed 'The Yetties', so relaxed and presenting just the right kind of programme for such a gathering. Dave Trenow and Dave Hislop were together again losing none of the old rapport with their audience. On the dance side the Massed Morris had lost none of its magic, so what if some of the leaps weren't quite so high as before! Mike Garland and son danced a Morris Jig superbly and Pat Tracey danced with a precision and technique that fills me with admiration. How she manages such impeccable performances and still SMILE continues to amaze me. The Handsworth Sword Dancers echoed the precision of the dance in their display and remain one of my favourite traditional teams, from way back when I first saw them at the Albert Hall.

Running as a thread throughout the whole day was the music which kept all our toes tapping, played individually and collectively by many musicians, who enhanced our enjoyment and who obviously enjoyed playing together informally in the best folk tradition.

On an even more personal note it was especially pleasant for me to be accompanied by my family and grandchildren, a fairly rare happening these days. Judging by the intense concentration whilst watching the morris and the loud and enthusiastic attempt to join in with The Yetties' choruses, we have at least one possible Morris man and folk singer coming up and, after all, that's what its all about!"
Dorothy Beckford. 1989.

The report written by Barbara Ginn for Dance & Song was not printed, the only copy was lost.

We stayed the weekend with Griff and Nanette Jones. The van was not ready, despite all my efforts, but we did have the electric wheelchair. We were determined that Peter should use this instead of the DHSS chair, partly because it looked so much better, but also to show what the Benefit money was being used for. So I towed a trailer containing the wheelchair down the M.1 six weeks after passing the driving test.

It was not all plain sailing though; there was a small step to Griff's front door, Peter thought he could manage it, couldn't and fell heavily. It was a fore-taste of what was to come.

For four days after Golden Oldies we were on a high, we had many letters of thanks from people who felt refreshed and filled with renewed vigour to continue after being disheartened by the farce that was being carried on in the EFDSS. Then we literally came down to earth with a bump. On Wednesday Peter got up from lunch and walked across the room with his frame, as he did every day, on the way his leg gave way; he fell badly with his leg buckled under him, badly spraining his knee and ankle. He could not put any weight on that leg so we had to face problems we thought were a little time off to get him around the house. We discovered just how small the loo is when one tries to get two adults and a wheelchair in it!

Giles and I spent the weekend clearing furniture into the portacabin so we could manoeuvre the wheelchair around the house. The portacabin was becoming full of our furniture and the house full of Peter's equipment. Both of us doubted Peter would walk again; deterioration had been so rapid since Christmas we felt sure that by the time the sprains mended MND would have taken over. It was a depressing time.

EFDSS, EXTRAORDINARY GENERAL MEETING

It was made worse when a few days after the fall we heard that an EGM had been called by members of the EFDSS Rescue group, who wished to sell Cecil Sharp House. They proposed to remove most of the current NEC as Directors, replace them with 'Rescue' members and appoint an Administrator under the new Insolvency Act to effect a reconstruction of the Society, although they did not explain how an Administrator would be paid.

There had been uproar in the Society when 558 ballot papers for the 1988 NEC election were found to be photocopies. The Electoral Reform Society had been asked to investigate, paid for personally by Ursula Vaughan Williams. News of a 'rigged ballot' made the national newspapers, including an article by Bernard Levin, although the photocopies made no difference to the outcome of the election; the Friends of the House side still polled most votes. To our simple minds the outcry was a red-herring but accusations of foul deeds by both sides closely followed. Bits of paper flew through our letter box stating 'facts' until one did not know what to believe or who was manipulating whom. We had naively thought that Golden Oldies had heralded a time of reconciliation and renewed hope for the Society. Peter was very upset that the fighting was becoming ever more nasty; we could only see that some Members were out to destroy the Society completely

both morally and financially, which side we could not tell.

I was incensed that one of the reasons given for calling the EGM and removing NEC was "Mistreatment of staff." The 'Friends of Cecil Sharp House' NEC had made the Manager, John Seabourn, appointed by the 'Sell CSH' NEC, redundant. After only a few months in employment with the EFDSS he left with £20,000, a year's salary, as per his contract. This compared with Peter's 'fair and generous settlement' of £9,650 and no hope of future employment, unlike Mr. Seabourn, who was younger and a qualified accountant during the Boom Years.

That the people who had sacked my Peter were quoting 'mistreatment of staff' as a reason for disqualifying people from Directorships, which would have serious consequences in their business lives, made me very angry in view of the way that Peter had been treated by the same people. I decided I would attend the EGM, even though it was declared illegal. Up until the last moment Peter was not going to go. I was very determined I was not going to stand by again and say nothing. Peter decided to come too .

The hall in Coventry was full of Members on the 'Rescue' side. Although I had not prepared anything to say, when John Seabourn's redundancy was quoted I declared (at least, I intended to say), to the meeting, that "if mistreatment of staff was to be cited as a reason for removing NEC members then other NECs were also candidates. Most members of staff had been treated unfairly in the past, including Peter." I received a round of applause, which I took to be support for Peter. They could hardly do anything else as he sat in his wheelchair.

A few weeks later Peter wrote a report on the meeting, intending to send it to Dance & Song, however he did not have the confidence. I include it as in the future, when the history of the EFDSS is being rewritten, we were there, prejudiced in our own way, but not of either of the opposing sides:

ILLEGAL EGM, COVENTRY

One way of ensuring a good attendance at a meeting is to declare it illegal. On the 15th July I joined many other members of the EFDSS at a 'private' meeting, called by Miss Janet Wood and others, at The Central (Methodist) Hall, Coventry. The purpose was to consider the very serious matter of removing Directors of the English Folk Dance and Song Society and to consider a resolution under the Insolvency Act. Out of 319 members present it appears that about 299 were determined to vote out the current members of the NEC. The mood was set and any debate seemed irrelevant. Frank

Rawson, who came as 'Communicator' for the NEC, stated that the meeting was illegal and remained as an observer, willing to answer questions. Although his services were not called upon he was warmly applauded later for his bravery in attending. A Daniel in the Lions Den!

Because I've been around a bit it was not surprising that I knew most of those present. I knew them as hard working folkies in local situations throughout the country. This was a rally of the Rescue Group, the party in opposition. Had the other lot been present I would have recognised them also as hard working folkies.

To-day's saga began back in April when the NEC, in response to a proper requisition fixed an EGM for mid October some 5 months ahead. This would have the effect of negating the resolutions proposed, so the requisitionists opted to arrange their own date. However this meeting was declared void because the NEC had fulfilled the legal requirements for an EGM.

I came to listen, hoping to see fair play, yet still to remain independent of all pressure groups. In the absence of the defendants and the dis-enfranchisement of many members the voting out of the current NEC was predictable and one sided, to say the least. As Company law was being used I would have thought that mis-management had to be proved. Much had been written in the Rescue newsletter about particular incidents and situations all of which will have another version. The proposer and other speakers didn't convince me of mis-management but I was in sympathy with someone who pointed out that our normal democratic election in November was a better way of delivering a verdict on the current NEC.

Company law also allows a group of members to replace those ousted with their own nominees. We were presented with a package of seven, two of whom could have still been part of the Management; they had resigned. In the absence of any election address or statement of intent it was suggested, by Gordon Ashman, that 'you will just have to trust us.'!!

The special resolution which seeks to reconstruct our Society under the Insolvency Act 1986 was of interest to many, including myself, who realise that the Society's present existence must be at an end. Apart from the resolution itself no qualifying notes had been written and circulated in advance. The proposer explained that the Act was new and could help Societies like ourselves who were in difficulty; he felt it was the best route to take. Such a route involves the appointment of an Administrator but questions relating to the financing of such a post were only vaguely answered. Although there was some enthusiasm for an independent person to 'sort us out,' the discussion was inconclusive and limited in time in the interests of getting out of the hall. I thought that the subject deserved a much wider debate and was happy when a suggestion was made to adjourn. However, the proposer insisted that a vote be taken on the resolution from what I judged to be a reluctant audience. It was carried easily enough on a show of hands.

So the Management are instructed "to take such steps as are necessary to seek an order of the High Court (Chancery Division) under SS 8 & 9 of the Insolvency Act 1986 to appoint an Administrator to effect a reconstruction of the Charitable Company in such a way as to permit the continuation of its charitable objects, including the continuation of the nationally important Vaughan Williams Memorial Library, and for the order to authorise the Administrator to deal with all property held subject to special trusts, subject always to the consent of the Charity Commissioners."

At that stage I had to remind myself that this was not a legal meeting of the EFDSS. I also pondered on the thought that had it been a fully representative meeting we wouldn't have even got around to discussing this resolution.

That time in EFDSS history was all very nasty; we found the bits of paper which came through our door, with either side accusing each of dire deeds, strangely therapeutic. We could rant and rave about both sides' stupidity, thus getting rid of the intense frustrations caused by MND. We almost enjoyed what was really the death throes of the Society which had been our life.

HOLIDAYS and HELP

FELIXSTOWE FESTIVAL

In May we decided to go to Felixstowe Festival, to be amongst friends. This was a sad time for the Festival as Phil Woodgate, the Director of Felixstowe Festival and friend, had recently died of cancer.

Felixstowe Committee very kindly organised and paid for us to stay in a posh hotel, quite a change from the windswept campsite we used to stay on. It was difficult with Peter unable to stand on his sprained leg and the van still wasn't ready so we had to use the manual wheelchair. Peter was also needing help with cutting up food and lifting cups to drink and we weren't quite used to performing these tasks in public. Diane had brought a commode on casters which could be pushed over the toilet, to cope with the latest problems presented by the fall, and a 2-handled light weight mug, which we took with us. In the new Leisure Centre, which replaced the Pavilion, we came across a planner's idea of a toilet for the disabled. It had just one door from a very public corridor; the carer having manoeuvred the wheelchair into an awkward angled space and transferred the occupant, was then forced to stay in the toilet as opening the door would expose the user to public gaze! Despite the problems, we enjoyed being back in Suffolk.

NAIDEX EXHIBITION

RADAR put on a major exhibition (Naidex) of equipment and services for the disabled each year; it is very worthwhile going even if you are not disabled. We were well into equipment by now and in May we went to a Naidex in Manchester. Peter spent a long time at the Possum stand. Possum is an "Environmental Control System. A single switch can control up to 20 mains electric appliances per room in up to 3 rooms. It is available free from the Department of Health to patients so paralysed or disabled by disease, injury or congenital defect that they are unable to carry out simple tasks at home, such as switching on a light." *In May Peter could not do this as he could not walk and he had not the strength in his hands to press a light switch. We arranged for a visit by a Possum assessor. Peter was very interested, this would give him greater independence.*

VAN

On Friday 26th May I drove the Orion into Sheffield and came home alone, very nervously, with the new van.

That evening we heard on the news that Don Revie, the football manager, had died of Motor Neurone Disease. Peter had followed his progress; from the little that was shown on TV it appeared that Peter's MND was similar to Don Revie's and we assumed we were not long behind him; yet in May 1989 we also assumed we had a long way to go. Peter was very shaken by the news.

The next day we set off to the Gower Peninsular in South Wales. Peter had chosen a holiday bungalow from the Hoseason's brochure because it was advertised as having a ramp and suitable for disabled. He had fond memories of an early Folk Camp on the Gower and wanted to return. The van had to be run in, so we went slowly and I had trouble getting third gear, which was pretty hairy at times. Peter never complained.

'HOLIDAY'

When we got to the bungalow we found there wasn't a ramp and the door was 10" off the ground. The only way to get Peter and wheelchair in was to back the van up to the door, Giles put the van ramps into the doorway and Peter reversed straight into the hall. All this with a brand new vehicle.

The 'holiday village' was not what we were used to, rather austere and not in an attractive area. There was a swimming pool, but we could not get Peter in it. We went to beaches but Peter could not go on in the wheelchair. Coping with not standing or being able to sit up without all the equipment, especially the bed, was very difficult and exhausting. On drives Peter navigated, something he was not used to, so we ended up attempting to go along footpaths in the van! The holiday was not a success and we came home early, to everyone's relief. Holidays were lost to us.

DAILY LIFE

We came back to a routine of getting Peter up, washed and dressed, breakfast prepared then sat at the wordprocessor on the Mangar Buggy while I took William to school. Once the WP was switched on and paper in the printer Peter could manage, typing with two fingers. We had bought a sheet feeder for the printer so he could print several sheets without help.

At lunch-time I would push the Booster up to the dining table and prepare his lunch. He could pick things up if not heavy and I had cut his food. After lunch he usually went to bed so I pushed him through and transferred him onto the bed, lifting his legs on. Later he would go back to the wordprocessor and it would all be repeated. At night he would need turning 2 or 3 times to get comfortable or the duvet retrieved if it had slipped.

Toileting necessitated transferring Peter from the Buggy to commode which I then pushed over the toilet. Twice a week we went to hydrotherapy at Firbeck, now using the hoist to get him into the water.

IN-GROWING TOENAIL

When Peter was unable to walk his feet began to swell due to his inactivity. I told him his shoes were too tight but he persisted. The pressure caused an in-growing toenail necessitating surgery. Dr. Proctor did this under local anaesthetic at the Health Centre, not a pleasant experience. Do not wear tight shoes if your feet swell.

The District Nurse came to assess our needs when the toe needed dressing regularly. I expected that they would see the difficulties we were in and assign someone to assist; they said I was coping. To those in a similar position tell the Authorities when you need help, it is rarely offered. Nurses only came to dress Peter's toe, not the rest of him, as I needed.

HELPING HANDS

By this time we had lost contact with most of our local friends although folk friends still phoned or wrote or visited. We became more reliant upon the Coward family living opposite, especially in emergencies such as a fall. In all the times when we have needed help it has not necessarily come from the expected source of family and friends but it has been forthcoming. Such were the Cowards and then Helping Hands.

Two friends had set up a business to do cleaning, shopping, babysitting, anything that was required and posted notices through doors. This seemed too good to miss, my house was a tip, I had little time for housework. I booked them to do some cleaning. When they turned up I found I knew one, Cath Holmes, from National Childbirth Trust days. It turned out that Cath was a Nurse and did not mind taking Peter to hydrotherapy, including drying and dressing him, which I dreaded it was so tiring; so I stayed home one of the sessions and did the cleaning. Peter wasn't nagged, we both had a break from each other and it proved the start of a very valuable friendship with Cath.

By the time Cath joined us the sprains from the fall had mended and to everyone's surprise Peter could stand again and walk a few steps with the frame. We really thought that MND would have destroyed those muscles as he had not been far off before the fall. Even Jane Petty, the most experienced person we knew of MND, was amazed. It certainly appeared that the progression of the disease had slowed in comparison with the previous few months. Whether it was due to taking the amino-acids we can never be sure, but we didn't feel inclined to stop.

FOUNDATION FOR COMMUNICATION FOR THE DISABLED

After the Possum Peter turned to looking for alternatives to the wordprocessor for the time when he would no longer be able to operate the keyboard and possibly be unable to speak. The wordprocessor supplied with Possum would not be adequate. We preferred to prepare for problems, many people with MND would rather not and cope without many of the aids available.

Colin Matthews, a voluntary worker for Peter at Expo, had taken a new post with the Spastic Society as Adviser on Technical Equipment; he arranged a meeting with speech therapist, Liz Panton of Newcastle Communication Centre and Paul Hawes of the Foundation for Communication for the Disabled, Surrey. Diane Peake also came. The advice was to replace our PCW with a PC, IBM compatible in order to have ease of starting up and software to operate a single switch. This entailed an outlay of £1,000+.

We came to no conclusion as Peter could still use the PCW with help and if we had a new machine he would have to learn a new system; the last one was infuriating enough! However I strongly recommend contacting the Foundation for advice. They were considerate, helpful, at no time did we feel under any pressure to buy; Paul went to great lengths to find the right equipment for our needs and, what was nicest, disability was treated as normal. We were not labelled as having 'this disability, therefore that happens', Peter had 'certain problems, how is it best to solve them?' In other words he was treated as an individual, quite rare when one is disabled. One of the most annoying aspects of having MND was the way some professionals would arrive without an appointment, expecting us to drop everything to see them. This was not the case with either Diane Peake or Jane Petty, who made proper appointments or phoned first. The Technical Officer, however, regularly called unannounced. Twice we were out; he then phoned to complain; our lives were not our own! Do not be bullied, without the disabled they would not have a job.

TRIPS OUT

By July we were settled into a sort of routine and MND was not nearly so rampant. We had trips out in the van including the illegal EFDSS EGM at Coventry, Stainsby Folk Festival, Rother Valley Park and the Great Yorkshire Show. Here we were quite shocked to see a large number of young people in manual wheelchairs who were parked while their carers went elsewhere and could not move. It quite upset me. Peter was able to take himself where he wanted; we had to look for the easiest routes and check that he was OK but it was a good day out. We really appreciated the van having cooking and eating facilities and the toilet on board. There was a tremendous contrast in the quality of life between Peter and those young adults confined to being pushed, maybe for years.

CARAVAN

Giles and I found time to make progress with the portacabin, moving the Nursery equipment out of the caravan and rearranging furniture. This was fortunate because one morning I looked out and the caravan had vanished. Rather stupidly I ran down the drive expecting to see the caravan across the road in the hedge! We did not see the caravan again, with it the cushions for the van and a lot of camping equipment. We were very sad as we were fond of the caravan, few had been made and it had been ideal for our needs before MND. However its loss did solve the question of whether I would ever tow it. We bought a large lightweight tent instead, which the wheelchair could go in. We did get insurance on the caravan but nowhere near what we would have needed to replace it.

INDEPENDENT LIVING FUND

I had hopes in July of opening Nursery in October but it was also becoming clear that I would need help for Peter while I was working. Diane Peake came with a leaflet about the Independent Living Fund; this was a charitable trust to help very severely disabled people with the costs of employing assistance which they need to enable them to live independently in the community. It was Government funded, administrated by independent Trustees, set up in 1988 following changes in Social Security legislation. In 1989 very little was known about it, we were very lucky that Diane picked it up. We put in an application, it sounded too good to be true.

MARY MARLBOROUGH LODGE, OXFORD

Jane Petty, aware of our interest in equipment, suggested that Peter might care to go to MML for assessment, this would entail staying in the hospital for one or two weeks. We agreed as they might come up with something useful and the boys and I would get a break. Our GP referred Peter. We were given a date, 13th August 1989, following Sidmouth. Meanwhile Diane provided a swivel seat to fit on the bath as transferring Peter from chair to Booster in the bath became more difficult so he could have a shower. Bathing days were over.

SIDMOUTH

After the holiday in the Gower I was not keen to go away again but Peter wanted to go to Sidmouth. I couldn't refuse although I drew the line at camping. We booked a family room in the Bedford Hotel, on the Esplanade. I explained our problems and they assured me that despite there being steps the staff could manage. I was still doubtful but booked for 4 nights. We took the manual wheelchair for use in the hotel, which was fortunate because the joystick control on the powered chair gave up the second day. The staff in the hotel were wonderful, carrying Peter up and down steps and assisting when he fell. We were in a downstairs room and saw lots of friends passing the french windows. We did have problems with the bathroom; Peter was still walking with the frame, just, but there wasn't enough room for the frame in the bathroom. It took a lot of manoeuvring to get to the toilet and some very dicey moments.

To my great surprise we all seemed to enjoy Sidmouth. People helped push Peter, the organisers gave us a car pass to park at the arena and attempted to mend the joystick. Giles could go off on his own, I even left Peter on his own in the Church one evening, collecting him later. The weather was hot and it was lovely being waited on in the hotel as it was very tiring seeing to Peter in the day and having to turn him several times at night.

One of Peter's visitors was Hilary Warburton, one of the EFDSS NEC members. She surprised us by asking Peter to run a Christmas event at Cecil Sharp House on behalf of the Society. We took it on mainly because it seemed churlish not to, at last Peter had been asked to do something. It was not ideal, working at a distance and Peter increasingly handicapped.

Peter was pleased with the way Sidmouth Festival was developing and on our return sent a few suggestions to Steve Heap, Director.

POSSUM

We returned early as the Possum assessor was coming on Friday 11th. August. Diane, Ray, Hellen Critten from Possum and Dr Mahoderon, Health Authority Rep. (who sanctions what is recommended) attended. We asked that we had controls to cover alarms, bed, wordprocessor, telephone, radio, television, lights, curtains, intercom, electric fire and fan.

The suggestion was that we would have Possum in both the front room, Peter's bedroom, and in the extension, where he worked at the wordprocessor. This entailed fitting new electric sockets and lifting the carpets in each room. The house was already full of equipment and the portacabin full of furniture. I persuaded Peter to confine Possum to the front room *and we move the wordprocessor in there, so everything would be to hand. The front room had to be re-arranged anyway to accommodate Possum. I was beginning to understand why many disabled did not go in for equipment; it can take over one's life!*

MARY MARLBOROUGH

On Sunday, 13th August we packed the van again with all equipment, tents and luggage and set off for Oxford and Mary Marlborough Lodge for assessment, with some trepidation; we were not sure what we had committed ourselves to. I must have been in a state as I left my handbag behind with all my money and credit cards. I rang our neighbour, Don Coward, with Giles pocket money; Don went out of his way to bring my purse to Oxford on one of his deliveries.

Peter was put in a room on his own. Tired after the journey we put him to bed. We had to order more pillows in an attempt to get him comfortable, he was used to the electric bed being raised to support his legs, helping to prevent cramps.

Spouses were expected to stay but I had decided to take the opportunity to visit Mum and then go home to sort out the house in readiness for Possum. We camped one night then went into MML for the day to check that Peter was alright. He had met another man, Lesley, the first person we had known personally with MND. He could walk quite well but he could not hold his head up or feed himself. Peter compared notes and realised how fortunate he was. Lesley had been a highly paid Manager, so was not without money, but he was virtually housebound and only had a manual chair, so had to be pushed everywhere. He had hardly any equipment and spent his day sat in the garden or watching television. He did not even have a computer. His wife could not drive and would not learn as she had had a breakdown due to the stress of coping with MND. We felt very sorry for them. There were others even worse. One woman had been a professional pianist and lost the use of her hands. She saw no point in carrying on and just wanted to die. We were quite surprised to find how people reacted so differently to the disease. There were five MND patients amongst a variety of disabilities.

I showed the nurses in charge how to make Peter comfortable and the exercises to keep joints mobile and hoped he would be alright. We arrived at Mum's late that Monday night. We hadn't seen her for over a year as there was no way we could get Peter into the bungalow. We spent a few days taking Mum shopping and out on trips, returning to Oxford for the weekend.

Peter had not slept comfortably out of his own bed and he had fallen when a nurse took him to the toilet so now two nurses took him. He enjoyed the company

and found the advice useful. We camped for the weekend and on Sunday we took Peter to the campsite. It was by the river and very peaceful. A happy day.

We had a report from MML which gives an independent assessment of the stage MND had reached at the time we went to Oxford:

DISCHARGE REPORT

Nuffield Orthopaedic Centre, Headington, Oxford OX3 7LD.

NURSING; Mr Dashwood is dependent for all care except feeding. Continent, needs help to transfer.

LOCOMOTOR ASSESSMENT; Can walk with a rollator frame but feet tend to drop. Muscle tone reduced in all limbs distally more than proximally. Power: shoulders grade 4; elbows 3+; wrist 2. Hips 3+; knees 2+; feet 1. Contractures — minimal tightness of finger flexors. Spine straight. Has hydrotherapy twice a week.

TREATMENT: Flowtron tried to decrease ankle oedema *(boots which vibrate to disperse fluid)*. Below knee Sigvaris *(elastic)* stockings to decrease swelling. Ankle/foot orthoses were considered but are not suitable due to swelling. ESP boots *(soft with velcro fastenings)* supplied. General mobilising and active exercises. Stretches for hands. Foam roll to help keep fingers straight. Collar given *(to support head)*.

TRANSFERS: Has help from one person to stand and turn. Mangar Booster Bug assists his wife with transfers. Turning disc tried, successful *(not with his wife!)*. Medesign sling tried, not suitable. Information on Isis portable hoist and Wessex gantry hoist *(to help with transfers in the future)*.

WHEELCHAIR: Has an 8L *(manual)* chair. Issued with 109 wheelchair *(electric indoor)*. Back rest extension — 12", arm rests raised 2", comfort strut and tray ordered, right hand control, Zimmer ejector seat and Sumed cushion *(contained a gel, to prevent pressure sores)* ordered.

PERSONAL CARE: Dependent for most aspects of personal care. Teeth; uses electric brush, independent if switched on. Feeding; manages light cutlery, beginning to be difficult. Given right mobile arm support with T-bar and spork. Drinking; requires cup to be half full and large handle.

WORK & LEISURE: Enjoys reading — difficulty turning pages. Shown techniques using paper clips, rubber thimbles. Information on Wroe *(electric)* page turner. Enjoys sketching — fitted with right mobile arm support with pencil holder. Uses word processor.

COMMUNICATION & ENVIRONMENTAL CONTROL: Shown PSU.6 *(Possum)* control system which is to be installed at home. Given information on compatible printers and computers for PSU.6.

TRANSPORT: Has van with drive-in for wheelchair.

SPEECH: No problems eating or swallowing, speech 100% intelligible.

PETER'S REPORT ON MML:

I needed advice on all aspects of MND including equipment, exercise and general care. I was in Mary Marlborough Lodge, Oxford for 10 days. It was useful to meet other MND patients and discuss problems with them. All four had been affected in different ways.

I am grateful to the centre for equipping me with an electric indoor wheelchair and making useful adjustments to it re seating, height of sides and the fitting of a tray and a feeding arm as my arms were too weak to lift utensils. A combined fork/spoon was fitted as an extension to enable me to pick up food from the plate. It was noted that I was interested in drawing so I was given another feeding arm adapted to hold a pencil so I could draw. As arm muscles became weaker this proved invaluable for pressing the keys of the word processor, eliminating the need for single switches.

For independence about the house a compact and manoeuvrable electric chair, which should get round most corners, is a must. Seating can vary but mine is quite comfortable with a Sumed cushion. We were also given a spring loaded ejector seat which was not successful as it tended to stand me up at an insecure angle; also the spring didn't always work immediately but hit me behind the knees on the way up!

I was fitted with elastic stockings to reduce swelling in ankles and had physiotherapy sessions to assist in the process.

I am quite certain that the centre can assist the 'straightforward' disabled such as those who have lost limbs. I came away unconvinced of the centre's ability to understand and give more than minimal help to those with MND and similar conditions."

He was never satisfied, he had far more help than most people in his situation!

On Monday I returned home with the boys leaving Peter for 5 more days. I tidied the garden and re-organised the house, again. The door between the front room, Peter's bedroom, and the dining area had been blocked off when we used the front room as an office and shelves put in, hidden by a curtain. Giles and I had to find homes for the things on the shelves and unblock the door so Peter could get into the dining area without going through the hall. We then moved the wordprocessor into the front room, with all the ancillary equipment, paper etc. On Friday 25th Don brought Peter back in his van, along with sundry equipment and the fourth wheelchair!

EXPO 1989

On Saturday 26th August we packed the van again, this time for Peterborough and Expo. It was to be the last; the Showground had been booked for an International Landscape Exhibition in 1990 and Expo organisers had not found a place to relocate.

Peter had sent out the detailed working programmes in July, before Sidmouth and asked Peter Davis to be in charge over the weekend, in case we did not make it. He was still expanding the show; in addition to the regulars, The Yetties, Squarecrows, Rhona Baldrey's Irish Dancers, John Tether, Peterborough Morris and Cross Key Clog and song evenings hosted by Brian Kell, Peter introduced Jazz dancing with the Jiving Lindy Hoppers and an additional Compere/performer, Stanley Accrington. Other teams included the Tatry Polish dancers from London and the Grand Union Rapper Team from Bedfordshire. The Wolsey Folk Group, from Ipswich, came to the first Expo and the last. As usual the celebrations began on Saturday evening with a concert, dance and fireworks.

This time we had no choice but to camp. I was quite prepared to go home on Sunday, we had not tried sleeping Peter in the van. Friends helped put up the tent; we had the big wheelchair and a high seat for Peter and kept the toilet in the tent, with seat; but MND had progressed since Sidmouth and I had difficulty getting him up on my own. Peter Davis had increased duties.

To get into the van Peter drove the wheelchair up the ramps, then I transferred him onto a seat. I would put the chair into manual and run it out to be stored in the tent. I then had to make up the bed, get Peter washed and in a track suit for sleeping and made comfortable. William was to sleep in the tent with Giles but wanted to stay with us so slept on the front seats, a mistake; in the middle of the night he fell off the seat knocking the horn. Half the Folk camp rushed to see what the emergency was! To my surprise, apart from this incident, we had a relatively good night. I had to turn Peter several times, but we did sleep.

Expo was quite good, we were amongst friends who knew us before MND and whom I could trust to look after Peter, especially the Scotts and Davises. I went round the site with the boys, which was relaxing. We were all together and doing our own thing, almost normal. If people found it difficult seeing Peter they did not show it. In himself he was no different and bombed around in the electric chair.

Sunday night was a different matter. I could not get Peter comfortable and we hardly slept at all, so Monday was a trial. I was very glad to get home.

In November Peter wrote to all who had been involved:

"I would like to express my thanks to all who contributed to the Expo Folk Show over the course of 11 years. Like me, you will have your own memories of the happy occasions in the barn and the distractions around it, be it the Fun Fair or Fireworks, the Sealed Knot, Real Ale or the Red Arrows. In recent years the main event has run down but we maintained our audiences and interest to the end and went out on a high. There was a suggestion that the Folk Show could be set up elsewhere but I'm afraid that I cannot contemplate taking any initiatives in that direction. I am feeling the effects of Motor Neurone Disease more so in recent weeks. Janet and I are having to face new situations almost daily."

The end of Expo closed another chapter.

FURTHER DECLINE and the EFDSS

We had hardly been home in August with visits to Sidmouth, Oxford, Poole and Peterborough but we were aware that we were on another downhill slope and September saw a rapid increase in 'losses'. I could no longer stand Peter from the wheelchairs or stairlift, on my own; only the Booster chair and bed took him high enough. We sent the MNDA easy chair back as we had the bed for resting; someone else would benefit from the chair. As more leg muscles were lost so the days of any walking were over, other than in water. Peter could no longer dial or hold the phone; he was down to one finger on the key board; he tired very easily and usually had a sleep in the afternoon; he needed a lot of exercising or his legs cramped.

NURSES and HOME HELP

Getting Peter dressed posed serious problems. In Oxford he had two nurses to transfer him, I decided enough was enough and wrote to Dr Proctor to ask for assistance. Dr Proctor responded immediately and we were reassessed by the District Nursing Service on our return from Expo. This time a Sister came. She was most sympathetic and allotted us calls twice a day to get Peter up, washed and dressed and the reverse at night. She also referred us to the Home Help Service which gave us 4 hours per week cleaning, usually a low priority.

We felt many of our problems would be solved as much of the physical strain of MND would fall on others, in fact we changed one set of problems for another. We found the invasion of privacy one of the most difficult to cope with, along with not knowing when a nurse would turn up. They could come anytime up to 12 in the morning and after 6 at night. Sometimes it was 11 am and the morning was gone and 7.45 pm, so Peter was in bed before William. It was not good for morale.

Another problem was that we did not have the same nurse each day, so each had to be shown what needed doing. One came to 'assist the wife', which entailed ME getting Peter washed and dressed while she lent a hand occasionally. I wasn't having that and found urgent things to do when she came.

There were a disproportionate number of nurses allergic to cats, which was difficult with us having two. One Sister had a cat phobia and would call out, "Is it alright to come in?" from the door; we had no idea who it was and would say "yes", only to find the nurse disappearing in hysterics because a cat was in sight. There was a nurse who would not have gone amiss in the wrestling ring, Peter was not sure if he hadn't been

after her visits. It did not help that her car regularly broke down when she got to us. Later I would send her away and get Peter ready myself until we asked that she was not sent to us. Others were efficient and friendly; two I knew personally, Jean Blackburn and Hellen Adamson, as they had sent children to Playgroup.

The Sister recommended use of a sheath attached to urinary bag at night to save getting Peter to the toilet. The sheath had to be fitted every night. Jean Blackburn had the unenviable job of showing us how to put it on. A sense of humour and lack of embarrassment is essential to coping with MND! Having the sheath saved us getting up in the night but created other problems in that sometimes it leaked or we could not get it off in the morning, or on at night! There were lurid descriptions from the night nurses of other patients.

Two of the Auxiliary nurses became regulars in putting Peter to bed, which was a relief as they knew how to deal with him and were able to adapt to changing circumstances. Occasionally we had a male nurse. One would expect that Peter would have liked this but he lifted using strength instead of technique, which did not give Peter confidence, Peter had less control. The best of all the nurses was Sister Guy, a ray of sunshine. When she arrived on a morning visit the day improved immediately. We reckoned she should come on prescription.

Although we were allotted 4 hours Home Help household duties we rarely got them as my Home Help, Aileen, would be sent elsewhere on emergencies. She was a wonderful cleaner, however, and it was amazing what she could do in 2 hours. She did find coping with Peter difficult, knowing he was going to die, and would talk in whispers. She was particularly surprised that Peter knew his illness was terminal. We found this attitude oddly amusing.

REFLEXOLOGY

I retained Cath of Helping Hands for at least 4 hours per week to help in the garden, cleaning or whatever I could not do. She would help me get Peter back to bed and started massaging his legs to prevent the cramps. This hurt Peter as the muscles had gone so she started practising Reflexology techniques on him, massaging his feet. Cath had been trained in Hong Kong by a Chinese practitioner. The effect of reflexology was to relax Peter and prevent the cramps and other aches and pains. Frequently it sent him to sleep minutes after she started.

September was also a change for the boys. William went into the Junior School. I was worried that he would find the more formal style of teaching difficult to cope with but he is very capable and seemed to enjoy the challenge.

Giles left his protective School for Physically Disabled Children to take a Foundation Course at the local College. This entailed catching a bus instead of being collected by taxi and getting himself around, organising his own lunch and generally being independent. The first week he was amazed that he could choose his lunch in the cafe, take sandwiches, buy fish and chips or even not have anything at all! At school everyone had school dinners.

RESEARCH INTO COUNSELLING

All the rapid physical changes were putting a strain on us emotionally. Towards the end of September a researcher for the MNDA came to ask how counselling could have helped us at diagnosis. It was not a good time to come, we had put the traumas of diagnosis and the depression behind us, talking about them opened old wounds while we were trying to come to terms with new ones, we could not cope with both. Also, I think it would have been better if we had seen her individually so we could have talked openly about our problems. Although we were both fighting the one disease many of the problems we faced were quite different. All the physical work and organisation fell on me. The techniques we had used to get Peter dressed, fed and toileted had become redundant and we had to experiment with new methods which did not always work. Time consuming, exhausting and frustrating, every movement had to be considered. I was also torn between the needs of Peter and the boys, at 7 and 17 they needed a lot of attention. With disturbed nights getting up to turn Peter, I was at a low ebb, there was no time left for me as a person, so when we were asked if I made any time for myself, I replied: " When I get really tired that is what I yell about." Peter's reply was: " Yes she does, she falls asleep on the settee after dinner." I could have hit him!

On the other hand, Peter had to cope with not being able to do anything for himself. I cannot even imagine it and I lived with the disease. He felt guilty. He also had no one to talk to who could really understand his problems. The one thing he could still do was work the word processor, it became his life. He spent hours writing his life history, organising the Christmas event at Cecil Sharp House and letters. He used it to cut himself off from the guilt. He told the researcher: "I just blame myself that I can't do enough, I have a conscience about it. I don't think about the garden or physical things at all. Everything has fallen on

Janet. In my own mind I don't think she's got time to do anything. Situations become more acute. Janet flies off the handle much quicker, the children suffer from that and I withdraw."

In doing so he cut himself off from his family. I would have to get very cross in order to get him to talk or read to the children. Then, later, he was surprised that they no longer came to him with their problems. After days of ignoring us, he would suddenly expect the boys to talk to him and they weren't used to it. Someone said that they worried if they didn't see Peter smiling, because he always did, William retorted that "WE worried if he did as Dad was always grumpy." I think Peter thought it a joke but there was a lot of truth in it.

The researcher asked if the disease had brought us closer together? At that stage we had to say No. In many ways it was forcing us apart because we could no longer walk or garden together, we had to do things on our own. We found this hard and I stopped gardening because I missed Peter being with me. It would annoy me intensely and quite irrationally that Peter was in the house and not be able to help. When he was away in Oxford I coped much better, that was more normal for us, just as if he was away working for the Society.

The boys had to cope with all the changes too. Giles particularly missed going out as we used to, to castles, museums and on walks. Any trip took tremendous organisation, ten times worse than taking a baby.

Schools had reported that the boys' school work was not suffering. At College Giles found the tutors sympathetic and willing to listen to him about the problems at home, whereas William's teacher, with 30 in the class, had less time. William said he did not talk about his Dad because "No-one understood." They were both aware of the consequences of the disease, although we had not told them directly. In the summer, when we were travelling, both had remarked, "When Daddy's gone we shall be able to ..." It was done naturally, not a big deal. When William first said it I looked in the mirror to see Peter's reaction. He looked rather surprised but nothing was said. The remark did not need a reply and we kept the conversation light, accepted the fact. I think it helped Peter in the long run.

We did not discuss Death much, to live life as if we were about to die would have meant defeat. We knew it was there, inevitable. We tried to make the most of what we'd got.

HYDROTHERAPY

The physical changes also meant Firbeck could no longer cope with us, they did not have the facilities for someone as disabled as Peter had become. Jane Petty referred us to the Physiotherapy Department at Rotherham General Hospital, which had a small pool for exercising. Their main patients seemed to be arthritic, many having hip replacements.

There were only 1-3 people in at a time and a permanent nurse to help me get Peter dressed. The round trip could still take up to 3 hours, though, for 20 minutes in the water, as it took longer to get Peter ready. The days of Cath taking him were gone, the van, with its ramps, was essential. Reliance upon ambulances would have been impossible, Peter was usually very tired after hydrotherapy, waiting around for an ambulance, for maybe hours, would have finished him off. The effort of getting him there was worth it and I resented it less, he wrote later: "The water gives sufficient buoyancy for me to be able to walk a little and I am able to exercise leg and shoulder muscles under supervision. It is a good confidence booster and I would recommend it to other MND sufferers."

Occasionally, on good days, we took a picnic to Ulley reservoir, where we could pretend we were in Scotland, or to Wentworth Garden Centre.

NURSERY

The opening date for Nursery looked as far away as ever. We still needed mains services to the cabin. This entailed digging a trench down the garden for water, electricity and drainage. Peter was still doubtful that I had time to take on the extra work so I encouraged him to take a part and he hired a digger to dig the trench. Unfortunately he forgot to ask the size of the digger; which was how we came to have a huge JCB transforming the garden into a moonscape in September. We needed a 2 ft. deep trench, we got one 4 ft deep that William could stand in and not be seen! I had to hire a lorry to take away the surplus earth when it wouldn't all go back!

Our local handyman connected the services to the portacabin, put in a toilet, sink and cupboards, fitted gates to the garden for security and I ordered a garage to stand next to the portacabin. It was too small for the van but essential as a store for all the things currently in the portacabin!

I fitted carpet and cushion flooring in Nursery and we gradually got things into place. Various friends agreed to act as emergency supervisors, so in October Social Services registered us for 6 children per session, 10 sessions per week. I arranged insurance to begin January 1990.

INDEPENDENT LIVING FUND

Also in September the Doctor came to assess us from the ILF. We were prepared with all relevant information on income and expenses, as the Fund is means-tested, and on what assistance Peter needed compared with what help we received. We did not hear until late October the results of our application.

PROGNOSIS FOR WINTER 1989/90

Peter began having difficulty with breathing in September he was therefore at risk from a chest infection which could turn to pneumonia. This could be treated by antibiotics but I was warned it is frequently fatal. I ensured that anyone with an infection did not go near Peter, including nurses, who were turned away if necessary. He was also moved a lot, in and out of bed, going to hydrotherapy and on trips. Immobility encourages fluid to collect in the lungs and increases the likelihood of pneumonia. He also did deep breathing exercises and moved himself as much as he was able. The District Nurses and Home Help, I learnt much later, were told they would not be needed after Christmas. Fortunately no-one told us until much later.

RESPITE AT CLAREMONT HOSPITAL

At the beginning of October Jane Petty told us about respite care at a private hospital in Sheffield, run by nuns. They kept two free beds for MS and MND patients to give families a break; Jane was willing to refer Peter. He said we were nowhere near that stage yet; I felt differently, full time caring was very wearing and the boys had not had a proper holiday. I asked Jane to go ahead for the half-term at the end of October and told Peter. He accepted this although it must have been a worry to be away from his equipment and all those who knew his needs.

We took Peter into Claremont on Sunday 22nd October with his computer. His room overlooked the grounds with lovely trees and squirrels. There was no communal area, so I thought he might be rather lonely but nurses went into chat during the day; they seemed interested in the computer and the way he was coping with his disabilities. Peter liked the service, including tea from a silver pot and china cups, it was more like a hotel; although one problem was the shortage of night staff, only two for two floors, getting turned at night was not easy, Peter could not have gone there as he became more disabled.

When we came home my mother gave us money so I could buy some china cups as Peter said the tea tasted better from them. It was difficult to find some that he could hold, have only half filled and still get some tea.

The boys and I set off for York on Monday. We visited museums, the Cathedral, shops and went on a river trip, seeing a kingfisher. We walked miles, which we were not used to and were exhausted. On Thursday we went north to see Rievaulx Abbey, stopping at Helmsley, spectacular in the Autumn colours, it was lovely to be out in the country. William spent his time chasing about making a lot of noise, enjoying the freedom. We returned home via Sutton Bank, a 1 in 4 spectacular hill, to a bouquet of flowers and card from Peter. He had missed us.

On Friday I cleaned the house in readiness for Mum's 70th birthday party. I had invited fifteen members of her close family and collected her in Sheffield on Saturday. Rosemary was doing the catering and Cath the cake. The boys and I fetched Peter after Sunday lunch in order to have time to get everything ready. Peter was tired by the number of people and I put him to bed after tea. Mum went with Irene's to stay a few days.

POSSUM ENVIRONMENTAL CONTROL.

On Monday Possum was fitted, a mammoth task. We had been told that the fitters would be here by 9 am, by which time we had to have another fuse box and electric socket fitted and an electrician on call. Our handi-man came at 8 am and we moved Peter into the extension. Possum didn't turn up until 11 am. I was not impressed.

They said they would be finished in 4 hours which overran hydrotherapy time so I had to leave them to let themselves out. When we returned we found an awful mess; there were bits of cable all over the carpet, the wires behind the main control were like a plate of spaghetti, plaster dust from where they had drilled into the wall had not been cleared up. I had to pay Cath to come and clean the next day and some one from Possum came eventually to sort out the wires. We really could have done without the extra work. Possum apologised saying it was a new fitter but when dealing with the severely disabled one would expect a better check. I was glad we had confined Possum to the front room!

Despite the problems with installation Possum did prove invaluable. Peter wrote in January 1990:

"The Possum Environmental Control equipment enables me to operate independently, via a flat single switch and a monitor, the useful facilities around me; it includes answering and making calls on the telephone; bed raising and lowering; a lock on one outside door; intercoms on two doors and to Janet's and Giles' bedrooms; radio; lights; fire and word processor. I shall soon also have a curtain control and a page turner."

Later we realised we should have fitted an intercom into the living room so Peter could call night nurses or alert us in the day. At the time Peter could yell, he couldn't for long. The telephone worked on a microphone and speaker system, so it did not have to be held but the sound quality was poor and people on the other end often did not hear what Peter said. The intercoms were very effective; one by my bed would go in the middle of the night and I would be half way down the stairs before I opened my eyes, the call was so loud and urgent. I don't think I ever got used to it. Occasionally Peter would press the switch on the wrong line and set off the alarm by mistake. I would race downstairs and he would unconcernedly say sorry!! This did not go down well when I could be called out of bed three times a night when he genuinely needed help.

The Health Service offered us Night Sitters, Auxiliary Nurses, once a week to give me a break. I was not at all happy about a stranger in our house at night but agreed to try it. The first one went home after two hours as she was allergic to cats, the next two both smoked, Peter was having difficulty breathing! We stopped having sitters.

INDEPENDENT LIVING FUND

In October we were granted 24 hours care per week to be paid for by the ILF. They assessed us as needing the extra hours care whether I worked or not. There was no indication of what rates to pay carers, we had to find them, organise times, pay them and reclaim the money. We sent the names, addresses and qualifications of the people employed and invoices. This was a time consuming exercise which Peter would not have been able to do on his own and one needed substantial capital as the invoices were paid, initially 2 months, then 1 month in arrears.

Although the award was backdated we did not know if it would be granted so we went without help to which we were entitled and which would have made life more bearable, for 5 months. The procedure needed to be quicker and people be more aware that they might qualify. However, it was well worth the effort as we were now in charge of much of the care Peter needed. MND takes away control of one's body, it is essential to retain control of the environment. The money from ILF was a Godsend, without it and Possum Peter may have been in hospital and probably dead soon after Christmas.

We were fortunate in knowing a few local nurses through the original Playgroup, Cath Holmes I paid already. Hellen Adamson, one of our evening District Nurses, started helping in October and Jean Edmondson in November. They assisted with getting Peter on and off the commode, in and out of bed, dressing, sitting, getting him in and out of the van and the house twice a week on hydrotherapy days. They helped transferring Peter onto the stairlift, then to a chair, finally a shower chair in order to give him a shower and to be on call when I was out shopping or taking William to swimming and violin lessons. They were invaluable and lived near enough to come in an emergency in addition to Rosemary & Don Coward, who still came voluntarily.

NIGHT CARE

By November Peter needed two people to move him much of the time. There were a few awful nights when he called me down to turn him as usual and I could not get him comfortable so neither of us had much sleep. His condition had deteriorated so he could move himself even less and I had not the strength to lift him. I asked for a reassessment by the ILF in order to employ Night Duty Agency Nurses. They would come for 10 hour shifts on Sleeper Duty, ie. they would sleep but get up when Peter needed them. The first call was free, subsequent calls cost £2.30 each. We had been allowed 24 hours care per week, that didn't go far per night.

We did not hear from the ILF that we were granted the extra hours until January but started employing the Agency Nurses for 5 nights per week from November as an absolute necessity if I was to sleep. I was still on call at weekends and if I was needed. Peter usually needed assistance 3 times per night for turning, massage to ease the aches and cramps, or a bottle. We had stopped using the urinary sheaths attached to a bag, a bottle was much easier when someone had to get up to him anyway. Giles and I moved the folding bed into the extension for the nurses to sleep on.

The first week we almost thought we had made a mistake, one of the Agency nurses turned up with her slippers, dressing gown and curlers. She was near retiring age and we were doubtful that she could lift Peter; she assured us she would be alright. Neither of us took to her and I felt a traitor leaving Peter to his fate; she talked non-stop, which drove Peter batty. In the morning, while she should have been standing him up, she dropped him. He fell backwards, hitting his head on the metal chair, causing a nasty gash and dazing Peter. He did not fall once when I was moving him. That nurse did not come again; we suggested she did not go to any similar patients.

We were more successful with others, many of the Agency nurses became good friends. Anne Guest and Frances Turner were sympathetic and exuded confidence, Jayne Cookson was bubbly and took an interest in Folk, we looked forward to their visits, Diane Chambers became an essential regular and friend, volunteering to come night after night when the Agency could only find new ones who did not know our routine. We could not have managed without her dedication. We did have quite a fight with the Agency to have the same nurses. It became very difficult and traumatic training new ones as the disease progressed. We wrote the following as a guide line for nurses as to the normal night-time routine:

GUIDE TO PETER'S ROUTINE

10 pm Night Sleeper arrive. Put Peter to bed. Raise bed to sitting height and bed head to support. Lift Peter out of chair to standing. Janet will assist. Sit P. on bed, lift legs onto bed. E45 cream to heels, massage feet to warm. Bed socks on. Stretch and exercise legs, fingers, arms and shoulders to keep joints supple. E45 cream to prevent pressure sores. Place table at foot of bed to act as a bed cradle to stop pressure from duvet. Peter cannot bear any weight. Place red / white sleeping bag over table and Peter. Place green duvet over table and tuck into mattress. Place purple sleeping bag over Peter. Hot water bottle near feet. Urine bottle, needs assistance.

Sometime between 12.30 and 2 am on request: Urine bottle to Peter. Remove hot water bottle. Turn Peter on to left side.

Sometime between 3 & 5 on request: (doesn't always happen). Turn Peter on to his back.

6.30 am. Nurse to get up. Give Peter half cup of hot water. Make tea (2 tea bags). Give Peter Amino Acids with fruit juice, shake well. Get Peter up. Can stand from raised bed using frame, press knees to lock. Will sit in wheelchair for tea (not full cup). Washing and dressing. Use flannel and blue towel for top half. Sponge and brown towel for bottom half. E45 Cream. Peter will stand at frame for bottom half washing, Janet will assist in standing Peter up. Clothes put out for dressing. Put elastic stockings on. Tray slotted on electric chair for breakfast.

TOILET: Bring commode chair from hall to front room. Janet will assist standing to transfer from chair to commode. Pull commode through hall to toilet, open door wide, open window, lift toilet seat, push commode over toilet. (Council had promised to widen door, but never did.) On to frame and to indoor electric chair. Janet will assist.

We cancelled the morning District Nurses but kept the evening ones to wash Peter. Giles enjoyed meeting the nurses but William found all the strangers very difficult to cope with; Peter, William and I did not entirely come to terms with the lack of privacy. On Christmas morning we had to stop opening our presents because the Nurse arrived.

EFDSS. ANNUAL GENERAL MEETING

By late 1989 the EFDSS battles were less severe. The two factions came to an uneasy truce as the whole of the NEC resigned, most standing for re-election. This gave the membership the chance to express their opinion democratically by voting for those who either wished to sell the House or keep it. The AGM was held in Sheffield in November so we decided to attend. Our first AGM since redundancy.

The NEC which resigned were against selling; they were returned overwhelmingly, much to everyone's surprise. We feared it was the worst decision personally for Brenda Godrich who has a full-time and very responsible job; she now took on running the Society as well in her spare time. Brian Heaton, Peter's long-time friend and ex-EFDSS staff, stood as an independent candidate, polled most votes and was elected Chairman, despite not having been on NEC before.

We quite enjoyed the AGM. It was interesting to see who would not speak to Peter. He deliberately parked himself near some of those most violently in favour of selling the House, knowing that they regarded him as part of the Opposition. He took satisfaction in seeing their embarrassment at having to acknowledge him.

We expected that the AGM would be enough for Peter as he was normally in bed by mid-evening, but, despite aching legs, he was enjoying himself and wanted to stay for the evening Gathering. He was one of the last out of the building. He revelled in being amongst friends. At one point in the evening Hilary suggested she push Peter in his chair so we could 'dance'. In fact the chair was electric so Peter could manoeuvre it on his own, but I could not bear the thought of dancing with a wheel chair. It is not a rational reaction as I did not mind walking with Peter in a wheelchair. Dancing is so much more. We both felt the same.

Brenda and Hilary stayed overnight with us, helping to get Peter to bed. With the inevitable discussions the next day and the Christmas event coming up, he was feeling more involved with the Society again.

XMAS EXTRAVAGANZA

Autumn was spent organising the Christmas event at Cecil Sharp House for the EFDSS and the trip to London to attend it. I'm not sure which took more organisation! We relied upon equipment making a night away impossible. Peter Davis agreed to share driving the van into London, so I would not be too tired; we arranged to meet them half-way. We ordered Agency nurses for Friday and Saturday nights to help get Peter ready and back to bed. Hilary organised people to lift Peter and wheelchair into the house and I sorted out equipment and food Peter could eat easily. Anne Guest was on duty, we planned to ring her on the way home so she would be ready to help me get Peter out of the van and into bed.

Saturday morning she got Peter up, washed, dressed and fed while I organised the rest of us. We set off at 8.30 am, a terrific achievement, in freezing weather, elated that we were on target to get to London soon after the event started. Fifteen miles down the M1, as we were going up a steep hill, the van began to lose power; I pulled onto the hard shoulder and the van stopped. Giles and I walked half a mile to phone the RAC. When he eventually came the RAC man couldn't locate the fault. Peter was cold and aching and we had lost too much time to get to London. The van recovered enough to get us home but the Davises were left waiting at a motorway service area until we managed to contact them via the House. A year later I discovered that the van has a valve which must be opened in winter to allow more petrol through or it freezes. This had not been done, despite the van being serviced by a Renault dealer shortly before the excursion to London. Frozen petrol was the cause of our 'breakdown'.

We were very disappointed to miss seeing the many friends who attended, however, come the evening, we were quite pleased to be in the warmth instead of ploughing up the motorway.

In retrospect it was probably a mistake to take on the event; there was little time in three months to create interest and many people were involved elsewhere in other Christmas events so attendance was low, but it was novel to be asked by the NEC of EFDSS to do something.

1990

NURSERY

In January I opened Nursery for two sessions a week with a total of 6 children, at £5 per session per child. This was not a great contribution to our finances but it helped to keep me sane. It had taken a year to organise and around £5,000 from the redundancy money. Initially, I organised nurses to be on call when Peter needed help; Peter could summon assistance via the POSSUM telephone. Later, nurses stayed all the time I was out of the house, as Peter could not be left for fear of choking and he needed frequent massage to prevent aches and cramps. Jean, Hellen and Cath became very organised and frequently did the ironing or other household chores while 'Peter-sitting', which was a great help.

CATH

Just before Christmas, Cath was told a spot on her leg was skin cancer, which she had removed by laser treatment over several months. Cath could not work during this time or stand for long. It was a terrible experience but helped us as I could call on her to relieve Peter's aches and breathing problems at very short notice, which would have been impossible if she had been working. She could sit and massage Peter's feet without problems. This changed Cath's life too. I told Jane Petty how her reflexology helped Peter, Jane asked Cath to a lecture which led to her doing reflexology on a permanent basis, helping many people in pain.

HOIST

After Christmas MND took off again, this time the thigh muscles had wasted completely so Peter could no longer stand. Moving him involved a lot of organisation as I had to have nurses on call to help me with transfers, perhaps 10 times per day. I could not have kept this up, Peter was too heavy for me to move so many times. Our Occupational Therapist came to the rescue with a wonderful electric hoist which transferred Peter at the touch of a button. Peter was not over enthusiastic; he had confidence in me and felt very vulnerable swinging in mid-air; but it enabled us to transfer him easily, preventing him from becoming bedridden and developing pneumonia, as had been predicted. We could also transfer him into the outdoor chair so we could take him out; he wasn't housebound either. Peter wrote about the hoist for research:

"A hoist has been supplied by Social Services. This is on an overhead gantry supported by A frames and is electrically operated. The hoist is produced by Wessex Medical Services of Romsey, Hants. Transferring can now be effected by one person. A net sling has been supplied and it is essential to position this correctly round the back and under the legs. No transfer provides maximum comfort but bad positioning can make it worse. Protection is needed for the thighs to stop the net cutting into flesh. When transferring to wheelchair, commode or bed it is necessary to land the patient precisely because it is unlikely that a single carer would be able to move the patient once he has settled. A push on the knees at the last moment can be vital to get the angle right."

CATS

For some time our female cat, Tamsin, had taken to sleeping in Peter's room, this did not please many of the nurses. She was not allowed on the bed when Peter was in it, if she sat on him she was too heavy and Peter had no means to remove her if no carer was around, so she slept on his indoor wheelchair, which was kept next to the bed. As soon as she heard the hoist going to lift Peter she would sit up and stretch; at this stage the nurses would shoo her away so Peter could sit in the chair, those who knew better left her for as Peter swung in mid-air, Tamsin would daintily walk to the warm place he had left, curl up and go back to sleep. When he returned to bed she woke up as soon as she heard the hoist and waited until the chair was unoccupied and carefully returned to it in time for Peter to descend to the bed. She was not often far away from him and became very protective. When Peter was very ill and we had to call the doctor Tamsin pushed her way between Peter and Dr Clark, biting him as he was giving Peter an injection! She also liked to bring presents. Our big cat, Tamlyn had discovered he could open the toilet window by lifting the two latches so both cats used the window as a cat flap. It could be alarming if one was sat on the toilet to suddenly have a cat jump through the curtains, even worse if it brought something with it! Tamsin brought any amount of mice and birds in. Few nurses, even Cath, would rescue them so would rush to find me; unfortunately, it was too late for many and Peter became used to crunching noises as Tamsin ate her catches under his bed. After he died she transferred her dining area to William's bed room, although we still have Peter's bed.

GENERAL LIVING

There were some warm days in January and February when we went to Roche Abbey and Firbeck for picnics. Earlier in the winter I bought a sleeping bag to keep Peter warm in the wheelchair. We had bought a proper wheelchair cover but it tapered at the feet so was restrictive and was too small. We also used sheep skins to sit on, to prevent pressure sores, including in bed. I took photos on the trips as they were happy days out; later someone remarked what a broken person Peter looked confined to a wheelchair, but that is not how we saw them. Peter could still go out with his family into the countryside, to some extent under his own steam, by this time he was supposed to be dead. We saw the photographs as conveying triumph, not defeat.

The aches and cramps caused by lack of movement were worsening, Marilyn Smethurst, a physiotherapist I knew through Playgroup, volunteered to come and went through a range of stretching exercises with Peter. I can't say he looked forward to this, as the exercises hurt, but, along with the ones the nurses and I did three or four times daily, we kept his joints moveable preventing other problems, particularly with dressing.

For a long time it had been impossible to get Peter to the hairdressers so another friend, Cheryl Tuke, came to the house to cut and wash Peter's hair and beard after she had finished work. Her visits brightened his day as she is attractive and full of fun and made a big fuss of him.

When Peter could no longer stand on his own and his breathing worsened, the transfers to stairlift, which already necessitated two people, became too traumatic to continue. By the time we had transferred him three times we were all too exhausted to use the shower; instead I showered him at the hospital when we went to hydrotherapy and the nurse would help to dry and dress him. As the disease progressed it would take three of us. I then had to get him back into the van, lifting the ramps out and in, clamping the chair, before driving home.

I arranged for Jean or Hellen to meet us when we got back, to help get him into the house and bed, but it was still a very tiring expedition for both of us. On occasions the Nurses at hydrotherapy insisted I went for a rest on the bed. By the end of January it became obvious that our days of hydrotherapy were numbered but I did not have the heart to suggest it to Peter. His time in the water when he could stand, walk and feel 'normal' were very precious to him.

Early in 1990 Peter's breathing was causing him distress, bringing on the Irritable Bowel problems. It took him a long time to relax at night and breathe normally. He was offered tranquillisers but refused

them. Dr Proctor began calling monthly; he said he felt Peter would fight to stay alive because he had a young family and a younger man's life style.

To aid eating Diane Peake brought a Royal Doulton dinner plate with a raised edge to make using the arm support easier to use. Food could be pushed onto the 'spork' against the edge of the plate; thus Peter could still feed himself.

We had plans to do a follow up to Golden Oldies Folk Day based on encouraging young teams, musicians and singers but MND was taking over our lives and there was not enough time. Peter contented himself with writing about his childhood, letters to people and for research into MND. The arm support supplied by Mary Marlborough Lodge became very useful as Peter could use a pencil attached to the drawing aid to strike single keys on the keyboard. With a 'sticky keys' addition to Locoscript we did not need to buy another computer. In January 1990 Peter wrote:

"My life now centres round the word processor. Time is limited, however, as living with such a disablement as MND is almost a full time occupation. It signifies new routines such as an afternoon rest in bed and it takes that much longer to perform the simplest of functions. The twice weekly visit to the Hydrotherapy Pool is a 3 hour expedition. The philosophy of living one day at a time is to be recommended."

In February the inevitable happened and the physiotherapist brought our visits to hydrotherapy to an end. This was a bad blow to Peter and was the spur to starting a diary on the wordprocessor.

Indoor electric chair and word processor, April 1990

Peter at Roche Abbey, near Maltby, February 1990

PETER'S 'DAILY' DIARY

Monday Feb 12th. 1990. It is now 18 months since diagnosis and by own estimation I have had MND for approx. 3 years. I have reached the stage where I can no longer walk and standing up is a painful process. Although the hands and lower arms are weak I have still power in the shoulders. My breathing is shallow. The volume of the voice is low but I have no other speech problems. Legs ache often.

Hydrotherapy is cancelled tomorrow because Mark, the Trainee Physiotherapist, is absent and will be finishing this week. He has been vital recently in helping Sharon, the Physiotherapist, see to me in and out of the pool, to and from a lift. The suggestion is that this next session be the last for me as it is proving too difficult for all concerned! We would have come to a similar conclusion ourselves soon but it's hard to let go a service which has been so valuable and enjoyable.

Tuesday Feb 13th. A good night's sleep for me is to drop off between 11 pm and midnight and wake up 3 to 4 am and then through to 6 am. Thankfully this was last night's pattern. We've been using Agency 'sleeper' nurses for 3 months and we are now getting used to a 5 nights a week service. Many nurses have been sent, yet we are still getting new ones who need introducing to our routine, a tiring exercise for Janet and myself.

Aching legs are a regular feature and I have more resting times now on the bed, morning, afternoon and early evening.

VALENTINE'S DAY

For Valentine's Day I bought Peter a rose, he ignored the day. I had just spent five days searching for, buying and setting up a remote controlled hi-fi system, (with £600 just received from the Benefit Fund), on top of everything else I normally did. I was very hurt; I felt I deserved some recognition, especially as there may not be many more opportunities. The atmosphere was pretty frosty for several days.

Wednesday Feb 14th. We had a frightening few minutes when I choked at tea-time, apparently on a piece of apple which went the wrong way. It reminded us of those with the bulbar type of MND whose throat muscles are attacked in the first instance and who have difficulty in swallowing. There is no real sign that this is happening to me, although it can affect the throat in progressive cases like mine.

Thursday Feb 15th. Diane Peake, our Occupational Therapist, rang to thank us for our comments on the service and equipment we have received from Social Services to date. She wants me to write an article for an OT magazine from a ''consumer's' viewpoint.

Friday Feb 16th So to my last hydrotherapy session. The act of standing was so painful that I was only able to do it for a few minutes. It was with some satisfaction therefore that I was able to agree with the decision to cease. It's the end of an era; just think that up to almost a year ago I was driving myself to the local pool to enjoy a daily swim.

Monday Feb 19th. We've just completed a week-end with sleeper nurses, the first time since the one occasion in December for the London trip. I suspect we shall keep up the full-time pattern; it means that Janet gets a good night's rest and I have a full day of options as usual. My periods of being up are getting shorter as my legs soon begin to ache, it means morning and afternoon rests on the bed. The big question now is how I can best operate the word processor from the bed.

Tuesday Feb 20th Last night's film about an MND sufferer, Steven Pegg, provides us, and others who saw, it with plenty of talking points. We were shocked at the lack of equipment for one who was in the advanced stages of the disease. It was more than full time for his wife and carer if the chap needs turning 8 times a night, as claimed. We thought of a few things which would make life easier for everyone:- a posture bed, a hoist, a Possum Environmental Control, a powered wheelchair and a simple ramp from his room to the outside.

Wednesday Feb 21st. Yet another new nurse (Cherry) last night, I'm sure she's very nice but I didn't take to her and then we discovered she is allergic to cats. Another!

We tried to work out a system whereby I can operate the word processor from bed as I'm spending more and more time there. After Cath and Janet spent an hour shifting things around we came to no conclusion and everything is back where it was.

Dr. Proctor called; he confirmed that the shallow breathing was directly resulting from the MND and not due to inactivity. I asked for his opinion because I cannot feel anything happening similar to all the fibulations which I experienced in the lower limbs earlier.

Friday Feb 23rd. Took a quinine pill for the first time last night, the standard treatment for relief of cramp. The cramp affects my right leg in particular and one can feel the knotted up tendon behind the knee which can often be relieved by sympathetic massage.

Denis Salt came to stay. Denis had lodged with Peter in The Cottage in Surrey during the late fifties, Peter had been his Best Man. I thought his visit would cheer Peter up, we saw very few people other than nurses and it was very good of Denis to give us his time. It turned out to be a mistake and I was very much at fault. I took the opportunity to sort out the portacabin and go shopping while there was someone to keep an eye on Peter, not realising how tiring it was for Peter to talk for so long. It had a disastrous effect on his breathing, causing a lot of stress. After this we were very careful about allowing visitors.

Tuesday March 6th. Still recovering after the visit of Denis Salt yesterday. It really was too much for me and the effort of talking has affected my voice and my stomach.

We called in Dr Proctor who diagnosed a tummy bug. By Thursday Peter was having real problems with phlegm in his throat which he could not dislodge as he could not cough. I phoned the surgery, it was suggested we try inhaling steam and menthol. I also bought a variety of preparations from the chemist to clear the throat, all to no avail. I realise now that because I did not panic I was not taken very seriously.

On Friday Peter was in danger of choking, I asked for an emergency visit. Dr. Burns, who was on call, came after 6 o'clock, too late to acquire a suction machine which he said Peter needed to remove the mucus; Peter would have to go into hospital where the machines were available. I was very much against him going, Dr Burns could not understand what I had against it; I couldn't say, "I don't want Peter to die in hospital", for that is what I thought would happen. Peter was in a very poor state. I had worked very hard and the family had made tremendous sacrifices to keep Peter at home, we had failed if he died in hospital. We did not agree to going straight away, Dr Burns said to ring him when we had decided. I rang Marilyn for advice, as she is a physiotherapist. She said we should go in. I rang Cath, I felt sure she would be on my side, but she said we had no choice, Peter could choke. I still felt that admitting him to hospital, to be without his bed and equipment, would kill him anyway. Peter was in distress from the fear of choking so was ready to agree to anything. Very reluctantly I asked Dr Burns to arrange a bed.

I phoned my sister to come over to look after the boys. She was out so I had to leave a message, but she had said she would come whenever I needed her. I phoned Rosemary to tell her we were going into hospital. I

knew she would worry at seeing all the activity. She was going to Youth Club but would be back soon after 9 pm if she were needed. Cath came to help. Giles guessed that the situation was very serious. I took William into the portacabin and explained that Daddy might not come home again. It was important they both knew what was happening. I cancelled the Agency 'sleeper' nurse, Diane Chambers. Hellen was the District Nurse that evening, she helped with Peter, then quickly finished her round so she could come to hospital with us. By 9 pm we were ready to go; Peter was all bundled up in his outdoor wheelchair, William was going to Jean's until Irene arrived, Cath was seeing Peter through the patio doors when the phone rang. Irene asked if she could take the boys to their house as it was more convenient. From the message she'd received she had no idea of the trauma here. I was in no fit state to make any decision but I did not want our boys in Grimsby if their father was dying and William had violin Saturday mornings, I did not want him to miss it, routine helps in crisis. I said I would ring back.

At this stage Cath proved a true friend and took control, William could stay with her. He seemed happy enough with that. Rosemary later offered Giles a bed. I phoned Irene to say we had arranged things so she needn't come and set off. It was the start of a new relationship with Cath, she became a friend whom I could trust and I needed someone I could count on.

On the ward Peter had been allocated a bed nearest the nurses' station; it did have a Spenco mattress, to prevent pressure sores, as I had insisted he could not manage without one, but the bed was impossible. Four nurses lifted him into bed, no hoist. Cath, Hellen and I got him ready and as comfortable as possible with pillows, which wasn't much. They then had done all they could so went home. Once alone Peter and I knew we had made the wrong decision in coming into hospital. The journey and discomfort was too much and we now both feared he would not survive.

I rang Rosemary to check on the boys, it was about 11 pm and Peter still had not seen a physiotherapist who would remove the offending mucus. Rosemary asked how was I coping? I wasn't. She came straight to the hospital. This was a great help, I was not much use to Peter in my current state; by talking through the situation with Rosemary I realised that the most sensible thing to do was to call Diane and ask her to look after Peter. She would have been working anyway and knew his needs better than anyone. Diane came, a life saver. When Diane arrived Rosemary went home. At about 1 am the physiotherapist arrived; she inserted a tube down Peter's nose to remove the mucus, an horrendous experience but it did stop him choking and he felt a little better. By 3 am he did not appear in immediate danger so I left Diane in charge and went home to sleep. It was very strange to be in an empty house. Diane had quite a night; there was no chance of Peter sleeping and getting him turned was a major undertaking; she had to search out the nurses, who had no experience of MND.

I had to be at the hospital for 8 o'clock, Saturday morning, when Diane went off duty. Although she had promised to call me if anything happened, I was quite surprised and immensely relieved to find Peter still with us. He had been sat in a chair by his bed, supported by pillows and was fairly cheerful. I was told he could not be discharged until a doctor saw him. We sat there for an hour by which time Peter was aching and needed to be moved. We waited another hour while Peter was visibly deteriorating. I phoned Rosemary to ask if they could come to look after Peter in the van while I drove him home, then discharged him myself. There was no point in waiting for him to die in hospital of exhaustion, he was no longer in danger of choking he would be much better off at home.

We got him into the wheelchair, Don and Rosemary helped him into the van. Peter looked awful. Rosemary sat in the back with Peter, Don drove their car back. They and Jean then helped me get Peter inside. We had to get him onto his bed to rest comfortably. Don dispensed with the hoist and we lifted him from chair to bed in one movement.

At least he hadn't died in hospital. We gave him a few days to live at most but he was not going into hospital again. On Monday morning I phoned everyone I could think of to ensure I had a suction machine. It arrived on Tuesday from the Community Physiotherapy Department

Tuesday March 13th We've been through a whole week of turmoil and to-day is the first day that I can feel my old self especially as I've had a good sleep. I think stress has been building up for some time and all that talking with Dennis Salt was the last straw. The Irritable Bowel problem reared itself to my great discomfort and the after effects are still with me. We don't accept Dr. Proctor's diagnosis of a tummy bug.

I have been aware that there was mucus in the back of my throat for some time but my cough is too weak to move it and now it often cuts off my air supply. I panicked then and was in great danger of choking but by slowly inhaling the obstruction moved. Finally we went to hospital to have the mucus suctioned out with a tube up my nose.

The visit to hospital overnight is an horrendous story, there was no chance of getting comfortable, never mind sleeping. In no way can I go into

hospital without an accommodating bed. Hope it's now behind us.

Yesterday and to-day have been busy with visitors to do with equipment. Steve Baxter, the Community Therapist, has delivered the suction machine for our do-it-yourself nose job if we should have a mucus problem again. Dianne Peake, our OT, has been in and out with little bits such as the ball bearing drinking straws and the rubber ring for the toilet seat. Sister Guy was a welcome caller and made a note of some of our nursing needs.

REFLEXOLOGY

On Wednesday morning Peter was not at all well. He had hardly anything to eat and was back in bed to rest soon after breakfast. He was withdrawn and needed quiet. Cath came routinely to massage him and, as usual, he fell asleep as he relaxed. Cath was most concerned about him. We were both aware of a difference, he had no fight left, it was all too much and he was drifting away. Cath stayed so that she would be here when needed, both of us were convinced we would be calling the Undertakers shortly. We talked in whispers at the other end of the house, so as not to disturb him. After about an hour we were stunned to hear Peter shouting from his bed, "When is someone going to come and get me up, then?!"

Talk about rising from the dead! If ever I needed convincing of the power of reflexology, that was it. He obviously felt much better; we could not write him off so easily, although we still did not give him longer than a fortnight, he was so weak. I did not resume the amino-acids or any other medication, stopped when he went into hospital, as it did not seem worth putting Peter through the effort of taking them.

Friday March 16th JANET'S BIRTHDAY. *Peter tried to make amends for Valentine's Day. He organised a surprise breakfast, cooked by Rosemary, a lovely card and present.*

Saturday March 17th. It's been a whole week since the hospital horror and we are only just getting back to normal. I've had some good sleeps during the week but have not succeeded in getting two good nights on the run. Bowel movements are getting back to normal which will be a relief to Janet and the nurses, as well as me, who are now accustomed to dumping me often on the commode at the briefest of warnings. I give notice now of when I want to cough. In order to make maximum use of my weak effort Janet presses on my tummy and we attempt to clear my throat with a co-ordinated effort.

LORD NELSON

The Youth Club Giles attends had organised places on the sailing ship, The Lord Nelson, for both able and disable-bodied people. Giles was offered a place and set off for Southampton with others from the group on Sunday, 18th March. As he was leaving Giles asked if his Dad would still be here when he got back on Thursday. I did not have a lot of hope.

Monday March 19th My biggest problem now is to control panic breathing. I tend to swallow a lot of saliva causing me to catch my breath.

The day promised to be fine but it remained cold so, unlike yesterday, which was lovely, I couldn't go out in the garden

Tuesday March 20th. The day promises much so hopefully I can go out.

The sleep pattern is improving once again, the best is from 11 to 1 ish and then again from 4 to 6, like this morning. The middle bit is unsatisfactory, although lying slightly on the tilt does relieve pressure on the bottom and despite an uncomfortable head position I can sleep for a bit. I'm going to try getting up in the night for half an hour or so. The frequent changes during the day from bed to wheelchair have avoided pressures so there's no reason why it shouldn't work at night.

I had great difficulty persuading the night nurses to get Peter up during the night. "Night time is for sleeping." They also threatened that he would catch pneumonia.

It's now 12 days since I took any pills or medication including amino-acids. I cannot say if it's made any difference or not. I don't think I've had any more aches through leaving off the quinine but the absence of diuretics probably means that there is a build up of fluid in the body. We shall never know if the amino-acids have slowed up the progress of the disease no matter if we resume or not.

We tried out the suction machine this morning without success. Helen couldn't fix the tube up my left nostril and then it seemed as though the phlegm had disappeared. So we don't know yet if it can do the job for us. Not warm enough to go outside.

Wednesday March 21st. We can now claim that Spring is here and with it an optimism of nice days to come. The foot of the bed is not rising. We have had trouble with this often before but this is the first time it has not righted itself. The bed is propped up on blocks thanks to stirling work by Janet and Don but I had trouble with the new angle in getting off to sleep. Paracetamol did the trick eventually and I had a very sound sleep.

Thursday March 22nd. *Giles returned from France to Southampton. Peter would have loved to go on a sailing ship, the nurses and I felt he hung on until Giles returned to hear about the trip. I phoned the Lord Nelson as it docked in Southampton to let Giles know his Dad was still alive. After Peter had survived those few days he seemed to have no intention of dying.*

PAGE TURNER

One morning, around this time, the page-turner arrived. Peter had asked for one on loan from the MNDA to operate via POSSUM. He had been unable to turn pages in books or newspapers for over 6 months but there is great demand for these machines and inevitably not enough to go round. I was somewhat taken aback by the size of the packaging; fortunately it came on one of Cath's days so she helped me. The ones we had seen at the Naidex Exhibition could take magazines and books; we had planned to position it on a table over the bed so Peter had something to do when he was resting. The one that was sent could take a full Sunday newspaper so was around 3 ft. wide by 2 ft high, made of solid wood and weighed a ton! Two of us had quite a struggle to get it out of it's box, no bed table could have taken the weight. If it had fallen on Peter it would have killed him! There simply wasn't room for it with the bed, word processor, POSSUM, hoist, wheelchair, commode, hi-fi, bed table etc. already in our small front room. Reluctantly, on Peter's part, we sent it back.

Monday March 26th We've had another traumatic session with the suction machine. I felt that there was some phlegm building up in the throat area and so we asked Marilyn and Cath to come. After much thumping of the chest and the back by Marilyn some phlegm came into the throat causing me some panic breathing. I couldn't bring it up so one assumes that I swallowed it. We then tried the suction machine but had no success getting the catheter through the nose and the experience of having it down the throat was even more frightening but Marilyn had just a little success.

The motor at the foot of the bed has been replaced and the one at the head, which is very noisy, also has to be renewed (too much to expect them to have more than one spare motor). We do regret not being able to meet Jane Petty, our physio from the Hallamshire, who, prior to succumbing to her own back problems, used to visit us and all other MND cases in the area. She is the one who has day to day viewing of the problems facing individuals. We feel she would have been a help in the breathing and choking experience. Tummy problems continue with frequent sittings on the commode.

Wednesday March 28th We can now pin down some of the breathing problems to the periods immediately after meals. I find myself continually wanting to swallow which makes my tongue and Adam's apple feel overworked. Smaller meals but more often, plus rhythmical breathing, is recommended.

Friday March 30th We get some things right only to be foiled by another problem. I've been getting up in the night recently for an hour or so, the break normally means that I can go back to bed reasonably tired with a good chance of sleeping the last three hours or so. Alas, there are occasions when I've had backache and this can keep me awake as it did last night.

Sunday April 1st. The night pattern of sleeping is now a real problem. I sleep for only an hour or so from about 11 pm to 12.15. I then elect to turn on my side just to give the bottom and back a rest. It is agony often and there's no question of sleeping but I aim to keep it up for 45 mins. Then I plan to stay on my back for 1½ hours but I gave up last night and got up into the wheelchair for a long session from about 2 to 3.30. I prepared for the last session in bed, on my back, by taking a paracetamol but this only helped towards a period of less than 2 hours. It's the last hour or so before getting up that is often full of aches and I can't wait to get up.

Monday April 2nd. Well, that was a better night in the sleeping sense in that I slept from 11 pm to 2.45 with just a short rub of back and bottom at 12.30. It always takes some time to get back to sleep after being up but I estimate another session of 1½ hours until 6.30. when it was time to be awake.

Thursday April 5th.

I wrote to Dr Proctor who was due to visit

"We seem over the worst panic but other problems are emerging:

CRAMPS: These were not so noticeable when he had other more pressing problems but are now back with us. He cannot swallow the quinine tablets. Jane Petty is back on duty and suggests baclofen/lioresal in liquid form (?)

BREATHLESSNESS: Particularly after meals. I'm giving smaller meals made easier to swallow, more often. He is making efforts to control the panic breathing but it does worry him at night. We try to avoid stress in the form of visitors, but this is particularly cruel.

SLEEPING: Will take no form of sleeping tablet because of the side effects and losing control. Takes one paracetamol when all else fails. Our regular night nurse reports he is getting 3-4 hours sleep per night. May get another 2 hours in the day. Doesn't seem particularly tired but Peter and the night nurse worry about this. He is turned, massaged, got out of bed, given cups of tea etc. etc.

He does suffer from severe back pain and sometimes his neck(!!), plus pressure, although has no sores. We have tried all sorts of support to no avail. Night time is the worst as he has little to occupy him and the nurse sleeps, is only on call. In the daytime I am around, which is probably more comforting, (could be doubtful!). Today is more problematic as the bed broke down and he had no sleep last night.

OCCUPATION: There is little he can do to occupy himself. Working at the wordprocessor or reading is too exhausting for long, which leaves listening to the stereo and TV. He has too much time to think. Even conversation with anyone other than his family is denied him. (I realise there is little you can do about this but it helps to complain.)

BOWEL: Spends nearly as much time on the commode as in bed!

OEDEMA: Ankles are very swollen. Retried the Frumil diuretic but it upset his stomach.

DISTRICT NURSES now call once a week for support but the evenings have been cancelled as there was not enough to do: it depended upon when they called! I was upset but we resolved it by having the Agency nurses come earlier. This has proved, generally, less stressful."

Dr P. prescribed an anti-depressant to help relieve the stress which was causing more problems with breathing. Peter was very suspicious. I went to the Library and photocopied a page about Imipranine and its side effects for him; it should be taken for several days before it has an effect. I felt he should give it a try if it would help his breathing.

Friday April 6th. Just recovering from the traumas caused by the bed being out of action. As forecast by Theraposture, the gear motor packed up Wednesday leaving the head at the topmost angle, the very worst of positions. I had a sleepless night, fortunately the bed was put right yesterday. Theraposture had let us down earlier by bringing the wrong replacement. We were unfortunate to have both motors go almost at the same time, only one of which was covered by warranty.

NIGHT-TIME

From around this time the Agency nurses found they were being called more frequently, may be up to 4 or 5 times a night instead of 2 or 3, Peter slept very little, was uncomfortable and needed reassurance. The duties gradually changed from 'Sleeper' to full 'Night-duty' at considerably more cost, paid for by the Independent Living Fund

HOUSE-BOUND

With all the problems caused by going into hospital and the bed breaking down we were finding life very difficult. Adding the risks of infection and the cold weather, it was impossible to consider taking Peter out and I could not leave him long enough to go far without him. When I returned from taking or collecting William from school, swimming, violin or from shopping I did not stop to lock the van but would rush in to check Peter first. Life was a little fraught.

When the Davises rang at Easter to ask if there was anything they could do I asked them to take the boys out for the day. The disease was very unfair on them, it not only took their father but mother too; Peter needed me more than nurses because I knew his routines and he trusted me. Peter and Angela came all the way from Northamptonshire to take our boys to Conisborough Castle and a Doncaster park. They also listened to them. Relieving the pressure on us for a few hours helped enormously. So much so that, although we had banned visitors as being too much for Peter, we both felt confident enough for me to cook dinner for their return, which was a success and a surprise for the Davises.

SMELLS

Cooking dinner by this time was quite a performance. Any smell would affect Peter's breathing and he could start choking. We became very sensitive to perfumes, if a nurse was wearing any, even a perfumed deodorant, they would have to be turned away. Our regulars soon knew.

I had bought an electric fan for Peter after the hospital adventure, to create air flow which helped his breathing. It became necessary to use this to prevent cooking smells reaching him. Cooking Sunday dinner was a nightmare. Before starting Peter would have to be put in his room, away from the kitchen, with doors and windows open for air, if it was warm enough. We could not close the door because there wasn't one between the front room and dining area. In the kitchen, windows were open and both extractor fans switched on. The electric fan was then positioned in the doorway to blow any smells away from Peter's room.

It would have been easier to not cook Sunday dinner, but Peter looked forward to it. We went through all this performance on the day he died because he wanted his Sunday dinner. It was lamb.

Friday April 13th. Started on IMIPRAMINE, an anti-depressant to-day. Sleeping at night is still a problem exasperated last night by backache. When this occurs the best position is flat out with a hot water bottle in the lumbar region but really it can only be fully relieved by getting up. Less than 4 hours sleep again and very tired and not easy to drop off during the day.

Saturday April 14th. In fact I did sleep for 2½ hours yesterday afternoon and had a good night in bed. Cath cured backache by massaging the right big toe and a spot on the instep just below the toe! Jayne, the night nurse, also massaged the feet in general and this seemed to lead to all round relaxation, hence a good sleep.

Tuesday April 17th. PETER'S 62nd BIRTHDAY.
A present was quite a problem, in the end I decided to get him an original painting so he had something to look at. I wanted to buy one of Barry Renshaw's, a professional artist and friend in the Folk world, we had admired his work at Amber Folk Festival. Unfortunately, Barry lives in Derbyshire, there was no way I could take time off to travel that far. I settled for a local, semi-professional artist, John Rudkin, who lives near us. I knew his wife, Audrey. I chose a painting of Scotland to remind us of holidays.

Wednesday April 18th. Stomach and wind problems have taken over recently and we've left off the medication to try and trace the cause and if it is related to the latest anti-depressant.

Peter was very reluctant to take any medication including paracodal and blamed any stomach problem on whatever he had taken. It was very frustrating but the choice was his, which was very important.

I have had three bad sleeping nights but it was all OK last night marking the return to duty of Diane, our most regular nurse. The stomach seems better to-day so perhaps we are in for a good period.

Tuesday April 24th. We've had several beautiful and warm days and it looks like continuing. It was in fact too hot for me to stay outside yesterday but it gives one a feeling of well-being. With no medication whatever yesterday the stomach has settled.

Saturday April 28th Back ache is the latest problem which affects daily and nightly routine. The pattern now emerging is that it is not appropriate to spend more than 1- 2 hours in bed day or night. Anything more and back ache begins. It hasn't happened yet but soon I can see me getting up twice during the night. It does seem that my sleep requirements are now very little.

CARER'S DAILY LOG

By May Peter was too easily tired to waste his energy on telling carers what to do, Diane Chambers suggested we start a daily log to help all people concerned with his care. We recorded Peter's problems and state of health and gave advice as we had little time to compare notes on change over of carers. We began on 4th May.

Diane recorded that Dr. Proctor had okayed 2 paracodals at night-time to help Peter sleep. I think Dr P. was at a loss to know what to do with Peter as he refused all medication. Jane Petty also called and advised that we should stop the physiotherapy on Peter's shoulders; as the muscles had deteriorated there was risk of dislocation.

FEEDING

We knew the shoulder muscles had gone when I began to feed him. I had been dreading this; taking the last vestige of independence from him. When it happened it wasn't nearly so bad as I thought, just natural that I should do it because Peter could not do it for himself; as with everything else I had taken over. There were bonuses; he was less breathless after meals as he did not have to put in so much effort and he got chance to catch his breath while I was eating; I lost weight. Friends thought it was due to stress, it was much more due to not being able to tuck into a big meal while my husband could not cope with enough to keep a sparrow alive, combined with lack of time. Once Peter had finished eating he would need something doing: legs rubbed, the commode, back to bed, word- processor or stereo set up, there was no time to wait while I had my meal.

We had presumed from the literature on MND that he would eventually be unable to swallow, as is the case with one type of the disease from the start, this strictly did not happen. I did prepare food that was easy to swallow because of the breathing problems, porridge, soups, rice puddings, scrambled egg, blackcurrant juice from our own blackcurrants, but he also had meat and vegetables in gravy, not minced up as for babies, which is the case for some MND sufferers.

He also had a fixation about his bowels; serious illness tends to concentrate the mind on the real essentials in life. He thus had a staple diet of prunes, figs and rhubarb! In the very last days Jane Petty advised we get Fortical, a food drink, on prescription. Peter enjoyed these and they boosted his nutrition.

Peter became very sensitive to taste besides smells, noise and movement. He disliked tap water, so we had a constant supply of mineral water in the fridge, along with ice cubes which we crushed to moisten his mouth

when drinking became a problem. He preferred lemon tea, oxos and chocomint to drink and found Tunes and Buttercup Syrup eased his need to cough.

DRESSING

Peter did not become completely floppy, as many patients. He kept control of his neck muscles, so his head did not droop and he could sit up and move in his chair, although he needed support. To ease dressing I bought very loose jumpers, keeping movement to a minimum. Soon after he stopped standing we abandoned trousers, we had used track suit bottoms, into which I had sewn zips, to make dressing as easy as possible, but pulling them up and down caused too much stress when breathing worsened. Peter was quite decent, encased in his sleeping bag. A favourite piece of clothing was a Granny shawl I had crocheted in a previous existence. Diane thought Peter liked it because it belonged to me, actually, it was practical, warm and easy to put round him.

'LIVING WITH DYING'

I coped with this stage by thinking of Peter as two separate beings. I had to take care of Peter's body in order to keep the real 'Peter' with us. I did not resent the extra calls on my time and energy as much as before, only when tired, which was too often, they were essential.

We watched a BBC series, Living With Dying, presented by Martin Lewis, whose mother had died of cancer in a hospice. Unfortunately the programme was transmitted when I had to collect William from school so I could only see the beginning. Dr Proctor frequently visited when it was on too, so Peter would miss it. It would have been very helpful to watch it together, on our own. I videoed it and watched it when Peter was asleep but did not have the courage to suggest we watch the video, it seemed as if I was wishing him dead. We were both anxious about this stage, unknown territory that was more difficult to prepare for than the previous stages in MND. On the programmes a young wife described her husband dying from cancer and how she had had to 'let him go'. I was not ready for that.

GARDEN

In May we had some lovely warm days. I had built a dry-stone retaining wall at the end of the ramp and made other small garden areas to hide the sides of the concrete; these I planted with annuals so Peter could look out of the patio windows onto some colour. As I planted them I had no idea if he would live to see them but if we behaved as if Peter was about to die the disease had won. Some were flowering before he died, not all. There was also a change which is harder to explain than coping with the physical aspects of the disease, an extension of the feeling that his body was separate from the real Peter. The previous year I had been unwilling to work in the garden because Peter was unable to help me, I both missed him and resented him not helping. This year Peter usually sat in his chair by the patio doors, watching me work and it was as if he was in the garden with me, helping. We did discuss plans for the garden but talking was exhausting for him, I did not need to ask what he wanted, I knew. This was not confined to just the garden.

Gardening was also good for Peter. The year before he had not come out to watch me as he was frustrated by not being able to help and felt guilty. Now HE seemed to feel he was with me. He forgot the disease for a while, rarely asking for his legs to be rubbed and moved while watching me, although he was uncomfortable after a few minutes normally. It gave us an insight into our relationship which we would not have discovered without MND, and for which I am very grateful.

Wednesday May 9th. I was reluctant to come anywhere near this machine during the very warm and unusually high temperature for the time of year. It did us all good and inspired Janet to get ahead in the garden which, apart from anything else, has been therapeutic to me. There is a suggestion that the warm weather will return.

Sleeping patterns have been varied but at present I'm getting up soon after midnight having rested my limbs but not really slept. After watching a film on T.V for an hour or so I take a double paracodal and return to sleep, often for several hours. This morning it was from 2 to 6.30 with just one turn at 4 and another short awake at 5.30. Backache is always a possibility as the muscles weaken. No medications just now and no tummy upsets.

NAUSEOUS

The next day Peter was not at all well, it was even too much for him to work the POSSUM switch. He felt light-headed so I opened the doors and windows to get as much air as possible. He slept very lightly so most housework was out of the question. I rang both Steve Baxter, Community Physiotherapist and Dr Proctor for advice on helping his breathing; I couldn't breathe for him. Steve suggested that Peter lean forward in his chair to relax the muscles to help breathing and said that oxygen was inappropriate, it was used when there

is difficulty transferring oxygen into the blood stream. I asked about the use of a ventilator, to make sure I had covered all possibilities. This would entail admittance to hospital for several days which was out of the question.

Dr P. told us Peter should lean back in his chair to enlarge the chest capacity and prescribed oxygen!! It would help relieve some of the distress for both of us.

In the afternoon Patrick Malham, from Handsworth, called. He stayed to chat to Peter while I took William to his swimming lesson. Jean was in charge and I told her to make sure Peter did not get too tired. I was surprised that Patrick was still there when I got back, Peter was feeling a bit better.

By evening he was not well again, feeling sick. I put him back to bed at 5.30 with a hot water bottle and he slept.

At 7.00 he woke and I got him up for tea of rice pudding and prunes. Just as I was serving the District Nurse arrived so we had to stop and get Peter back into his room to be washed and changed. He did not get tea until 8.00. Not an unusual occurrence. After this things calmed down for a couple of days, apart from back ache, particularly at night.

On the 13th he felt sick again. He could not settle when I put him back to bed at 9 am. He ached and had to be rubbed and resettled. He looked very weary. I discouraged him from getting up too early and he slept until 11.30 am while I tidied the garage. As it was Sunday the boys could alert me if Peter needed me.

When Peter woke it took him some time to come round, he was confused, but went on to eat a good Sunday dinner, even having seconds and a little wine. Later he took a trip round the garden and chatted to Don and Rosemary.

Tuesday May 15th Peter felt better today hence this entry, however it took 3 sessions to write this much, about 1 hour in all.

The condition progresses in some directions, almost un-noticed until one takes stock. The nurses are finding my legs heavy to bend and move and, over the course of many weeks, I am finding it more difficult to use the hands in controlling the direction lever on the wheelchair. The shoulder movements are stiff. The sleeping pattern has continued as before but I now find it difficult to relax and sleep at all when I first go to bed at 10.30 ish. The one night experiment when I took paracodal before going to bed didn't work and I was awake for hours. I am now sleeping a lot during the day.

My breathing has improved slightly — maybe I've learnt how to control it.

Wednesday, 16th May. *We hadn't taken Peter out on a trip since February. I decided to throw caution to the wind and take him out in the van while the boys were at school. We had prepared well; the outdoor chair had not been used for sometime so I had it on charge for the day and night beforehand and put the Spenco cushion from his indoor chair to help avoid pressure sores*

6.30 Diane bed-bathed and got Peter up, as usual

7.45 I fed him breakfast. Got William's packed lunch ready.

8.15 Took Peter to front room and transferred to commode.

8.30 Took William to school, Giles in charge of Peter.

9.00 When I got back I put Peter back to bed and he slept.

9.15 Hellen on duty. I took Giles to the Advertiser offices as part of his College course.

10.00 Cath arrived to help on our outing. Peter was still asleep. Cleaned up and prepared picnic.

10.30 Got Peter up and ready to go out by 11.15 Out to van to find the chair not working properly. (Transpired we needed new batteries.) Peter still determined to go so we put the chair onto manual and Cath, Rosemary and I pushed it into the van, up the ramps, bashing Peter's head on the way, badly grazing it. We had not allowed for the extra height of the cushion! Sensible people would have given up at this stage, we didn't. Cath sat in the back to steady Peter round bends now he had little control. The chair was clamped and Peter fastened with a seat belt but he still felt very insecure.

12.00 Lunch at the Garden Centre. We had taken fresh bread, jam and cheese which I had to cut up. There was little room in the van with the chair in so I did Peter's first which Cath fed him, then Cath's. By then Peter had finished and was ready to go, never mind that I hadn't had mine! He stopped seeing me as a separate person, rather as an extension of himself. This was fine, but I still needed to eat!

Cath and I pushed Peter in the chair round the gardens. He particularly wanted to visit the pottery in the Craft Workshops as I had seen an indoor fountain which I thought he would like. Looking at the path we took him down now I can't imagine how we did it, the chair is immensely heavy. However, the path became even steeper and I didn't think we could push the chair back so I went to ask the potter if he would bring the fountain to Peter. Instead HE pushed Peter down to the shops, then pushed him back to the van. We bought a fountain with money just come in from the Benefit Fund. We thought the sound of running water would be soothing, in fact it had a less desirable effect but proved quite a talking point.

1.30 Arrived home with Cath in a state of exhaustion. She was holding onto Peter when the table top, stored behind the front seats came loose so she was holding that up with one foot to stop it falling on Peter, while holding onto Peter when we went round bends. Adaptability is essential when coping with MND!

2.00 Peter back in bed.

3.15 Slept.

4.00 Up. Tea, bread, jam and lemon tea.

5.30 Commode.

6.00 Soup and bread.

6.30 Cheryl arrived to wash and cut hair. Peter breathless so she cut William's first. We should have asked her to come another day but did not like to when she had put herself out for us and Peter said he could cope.

6.50 District Nurse (Anne Middleton) arrived to wash and commode. Then Cheryl cut hair. Peter was fairly tense.

8.30 Stomach ache and choking.

8.45 I put Peter to bed as stressed. Massaged, applied heat pad to stomach, still nauseous.

9.30 Diane arrived and washed him. Peter very distressed, breathless and nauseous.

10.00 Into leather easy chair to try to get him comfortable.

10.45 Very pale. Contacted doctor.

11.45 Dr Clark called, gave injection to ease feelings of nausea. (Tamsin gently bit Dr C. while he was doing this.) Fluids only for 24 hours. It was a bad night but he was a little better by morning.

Thursday, 17th May *Diane had washed him in stages during the night. We gave splinters of ice cubes to moisten his mouth and mineral water, he felt 'woozy', but not as bad as the night before. He was asleep again by 9 am. I phoned the Surgery to say he was a little better and the Agency to cancel a new nurse. They were sending one in the day to be shown what to do so we had more to rely on. The Agency had expected that Peter would be in hospital by now, they kept asking Diane when he was going. This is what is generally expected, one dies in hospital, but Dr Proctor made it clear he would support our decision to stay at home for as long as we wanted. I was determined he would not go into hospital again after the March incident. We were alright if we had nursing support.*

Cath came to do her reflexology, his breathing was very shallow and he had no fight. He fell asleep listening to Artisan as Cath massaged his feet. When he woke he was cheerful, again! He got up and watched TV. In the afternoon we discussed whether the trip out had been worth it in view of how ill he had been afterwards. Peter felt it was, despite the apprehension beforehand and his lack of control, which was the worst of his situation.

Later Dr Proctor crept in, obeying notices on the door not to knock in case he woke Peter, he made me jump. He advised little food (Peter was hardly eating anyway!) for the next couple of days and to contact them if we were worried. I asked how long Peter could go on like this but he could give no timescale, "Peter was still here by sheer will power." Dr P. had expected pneumonia to set in since before Christmas.

Cath brought William home from school and did more massage, so he was well enough to sit by the patio doors and discuss the garden, a safe subject. Diane came on duty as we could not have coped with a new nurse. He had a good night.

Friday, 18th May. Peter was having trouble breathing so Giles took William to school and Cath came to massage. I managed to go to the shops. Jane Petty visited for the second time since her return to work, which was very welcome but tired Peter. When Don called later Peter refrained from talking. In the afternoon I ordered a Hi-fi aerial to be fitted because the reception on FM radio was very poor on Peter's system and he wanted to listen to radio, particularly to World Service in the night.

We had been in touch with Artisan; Peter very much wanted to hear them again live, their tape was one of his favourites. I had arranged with Jacey that they should come on 23rd May, five days away. In view of what we had just gone through I did not feel it was fair to let them come. Peter was even more sensitive to noise, Hilary has a powerful voice, they would have to sing from the end of the street! We might also have to turn them away if Peter was asleep or unwell, it was a lot to ask of people struggling to make a living. I cancelled.

Peter was disappointed and I am still not sure if I made the right decision. I felt that their coming could literally kill Peter, he was not strong enough to cope with visitors let alone singing. Peter might have died happy but I thought it was unfair to burden anyone with causing his death.

Saturday, 19th May. We had arranged for Diane Chambers to look after Peter while we went to Feast of Folk at Derby. Peter was not well enough to leave for such a long time so I took the boys to the Yorkshire Sculpture Park and Cannon Hall for a break. Peter was depressed before we left and not well while we were out. When I phoned Diane she was concerned about him so we hurried home. Our arrival home calmed Peter and he had a reasonable night.

The next day he was still suffering, tired and his voice very faint. Talking TO him was too tiring. In the afternoon we had to call Hellen to use the suction machine, only done when really necessary. In the evening he was still having trouble, choking, the only way to calm him was for me to sit with him. We looked at photos together. He was frustrated at not being able to turn the pages which caused one of the few outbursts of complaint during the whole time we struggled with the disease, "It is one damned thing after another with this thing!"

In the evening Anne Middleton, one of our regular Auxiliary Districts came but Peter felt too ill to be washed. Anne was upset, she had not seen him like this; he tried to be cheerful when anyone came. Later Diane had to use the suction again. Peter became frightened of choking and needed a lot of reassurance. When he did drop off to sleep he would wake with a start and wonder where he was.

TALKING BOOKS

As we had not acquired a page-turner I ordered a Talking Book machine for Peter, available to severely disabled besides the blind, to give him an alternative occupation. We had to tick 10 titles from a huge list so he could be sent 2 'books'. A special machine was sent, (without a plug — to the severely disabled!), to play the unabridged tapes; they could not be played on an ordinary cassette machine. They sent 'Wuthering Heights' and 'A History of Ireland', certainly not his first choice. We were not impressed by the sound quality and were amused to hear Jean Matthews reading the Bronte book. It was not her name on the title, but it sounded just like the wife of Nibs Matthews, ex-Director of the EFDSS.

Peter operated the machine from his bed once it was plugged into POSSUM. It was a great help, soon after switching on History of Ireland Peter would be fast asleep. It worked much better than the relaxation tape he normally listened to.

Monday, 21st May. Peter was worse. When he woke mid-morning he thought there were two of me! He was tired and did not even feel up to having Cath's massage. Sister Guy called, she warned us to watch for thrombosis in the calves, a sharp pain. When I asked about what the next stage would hold for us she felt Peter would go quickly from heart failure; kidney failure was another possibility, although "some people do hang on." She also said that Dr Proctor had told her last year that Peter would not live until Christmas.

Perhaps because he was so ill, Peter was very keen that I plant the vegetables, they had a future.

Dr Proctor visited and offered sedatives, which were refused as usual. By evening Peter said he did not feel 'right' and was 'very weak'. He needed frequent oxygen, massage, moving, continual attention. He requested that night nurses keep a check on him as he could not always manage POSSUM.

He was very sensitive to noise so I asked for talking to be kept low and to a minimum around him, it was very easy to chatter over the top of him when we were getting him ready; this was too tiring for him.

On Tuesday we listened to a tape of a Ewan MacColl song in order to write the words down. We had heard it on Folk on 2 played in memory of Ewan, who had written it when he knew he was suffering from heart problems. It was called The Joy of Living; (see Appendix v.) Peter wanted it sung at his funeral. I wasn't very good at coping with the sentiments expressed and was flippant when Peter may have wanted to be serious.

Thursday, 21st May. We discussed Mum moving up here. She had been finding her bungalow in Dorset too much to look after and my brother, who lived near, was considering moving to Australia. I had looked at sheltered flats being built near by, which might solve her problems. Peter thought I was taking on too much but I felt I did not have a choice. Mum arranged to come up to see the show flat at half-term.

Thursday and Friday nights were bad, the nurses were worried about him. On Saturday Mum came, stayed the night and we did without a night-nurse. I must have been mad because I took on two night duties as well as the day and seeing to Mum!

Mum was impressed by the flats and decided to put in an offer on one, subject to selling her bungalow. There was only one ground floor flat left. Sunday afternoon Irene and Geoff came; Hellen looked after Peter so I could talk to them. Peter did try to join us but could not cope with everyone talking.

Just because we were all tired after an exceptional couple of days the District Nurse who came that night was new. We could not cope with training someone, it was easier for me to get Peter ready. Fortunately the night nurse was Jayne, a relief to us all.

On Monday Peter was quite cheerful, the weather was warm and sunny so he was very reluctant to go to bed as usual, his body told him he should go but Peter did not want to. The body won.

After Mum had been I felt it was only fair that Peter should have the opportunity to see his family. I had not asked his sister to visit since a disagreement when Giles was a baby, although we had seen them when we went south and I did not refuse when she had asked to see the house when we moved north. I broached the subject with Peter; he did want to see Kit so I phoned her that evening to come the following weekend. In the afternoon Peter asked to use the wordprocessor! He managed a paragraph.

Monday May 26th It's a fortnight since I came to this machine and as ever we've had moments of crisis in between. This May Day Bank Holiday has arrived to find me in a more positive mood than of late and I think much of this has been helped by a pleasant blooming garden which I look out on from the back lounge. It shows that Janet has been able to spend some time and effort in making it nice but this has been restricted by my constant requirements. I think the impartial observer would note an unusual frequency of commode squatting.

This was Peter's last entry. We offered to type for him but that wasn't the same. He had to concentrate to keep breathing, any other activity, such as reading, eating, moving, talking, distracted. He could not breathe AND do anything else.

In the evening he sat in the garden, William sat with him and reported "Dad is much more cheerful." He also said he did not want to see his Dad die but wanted to see him afterwards. I tried to explain what it might be like although I had not seen anyone die either. William volunteered to sit with Peter if Jayne had to go home, she hadn't been well with hay fever and wake me if I was needed. I had arranged to take the boys out the next day so needed my sleep. It was half-term, in previous years we had taken our main holiday at this time, this year we were all just about housebound.

After a reasonable day Peter could not manage dinner and suddenly felt very tired. He wondered "What's happening?" and was worried about choking. After Jayne arrived I called Cath, going to her house to baby-sit, while she saw to Peter. Cath had been on a week-end course to study a technique to ease swallowing. I was unhappy at her being away for several days but it proved very useful. Cath stayed until after midnight. I did not get to bed until 1 am so was not pleased when Peter accidentally set off my intercom alarm at 4 am, even less so when Jayne got me up at 5.45 because she was going home with sinusitis. I had no more sleep. Peter was not well, he kept waking and staring around. I sat by him for reassurance and he did improve.

A TRIP, CURTAINS AND PANIC

Cath arrived to look after Peter while I took her boys and ours to Cresswell Crags. We eventually left near lunchtime, although I was very apprehensive about leaving Peter. We had a picnic, explored the cave area and looked at fossils. It was on the way back that Giles said, "What's that yellow paper under the window wiper?" Panic, it couldn't be a parking ticket. I found a lay-by. There was a message, "Phone home as soon as possible."

This was it then. He was dying, or dead, without me. How could I have gone out and left him?! Giles and William knew how worried I was. We had to find a phone. I got through to Cath dreading to hear what was happening. She said, "Don't worry. Do you know where the switches for the curtain pullers are?" What was she talking about?!!

I had been through hell in the last 15 minutes because the fitters from POSSUM had arrived, without an appointment, to fit the curtain rails so that Peter could pull his curtains via POSSUM. It was a bit late in the day! The rails had been on order for 8 months; the local branch of MNDA were contributing towards the cost and had periodically enquired what was happening. We did not know. We had measured the windows on at least three occasions and one set of rails had been sent which did not fit. I would have cancelled them altogether but the thought that they would be fitted, along with the belief that the page-turner would eventually arrive, gave Peter hope. Peter had insisted Cath try to contact me, he had no idea what conclusion I would jump to. He seemed oblivious to the fact that death was very close on several occasions.

We did not have the missing switches, they had not been sent. The fitter was quite nasty to Cath, who knew nothing about them; she searched the garage in case I had put them there. The service provided by POSSUM left much to be desired. Without the switches the rails he'd brought were of no use so the fitter left before I returned. Having them fitted on another occasion would be too much for Peter. It was too much for me now! I cancelled them and the page turner without telling Peter.

The day had been bad enough when the Agency phoned; they had not been able to find a nurse to cover tonight. I had had very little sleep, the house was a tip, I'd been out of my mind with worry, now it looked as if I was on night duty too. I seriously thought of leaving home!

Without that option, I cooked Peter the bacon sandwich he fancied, opening all doors and windows so he could still breathe, then got him into bed and comfortable only to have the District Nurse arrive to wash him, so had to get him up again! Nothing was going right, I could not get him comfortable again. Eventually I put him in the leather chair, bolstered with pillows but he remained uncomfortable. After an hour I had just decided to transfer him to the wheelchair when he fell asleep and the cat jumped on him! (She had not worked out the chair was out of bounds too.) I was willing to strangle anyone.

The Agency found a new nurse, Doreen, there was no way I could manage the night. Fortunately Peter was fairly well and said she had a light night. When I got up at 7 am Doreen reported that Peter had asked for the fire on and to be left alone for a while. He woke

up and I discovered the fire was full on, we never had it more than half on; he was nearly roasted. I had to be on watch every minute.

Doreen did not know our routines so I did most towards getting Peter up, washed and dressed. Peter was in reasonable spirits but annoyed with Doreen who talked a lot. I wrote in the notes, "Perhaps he might appreciate his regular carers a bit more!" The morning was reasonable, but by the afternoon both of us were suffering from the previous day. Everything was much worse if I wasn't coping. I was tired and depressed after the last few days. Being half-term my regular nurses were not available and I had the extra pressure of amusing the boys. Then in two days time Kit was coming, which was an even more depressing prospect.

I massaged Peter's neck to relax him and he improved for the evening and slept, throwing all routines out. He looked awful when he was asleep, with his eyelids half open and very pale. Fortunately Diane was back so he had a reasonable night. Diane reported at 3.30 am "All quiet in the house, but not outside! Male cat dominating his territory and in a big scrap whilst Tamsin watched. I chased them off, they're not waking Peter!"

BACK PAIN

Diane had been away a week, a long time in MND terms. Peter needed moving every $1\frac{1}{2}$ hours at least. Diane thought it best not to disturb him because he needed sleep but we suffered for it in the morning. Peter was in a lot of pain from his back, where muscles were deteriorating at different rates and unable to support him, the pain made him feel sick. I called in Cath to help. He eventually fell asleep after 2 hours spent trying to get him comfortable.

In the afternoon I could not leave him. Dr. Proctor arrived at my request and prescribed something to relieve the feelings of nausea. 'He could prescribe morphine if necessary. Peter should not choke unless he panics himself into cutting off his oxygen. He feels he is choking because of the lack of oxygen and irritation in his throat. I was to phone immediately.'

I saw Dr P. to his car. He said that Peter was alive because of the care and equipment I had organised. No one would have expected him to be still alive and that he would like to bring a few of his other patients to see how we cope and remain so cheerful. It was a boost to my confidence when I badly needed it.

That evening I told Peter what the doctor had said. He was amused by the thought that he should have died last Christmas, it cheered him up and we felt confident enough to chat about mine and the boy's future without him. He seemed to think that perhaps he did not have to struggle so hard, he had already cheated death by six months. Peter had no worries about William but wanted me to encourage Giles in singing, which he enjoys, perhaps a residential school to encourage independence. He also wanted us to go back to Scotland, which I thought would be very difficult without him. We discussed how I should rearrange the rooms once we no longer needed access to the front room. He said again how he liked me to work in the garden.

Diane was still on night duty. Giles told her that if his Dad had his mouth open he was asleep, which she noted. She had a cold night as Peter would not have the fire on.

FINAL VISIT

Friday, 1st June. Cath and Giles collected Kit from Sheffield coach station. Peter had eaten and rested well before her arrival. Cath had massaged and I primed the boys to chat to Kit while I kept Peter out of the noise.

She was very brave in coming to see him. She was in her late sixties and had not seen Peter since the onset of MND. However she was typical of the way many people cope with the disabled; she talked loudly and as if he were a child because he could hardly talk. It greatly upset me and I left her to the boys in the evening while Peter was resting. Diane was exceptional, coming early to see to Peter, then talking to Kit before we went to bed.

We really could not manage visitors so Kit only stayed the one night. Cath took her to the coach next morning. She was very upset on leaving. Peter was quiet after she had gone, but suffered no physical ill-effects. They had had several chats which pleased Peter. It was as if he was saying goodbye to his childhood, which Kit and Peter had in common.

He coped very well with seeing her. I did not. I was less than sympathetic in the afternoon, unreasonably blaming Peter for having put us through the trauma of her visit, although I had asked her. This contributed to his depression in the evening and night, although he told Diane that the breathing problems were getting him down.

Sunday was cold and raining. I did not feel well. The amounts Peter could eat were infinitesimal and took ages to consume. He knew I was busy cooking, seeing to washing and ironing and was very reluctant to ask for assistance. Not a good day. That night Diane reported he dreamt a lot, he called "Janet", instead of Diane, then, "Why am I here?"; later, "Are we going?" In the afternoon I had to ask our neighbour, a nurse in Intensive Care, to use the suction machine, our regular nurses being out. She had only used it on unconscious patients but was very good, getting a lot of mucus.

Monday, June 4th. I had definitely had enough. After an exhausting week I felt I could not go on much longer. The boys had no life, I just about managed to feed them but had no time with them; I was torn between their needs and Peter's, which were all-consuming. The boys could not even talk to their father because it tired him too much. I could see no end to this existence. Peter relied upon me emotionally as well as physically for survival, living through me. He seemed to have no intention of dying, still wanting the flipping page-turner! However his body was giving up and taking Peter, struggling, with it.

Sleep was becoming impossible for him. He had to have someone near him continually so he could relax but would jump awake, disorientated and frightened. He told us that as he woke he saw the room as if it were in miniature, so he did not fit in; or flat, like a cliff that he was about to fall over. He would concentrate very hard on the painting of Scotland until the room righted itself but it was very frightening.

He dozed in bed for a couple of hours then was up for three; 1 hour recovering from getting up, 1 hour to have a meal and a further hour to recover from the meal, with oxygen every hour.

On Tuesday Peter suggested he should go into a hospice so that I could have a break. There isn't a hospice in Rotherham. My nurses were back to normal, boys back at school and I felt more like tackling whatever else MND had in store for us. There was no choice; Peter was not going to hospital.

On Wednesday Dr P. called and suggested alcohol as a relaxant, if that failed he could prescribe a low dosage of morphine which would relieve the aches, pains and breathlessness; it would not be addictive immediately so he could stop but side-effects include nausea and constipation! I had to ring before Friday as he was then away for two weeks. As a last resort I should get someone infectious to cough on Peter!

That evening Patrick phoned to say Handsworth were dancing Morris locally, could they come and dance for Peter? The District nurse and I had just got him to bed but Peter wanted them to come so I phoned Cath to help me get him up and to relax him before they came; this would be quite an ordeal.

Peter enjoyed watching the dancing, on the lawn, despite his exhaustion. It seemed as if Fate was being kinder, he had seen his sister for the last time, now Folk which he so loved.

Thursday, 7th June. I tackled him about the morphine. He did not feel he had reached the stage of needing it but I thought he should try it. Marilyn came to do some physiotherapy and said she would recommend morphine for her husband in the same circumstances. Peter was afraid of the side effects, particularly as Cath had told him it would knock him out; he dreaded losing all control, which I could understand.

I rang Dr P. for confirmation; he thought Peter probably would react badly as he did to everything, but there was no alternative. He called later leaving a prescription for 5 mg morphine to be taken 6 hourly plus anti-nausea and constipation medicine, stemetil, to be started before the morphine. Peter agreed to start when Diane was on duty again. Dr P. preferred Monday when Dr Clark was on duty.

This proved to be an eventful day, after the doctor left Jean and I found the hoist was not working. Life was impossible without the hoist. I phoned the manufacturers who suggested pressing some switches on top of the 7' high gantry. I stood on a stool to try but nothing happened. Meanwhile, Peter was choking, Hellen was called to use the suction machine; then the three of us pushed Peter, in the sling, into bed. Wessex phoned Clark's of Sheffield to come out. I had another go at the switches, perched precariously over the bed. It worked, the hoist, which I was holding, moved and I nearly fell on Peter. Never mind joking about trying to kill him, I nearly did!

The engineer checked the hoist and left an emergency number.

Friday, 8th June. A massed attack on Peter, Jean Blackburn and Jane Petty both advised taking the morphine. I asked Jane how long he could go on in this state, she said "As long as he has the will to live, lose that and he will go very quickly. Could be 2 to 3 weeks, but breathing is a real struggle."

Giles went away for the weekend on the annual trip to North Yorkshire with Youth Club.

Friday night Elizabeth Stockwell was on duty. She had been before but not for many weeks so was not used to the routine or the signs of stress. She did not allow for recovery time, getting Peter up and washed at the same time. When I got up his breathing was appalling, the worst he had been. There was no way he could manage breakfast until after William had gone to

violin. He then had some of our first raspberries of the season with porridge.

He volunteered that breathing and apprehension are the worst aspects of the disease, besides having difficulty contacting us via the intercom and sitting up, needs more support.

Jean stayed while I collected William. In the afternoon Cath came so I could take William to the school's Summer Fair. It was very difficult to discern any breathing while he was asleep. Cath reported she had only left the room once to get a drink and Peter had wanted to know where she was going. She had massaged and administered ice chippings for over an hour. He had little contact with reality. When I came home he suddenly said "Raspberries." I asked if he wanted some? "NO!", as if I was stupid.

His breathing was erratic and hardly in existence. For the umpteenth time Cath and I did not give him long and she said to phone anytime.

An hour later he'd done it again, back to what counted as normal, relaxed and chatty; well enough for me to leave him to sort out the washing. Cath did not believe he could recover again!

By the evening he was back to choking, the suction machine caused more stress so he was in a bad way when Elizabeth arrived. I did not feel I could leave him. We could not get him comfortable but moving him in the hoist caused more stress and I feared it would kill him. We sat him up on the side of the bed to eat raspberries and ice cream and take some paracodal. He remained rocking backwards and forwards. Elizabeth asked if it was easing things, meaning the aches. Peter exploded with "NO, it's to show they BLOODY WELL HAVEN'T GOT ME YET!!"

We settled Peter back in bed, administered oxygen, then changed the cylinder to ensure there was plenty for in the night. The new cylinder started to blow out oxygen. It was around 11.30 pm but I phoned the pharmacist; we could not be without oxygen. He came with another cylinder and spare controls. Several attempts later we had a working cylinder available. I went to bed, shattered, at 1 am.

10th JUNE 1990

Peter was marginally less exhausted when I got up, Elizabeth had taken things a little more slowly. He had not been well in the night but refused suction as it had been so stressful last time. He was still struggling for breath and breakfast was too much. I put him back to bed and he got up much more rested. William was playing his violin which pleased Peter. The following Wednesday was William's 8th birthday, I gave him his present, a synthesiser, early to give him something to do while his Dad needed all my attention and Giles was away. I talked to Peter, we needed to discuss the diamorphine because he should take the stemetil today, to prevent nausea according to Dr Proctor, if he was to take the morphine tomorrow.

DIAMORPHINE

The information we had been given was that the morphine would relax Peter to ease the stress. Cath, who was against taking it, said it would knock him out so he no longer had control. I now know that morphine suppresses breathing, no one told us at the time. I believe it is essential to have all the information when making decisions, nevertheless, on Sunday morning we were both aware that although we were discussing taking or not taking the morphine, the result of doing so would be that we would be parted. We did not know if it would be by unconsciousness, sedation or death, but this was the next stage, quickened, if we agreed to taking it, by the morphine. Peter said, "What did we have? These few minutes in a day." The minutes talking with me were his life, the rest of the time was spent concentrating on keeping breathing. The equipment and nurses were essential but Cath kept him bearably comfortable physically with reflexology while I gave him the will to live through me. There were times when I felt if I had left him alone, as he would have been in hospital, not talked to him, he would have let go of life sooner and would not have struggled for so long. Perhaps it would have been kinder to let him give up but I could not let go. However much I complained about the situation I had sacrificed mine and the children's needs in order to keep Peter with me. The children temporarily lost both parents.

I agreed with him and said we were paying a high price for those minutes with the suffering of all of us, Peter, me, boys, nurses, we had to see Peter struggling without being able to help, was it worth it? I also told him that I was OK, now nurses were available again and boys back at school, if he wanted to carry on there was nothing I could not manage, although it was awful to see him suffer. Peter did not feel he was suffering, while he was, the need to breathe was so overpowering that he was not aware of anything else and he wasn't in pain. The aches and cramps "fall into place, they aren't important."

He decided not to start the stemetil but would wait until Monday, although I was dreading the next struggle it was his decision. It had to be.

I told him that Jane Petty had said he would die if he wanted to and let go. Peter asked "How do you do that?" I did not know. It sounded easy the way Jane said it but the bond between us was too great, neither was willing to break it.

He was tired, Cath came to relax him and we put him back to bed. I started cooking dinner. This was difficult because I could not stay with Peter, which he needed, and cook dinner. I gave him a choice of something I could cook quickly or Sunday dinner, he chose Sunday dinner despite the usual problems from cooking smells to contend with. There was no indication at this time that the day would be any different from the others but his body had other ideas. If Peter was not willing to give in his body would do it for him.

He suddenly started one of the worst episodes of choking we had encountered. I called Hellen to use the suction machine and sent William down to Jean's to play with Paul. Peter was already very weak and although we did remove some mucus we had to stop because we were all aware that the stress caused by having the tubes inserted through his nose and down his throat was killing him. We got him up into his chair. Hellen went to wash the suction machine, I massaged Peter's neck to try to relax him, using the technique Cath had shown us, Peter turned to me and said, "I love you." We were on the edge of another precipice; we could not go over this one together.

We phoned the surgery for an emergency visit. I was not keen on this as I knew Dr Proctor was away and Dr Clark, who was primed about Peter, was not on until Monday. I phoned Cath to come. She said could she come after lunch when her mother could look after the boys. We agreed this was alright. I continued massaging Peter's neck to prevent him panicking. I have no memory of whether we had dinner. William had his at Paul's. Dr Smaling was on call. He had no background information on us but could see the state Peter was in. He prescribed 5 mg diamorphine to be taken orally.

Rosemary called in to see how we were, I told her things were serious. She went to see Peter but he was concentrating on breathing and could not cope with distractions. When Cath arrived Hellen went home to have her dinner. I went to the Duty chemist to collect the prescription. Jean came after she had finished work to find out what was happening and stayed.

Peter agreed to take a little of the morphine, which he drank through the special straw, even this he found difficult but he slept for the first time in days. He was completely washed out. He would not let Cath move from his bedside, even to go to the toilet or get a drink. She and Jean stayed all afternoon.

A neighbour was cutting up paving slabs. The noise was too much. We tried closing the window to cut out the sound but Peter needed the air. I asked Mick if he could go round the back of his house to work as Peter did not have long and the noise was distressing him. He stopped.

I went to bed. I assumed I would be up most of the night and needed some rest. Diane was back on duty at 9.00 and we were arranging a rota with Jean, Cath, Diane and I so there would be two people on duty. Peter would not be on his own at any time. I did not sleep, I cried. This time was the worst of all; I HAD to let him go now yet I couldn't bear it. There are no words to describe the feeling, despair is too feeble.

Peter slept for a couple of hours then needed to get up. He thanked Jean for all she had done. He needed attention and ordered us around, get a blanket, hot water bottle, tea, homemade bread and butter pudding with rhubarb. Jean joked, "Is there anything else, Peter!" He was in good humour.

He ate a tiny amount of pudding. We massaged his fingers, which stiffened very quickly. Jean went home to get some sleep in order to come back later. Don collected Giles from the Youth Club trip. Giles came into Peter's room, by then Peter was back in bed and could not cope with much conversation. He said, "Hello, did you have a nice time?" That was enough.

Diane phoned to see how things were as she had been off duty for two nights. She came at 7 pm, early. By now Peter felt claustrophobic with too many people around, so Diane stayed mainly in the other room making drinks. Cath was not allowed to leave.

Tamsin chose this time to bring a bird in, disappearing with it under a chair in Peter's room. The bird was still alive and I managed to rescue it, but it was injured. I took it outside, Cath killed it. Cath could not rescue it, I could not kill it. The cat was not pleased but curled up in a corner of Peter's room.

Dr Smaling had phoned to see how Peter was and prescribed an injection of diamorphine because Peter had trouble swallowing the previous dose. The District Nurse who came to administer it was Anna, whom we

knew well and liked but I wished she had been Jean Blackburn who knew us better.

William came into the room to talk to me. Peter smiled. Both boys went to get ready for bed.

Cath was massaging Peter's neck, I was massaging his feet. Anna asked if Peter was ready, for the injection, but he said, "Not yet. Wait a minute." Peter was in control. He could just as easily have refused the injection. He knew what he was doing. It was around 8 pm.

He very quickly became unconscious. It was more than sleep. We put the oxygen near him, he hated having the mask on. I went to tell the boys that we thought this was really it; this time their Dad was dying, it would only be a matter of time, I would tell them if anything happened.

Cath was massaging Peter's neck. I held his hand. I had not realised how quick this would be and was upset at seeing Peter; he was an awful green colour, his mouth open and hardly breathing. I said, "I did not realise it would be like this, I don't like it."

Cath said, "You've got to let him go, it is unfair to Peter if you want him to stay."

This made me angry: "You don't understand, I CAN'T let him go." Peter started breathing again. His breathing improved enough for me to go to tell the boys that he might not be in immediate danger, he was a bit better, perhaps it would not be tonight.

While I was upstairs Anna arrived back; she had finished her rounds and came to sit with Peter. It was around 9.15 pm. She told Diane, "This is not right, he should be in hospital!" This upset Diane, the inference being that Peter would be better off in hospital as the nurses were better trained. The statement was so ridiculous that Cath and I ignored it. This is what Peter had chosen and the care he received bears no comparison to being in hospital. He was cared for by the three people who knew his needs because we had looked after him week in and week out and Peter trusted us above all others.

After seeing the boys I went to ask Diane to ring Jean to let her know what was happening; we had arranged for her to come up at around 9 pm. Diane was very concerned and told me to go and hold Peter's hand because the District Nurse thought it would not be long. By the time I was back by his side he had stopped breathing. I let him go by default; I was not there to keep him. I am actually quite proud of this, Peter could choose without my influence. Cath was with him, to relax him, so he could go peacefully and with dignity. If I had remained by his side I am sure I would have prolonged his life, but for what? When I reflect on Peter's death I feel it was RIGHT. Given the circumstances it could not have been bettered; it was the natural 'progression' in the stages of the disease and Peter had control.

Anna insisted that we put the oxygen mask on. This upset me, Peter could not bear having the mask on. She then shouted at him, "Come on Peter, BREATHE, BREATHE!" I could not understand why she should say anything, it seemed very unfair on Peter to call him back; what had it to do with her anyway, Cath, Diane and I were the ones who cared for him. Cath was furious, we had worked very hard for Peter to go as he chose, Anna was trying to take over. He did not breathe again. Anna asked me if he was still here. He wasn't. It was about 9.30 pm.

Tamsin woke up, walked across the room, jumped on Peter's bed and curled up at his feet. Anna moved to take her off but Tamsin knew she was not allowed on the bed when Peter was alive, she could stay. She remained at his feet through all the visitors, not getting down until all outsiders had gone from the house at about 1 am.

Anna took charge and asked if I wanted time alone with Peter? I was a bit surprised, there was no point, what was left wasn't Peter and there were things to be done. Anna phoned the doctor to come, I went to tell the boys that it was all over. A few minutes earlier I had told them their father was not dying so Giles misunderstood at first and thought he was alright. William cried when I told him. I asked if they wanted to see Peter, both had said they thought they would want to see him but they didn't. There were a lot of people around, which made it difficult. I did not stay with them because I had to prepare for the doctor coming. When I went up later William was asleep, Tamlyn on guard by his side. The cat looked as if he was not letting THEM get another one. I asked Jean to take photographs of the cats and Peter as I did not have a flash. I took some next day.

Anna arranged Peter's body. She asked how I wanted his hands, putting them across his chest. We put the bed head down but his mouth would not stay shut, not very flattering but he looked like that when he slept.

Dr Smaling arrived, rather loud and jolly and thrown by seeing Cath at Peter's bedside. Cath was Dr Smaling's cleaner, here she was in a very different role. He chatted to Cath. I thought this was somewhat inconsiderate, it was my husband who had died. I wished Dr Proctor had been there, but it did not matter much because it did not matter at all to Peter.

We had to pick up the death certificate the next day from surgery. We should call an Undertaker, he could not recommend one but they dealt with Bartholomew's a lot and found them satisfactory. This was fine, it was probably the nearest, I had looked them up in the paper

before. Cath phoned. Jean came up. I rang Rosemary, Kit and Irene, it was too late to phone Mum. I was on the phone to Irene when the undertaker arrived.

The man from Bartholomew's arrived carrying a cell phone. It was some time before I realised this was to phone someone to collect the body. Peter was not going anywhere tonight: I had looked after this body for months, it was to remain here one more night, not go somewhere strange. I was surprised and annoyed at the thought that it would be whisked away. Apparently it is very unusual to remain at home for long after death, just as one should die in hospital. I made the right decision. There were a lot more decisions to make, some I had worked out beforehand. When Bill Rutter died not everyone heard until the funeral was past and were disappointed they could not attend. I knew it would take some time for news to get round so set the funeral date twelve days hence, on a Friday. Some people would be coming a long distance, they would have Saturday to recover. This is a long time to wait for a funeral but was worth it.

It was only later I realised that Friday was the 22nd of June, 22 years to the day that I fell in love with Peter, at the Youth camp in the New Forest. There were other strange co-incidences; Peter was 62 when he died, I was 42; Peter was 42 when we married, 20 years before. 4 and 2 seem significant numbers. At 42 we both had a dramatic change in our lives.

Bill Rutter's birthday was 16th April (1914), the day before Peter's on 17th April (1928). Bill died on June 9th (1986), Peter died June 10th (1990). Fourteen years and four years separating each event respectively. June 10th was also six months after his last Folk event, the Xmas Extravaganza, 10th December, 1989. There was a strange comfort in these facts. Goodness knows what they mean.

The funeral date was relatively easy. Other decisions I had not prepared for; "What do you want Mr Dashwood dressed in?"

I had no idea! The Funeral Directors provide clothes, I imagined a shroud, like a sheet, I agreed to that. This was the wrong decision. When Jean and I went to see him laid out in his coffin, he was dressed in a pale blue, taffeta, frilly, dress shirt and waistcoat, with matching frill round the inside of the coffin. I presume females have pink! It looked terrible. Peter would not have been seen DEAD in this outfit. The thought gave us the giggles, which is why we came out of the Undertakers laughing. Decide what you want to wear before you die, even have a case packed! It was too late to change my mind.

Mr Bartholomew was there for at least an hour, seemed ages. He did not like the cat being on the bed, she might sit on the body and disfigure it. I also had to keep the body covered in case of flies. I had entered another world — of the mortician.

I agreed that they could take the body either before 10.30am or after 2 pm, the next day. They had a funeral at 12 noon. Cath, Diane and Jean were drinking tea at the other end of the room. Irene phoned back to find out what was happening. She insisted on coming over on Monday, taking time off school. She expected me to fall apart. She wasn't the only one, Dr.Proctor offered counselling once it was all over but it was the week before that I nearly gave up, this part had to be easier. It was ridiculous to break down now.

Cath at last went home to her boys. Rosemary came to see that I was alright. I offered Diane a bed for the night as it was now late and she had been expecting to be on duty. She said she could not stay with a dead body in the house. I found this odd, she had had some awful nights when Peter was alive, it could not be as bad now he didn't need her; also she was a nurse, weren't they used to this? She called a taxi. Everyone left by about 1 am. Tamsin got off the bed and went out.

I made sure Peter was covered, as I'd been told, switched off the lights for the first time for 5 months and went to bed with just my immediate family in the house. It was very peaceful.

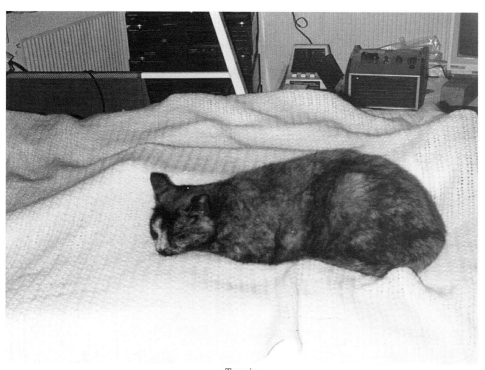

Tamsin

107

THE DAYS AFTER

I woke early. The house was quiet. I went downstairs and uncovered Peter. As I looked at what remained of him it was as if a part of me had been wrenched out. There was a physical pain far deeper than mere tears could erase.

Tamsin came in, ignoring breakfast she rushed into Peter's room looking for the bird she had brought the night before. When she couldn't find it she jumped back on Peter's bed and curled up in the same place at his feet. She stayed, only turning occasionally, until Peter was taken away in the afternoon. I had to lift her off the bed.

At 7 am. I thought Mum would be up and phoned her. Telling her about the previous night brought tears but I was also proud of the way we all, including Peter, had coped with death.

I left the curtain to Peter's room open and Peter uncovered so when the boys came down they could choose to look at Peter or not. We were so used to looking through every few minutes to see if he was still breathing, afraid that he wasn't, it was comforting knowing we no longer had to worry.

A few days before he died Peter insisted that I did not allow people to say his death was a 'relief', "It is NOT TO ME." 'Relief' is quite wrong, 'Release', maybe.

We had breakfast and I asked the boys if they had seen Tamsin? We went into Peter's room to stroke the cat. They visited her and their Dad several times during the day. I was very grateful that I had kept Peter at home, it gave us time to come to terms with the reality of his death, there was no mystery or fear. This was easier than the previous weeks had been.

I phoned school to say William would not be in and why. There were a lot more phone calls to make.

People arrived; Rosemary, Cath, Jean Blackburn, District Nurses, who had not heard, Aileen, the Home Help. She could not stay to clean because Peter had died. She was taken aback when I joked that Peter was still here, didn't that count? She was not happy that he was still in the house. There appeared to be a stream of women coming to see Peter; he would like that. Cheryl, our hairdresser, spent a long time with him, as did Anne Middleton, the evening District. They were both upset.

Irene came as promised, with Ruth. I did not like them sitting around so set Ruth to hoovering. It did not seem right to make such a noise but it needed doing. We closed the curtain to Peter's room because Ruth was not happy with it open. I was sorry about this, it was so nice to look through and realise we did not have to watch Peter every minute.

The men from Bartholomew's came mid-afternoon. I went into the room to watch them, Cath came with me. As they lifted Peter's body onto the stretcher Cath put her arm round me and said, "It will soon be over, this is the worst part." It wasn't. Allowing him to die was the most impossible act of caring for Peter. Now I remained responsible for his body and I wanted to make sure it was treated properly, but it wasn't Peter.

After they had gone we had to collect the death certificate and register the death. We went in Irene's car, I do not think I would have been safe driving; bereavement is a very unsettling state however well prepared one tries to be. Tamlyn tried to get in the car, they'd taken one of us he wasn't having any more going without him.

The causes of Peter's death given on the Death Certificate were:

a) Orthostatic Pneumonia;
b) Immobility;
c) Motor Neurone Disease.

The next few days were spent informing as many people as possible and arranging the funeral. I became attached to a phone. I cancelled the one session of Nursery I was running per week and postponed William's birthday party.

William and I went to see Peter at the Funeral Directors. The uncovered coffin was brought into a small, darkened room, like a chapel, before visitors were asked to go in. There is an overpowering smell of the embalming fluid. The body in the coffin was recognisably Peter, despite the fancy funeral clothes and the wasting caused by MND. The embalmer had consulted Dr Clark as to how the disease would have affected muscles. We put Peter's peaked cap by his hand so some of his clothing was familiar. His skin was cold, almost wax-like, unreal. William, aged 8, touched and gazed at the body of his father for a while, then said, "Can we see the others now?" He fancied a guided tour of the mortuary. Instead we received an interesting lecture on the embalming process. The embalmer was particularly proud that one of his clients had been to India for a month, to be seen by his relatives and returned in as good a condition as when he left, despite the heat and air flight!

I needed to have pictures of Peter around as we knew him, not with MND. I had copies of a photograph taken by Derek Schofield at Christmas 1988, in different rooms. At the time it was taken Peter could walk with crutches, he was still independent. William remarked,

"We could have kept that Daddy." He was not inclined to have the one we had just lost back again. He then asked when we would have a new Daddy? Giles was appalled by the idea; he had gained status and a role through MND, he was not keen to lose it. He also thought William was insensitive to my feelings. William was feeling deprived, everyone else had a Daddy. I was a bit surprised by the question but we sat down to discuss this. I pointed out that some father's don't want to see their children whereas William's did everything he could to stay with us. Then we considered all the fathers of his friends we knew, plus any other men we could think of, with a view to their being a prospective Daddy. We could not find one that William thought could replace his or that we would want to live with, so we agreed we wouldn't have a new one just yet.

FUNERAL

The disease had given us the opportunity to prepare. The Xmas Extravaganza was not Peter's last event, we had discussed what he wanted and he left notes on the wordprocessor:

Peter's Funeral
View to holding the entire thing at the Crematorium.
Book a double period 2 x 20 minute sessions.
How many does it hold?
Organ — any other instruments allowed?
Any music not allowed?
Scattering of ashes on Mother's grave.
The day thou gavest Lord is ended
The Joy of living
The life of a Man
Music: Princess Royal (3 versions)
Robin; Lay preacher
Peter Davis
Readings:
Kath says that the Rotherham Crematorium is very big and they will open the doors on to the garden for an overflow. There is a gallery for a choir or group. The car park is huge. They were not allowed to book more than one session.

From this and our talks I had to create a funeral worthy of Peter. I had given it some thought during sleepless nights, we did not want the usual morbid affair. Bartholomew's suggested I consult the crematorium, which is how Cath and I came to be shown round the venue; quite like old times. I noticed there was carpet at the front and remarked that it would make dancing difficult. The Caretaker was taken aback but gave no objection. I had not decided if I could cope with a Morris dance, but it was a possibility.

We rejected the vicar Bartholomew's suggested as he would not allow anything unconventional and asked Elizabeth Caswell, of the local United Reform Church, to officiate. We knew her personally. Peter wanted a religious service for his family. Elizabeth set exactly the right tone for the service and was a great help in sorting out the running order. The Committal was a particular problem, I had often helped Peter with programmes but the committal of a coffin had not been part of any of them!

Cyril Tawney and Artisan agreed to sing. Peter missed Artisan before he died, I hoped this might make up for it. Peter had also promised Artisan an event before MND took over; they got one in the end, not quite what we had in mind originally but Peter did get them free! I wanted them to sing Mary Ellen Carter, a rousing song but it contains the word 'bastard', I played it to Elizabeth to make sure she approved. She was quite happy, the song contained a Christian message.

Mum came up for the funeral as she also needed to sort out buying the new flat, staying with us. Kit and Derrick lodged with Cath's mother. Charlie was not very well so did not come. On the night before the funeral, just as we were going to bed, Tamlyn appeared through the toilet window carrying an enormous mouse. Tamlyn was usually too lazy to catch anything, when he did it was big, a blackbird, starling, even a stoat! He was very proud of himself bringing me a present. The mouse was still alive. I was used to this and fetched the dustpan to catch it; mice will run in thinking it is a safe hole so I can take them out and release them; a well tried routine. Unfortunately Tamlyn had caught a kangaroo. It ran safely into the dustpan, I lifted it up and the mouse immediately jumped out. It was now loose by the front door, I was afraid it would run up the stairs and shrieked for Mum to find a bucket to put it in. The mouse was jumping up the door by now, the cat furious in another room, Mum keeping out of the way. Giles woke up with all the excitement and from the top of the stairs looked down at the mayhem and said, matter-of-factly, "Are you having your breakdown now, Mother?" I assured him it was only a mouse I was chasing and he went back to bed. Somehow I captured the mouse in the bucket, covered it up, as the mouse was still jumping and let it go outside. By now it was nearly midnight and we had the funeral the next morning.

By one of the quirks of fate Peter's funeral was the same day as Kathie Mitchell's. She had been an Honorary Representative for the EFDSS for many years, living in Hull. She had died a few days after Peter but her relatives were unaware of the difficult choice they presented for some Folk people.

There were also many people from the South and East who would have attended Peter's funeral if the distance was not so great. Approximately 100 friends, relatives and nurses filled the crematorium, many joining us later for a buffet, prepared by Cath, and a dance in the Scout H.Q. Elizabeth and I timed the programme to the minute to ensure we did not over-run. I am pleased to say we kept to it exactly; Peter would approve.

With Artisan and Cyril Tawney singing I had an excuse to leave out the Joy of Living. I was determined not to cry at the funeral, Peter was unable to ensure the day ran smoothly so I had to do it for him, it was inappropriate to break down. I did not feel safe with that song so asked Bob Hazlewood to play it in Peter's memory on Folkwaves, Radio Derby, instead.

THE JOY OF LIVING
by Ewan MacColl

Farewell you Northern hills,
You mountains all, goodbye.
Moorland and stony ridges,
Crags and peaks, goodbye.
Glyder Fach, farewell,
Cul Belg, Scafell,
Cloud bearing Sullven.
Sun warmed rock and the cold
Of Bleaklow's frozen sea,
The snow and the wind and the rain
Of hills and mountains.
Days in the sun and the tempered wind
And the air like wine,
And you drink and you drink 'til you're drunk
On the Joy of living.

Farewell to you, my love,
My time is almost done;
Lie in my arms once more
Until the darkness comes.
You filled all my days,
Held the night at bay,
Dearest companion.
Years pass by and are gone
With the speed of birds in flight;
Our life like the burst of a song
Heard in the mountains.
Give me your hand then, love, and join
Your voice with mine,
We'll sing of the hurt and the pain
And the joy of living.

Farewell to you, my chicks,
Soon you must fly alone;
Flesh of my flesh, my future life,
Bone of my bone.
May your wings be strong,
May your days be long;
Safe be your journey.
Each of you bears inside
Of you the gift of love,
May it bring you light and warmth
And the pleasure of giving.
Eagerly savour each new day,
The taste of its mouth,
Never lose sight of the thrill
And the joy of living.

Take me to some high place
Of heather, rock and ling;
Scatter my dust and ashes,
Ffeed me to the wind,
So that I will be
Part of all you see,
The air you are breathing.
I'll be part of the curlews cry
And the soaring hawk.
The blue milkwort and the
Sundew hung with diamonds.
I'll be riding the gentle wind
That blows through your hair,
Reminding you how we shared
In the joy of living.

A CELEBRATION OF THE LIFE OF PETER DASHWOOD

22nd June 1990, Herringthorpe Crematorium, Rotherham

The last 3¾ years have seen the gradual loss of the man I married. Through redundancy he lost his job, through Motor Neurone Disease his ability to dance, garden, walk, write, feed himself and finally breathe. However we have never lost the essential PETER. As I have gradually taken over both our roles Peter has been there to advise and support. When he could see we could manage he had the strength to withdraw gracefully, quietly and with dignity. There are many people who feel privileged to have known Peter but none more than those who were present at his death. I hope he enjoys this celebration, he chose most of the music.

Handsworth Traditional Sword Dancers, Peter's last team, bore the coffin into the Crematorium to the music of English traditional dance tunes arranged and led by Brian Heaton. Cyril Tawney, representing the early Folk Revival sang "What's the Life of a Man".

What's the life of a man any more than a leaf?
A man has his seasons so why should we grieve?
For all through this life we appear fine and gay.
Like a leaf we must wither and soon fade away.

Robin Whittlestone, our best man, read from 1 Corinthians 15 v 42.44 and 1 Corinthians 13 on Love. Denis Smith, a musician and friend from Essex, played versions of the Morris jig "Princess Royal". Peter Davis gave the Tribute. Artisan, representing Folk of the 90s and whose singing cheered many of Peter's sleepless nights, sang "The Mary Ellen Carter" by Stan Rogers.

Rise again, rise again
Though your heart it be broken and your life about to end.
No matter what you've lost, be it a home, a love, a friend,
like the Mary Ellen Carter, rise again.
Rise again, rise again.
That her name not be lost to the knowledge of men.
And those who loved her best and who were with her to the end,
Like the Mary Ellen Carter, rise again.

This song, about a shipwreck and those who saved her against all odds, may have been a surprising choice but it typified the attitude we had to MND and Life in general.

Everyone sang the hymn "The Day Thou Gavest Lord is Ended" at the Committal. Peter sang this as a choir boy. Robin read a poem by C.Day Lewis

His laughter was better than birds in the morning, His smile turned the edge of the wind, His memory disarms death and charms the surly grave. Early he went to bed, too early we saw his light put out; Yet we could not grieve more than a little while, For he lives in the dance within us, smiles from the sky. *(Last line altered slightly.)*

The Minister gave a Blessing and we went out to Morris tunes, including "The Fool's Jig", which Peter used to dance. I could hear him asking for it to be played slower!

Mike Garland, Squire of the Morris Ring and ex-Eastern Folk and Men of Anglia, volunteered to dance at the funeral but I wasn't sure I would cope with someone else dancing and we were short on time at the Crematorium. He danced superbly at the 'Wake' afterwards

I had warned most attending that I would not wear black. What we had done in the last few months and days was a triumph over the disease; it wasn't Peter's fault that his body gave up. Wearing black, or even dark colours, was giving in to 'THEM'. I did not mind what others wore and did not want to shock people but I probably did. When I told my Home Help I wasn't wearing black she said, "You did really love Peter, didn't you?" !! Peter's family also found it difficult to understand, but many joined me; Peter Davis was asked if he was going to a wedding!

Sister Guy came to see me a few days later, she had gone to the Health Centre and told the other nurses, "That was the most wonderful funeral I have ever been to!" She attends a lot in her job. The nurses thought she was mad. Griff Jones made a recording of the funeral; we had to make several copies for nurses as well as relatives and friends. Giles played in a lot. There is a copy in the Vaughan Williams Memorial Library, Cecil Sharp House. Artisan created enormous interest, I had to send for their tape containing Mary Ellen Carter for lots of friends. Even when he was dead Peter encouraged people to Folk.

Dr Proctor returned from his holiday after the funeral and called to see how we were. He had tears in his eyes as I told him about Peter's last day. He had given us a lot of support. He seemed to expect me to be at a loss once I no longer had Peter to care for and again offered counselling but I felt quite good about how we had all come through this. Dr Proctor said he had not known anyone so calm; I never shouted or cried and we were always so cheerful. He didn't hear us when we were alone! I could not explain that although I miss Peter terribly I do not feel sorry for myself or bitter about MND. We knew the final outcome of the disease from the start; we did all we could to postpone it but death was the inevitable 'progression'. I had twenty-two very happy years with Peter, more than anyone else except his mother. Nothing can take them away and there is no point in regretting what I have not had; although at low times I am upset that William and Peter have missed William growing up. For myself, I took over so many of Peter's skills and roles in life, as the disease progressed, that he became part of me, and he is part of others to whom he passed on his love of Folk. 'THEY' did not get him.

IN MEMORY

Although many friends could not come to the funeral through commitments or distance we were overwhelmed with nearly 200 letters and cards and a total of £3,000 in donations. I asked for money to be given to the Motor Neurone Disease Association instead of flowers. Peter had not expressed a preference other than perhaps a book be donated to the Vaughan Williams Memorial Library. (This is it.)

We did not expect a large amount to be collected after the very generous donations towards equipment while Peter was alive. When it was apparent that a substantial sum would be transferred I asked that it be used for equipment for loan to MND patients rather than research. The disease can destroy physical abilities so quickly that one usually needs equipment at least a week before one realises, yet it frequently doesn't appear until 6 weeks after one has no further use for it! Few people on Benefits have the advantages that we had.

A year later I heard Donald Hunt, retired Manager of Halsway Manor, was in the closing stages of MND a year after diagnosis. He had equipment from the MNDA. I like to think that the donations from the Folk world in Peter's memory helped Donald.

Some money was given directly to the boys and I. We used it for hotel accommodation at Sidmouth and London, real luxury and provided happy memories. At Sidmouth Festival friends, who knew Peter long before I did, thanked me for looking after him. I thought this odd as I was his wife, until I realised that many people loved Peter. He had a charm which effected both men and women.

In November I bought an oil painting by Barry Renshaw. It is of a sunlit path through a wood, a man with a walking stick is disappearing into the distance.

There were several obituaries in Folk magazines. I asked Pete Shutler of the Yetties to write for Dance and Song. I sent him copies of Peter's writing, so much of what he wrote is contained in this book. See D. & S. October 1990. Volume 52 Number 3.

My favourite article on Peter was written by Colin Cater, a singer rather than dancer. Peter would have enjoyed reading this.

Handsworth Traditional Sword Dancers as bearers

POST SCRIPT: THE ASHES

After the funeral I felt I had done my bit and did not want to know about the Ashes, which Peter had asked to be scattered on his mother's grave in Lymington. But it was there on the computer, I would have to do it eventually. Fate struck again. Peter's brother, Charlie, died of heart failure after developing diabetes in February, 1991. This was a terrible shock to the family, two brothers in 7 months. We couldn't get to the funeral because of snow and Giles was recovering from an operation on his foot, so we arranged to go down at Easter for a joint ceremony of interring Peter's and Charlie's ashes in the grave.

We had to send Peter's ashes down beforehand. (I had imagined we would hand them over when we got there.) The Lymington funeral directors advised sending them by Securicor; this set up images of robbers attacking Securicor vans only to find them full of urns! Our Funeral Directors sent them by post.

On the morning of the service we woke to a freezing, howling gale and torrential rain reminiscent of the Dr Zhivago film. In the church were a few old ladies waiting to take Communion, one kept pressing a switch on an electric panel, 'click.... click'. Half way through the service it dawned on me that the 'clicks' were followed by a muffled 'dong'. She was tolling the bell!

Kit and Derrick and the three of us doubled the congregation; the vicar came in on crutches, with two henchmen, I presumed to hold him up if he fell which was quite likely, it being High Church there was lots of bobbing up and down.

After Communion Giles limped up the path to the grave, the vicar went in a car and we all tried to avoid being blown over. The Church did not allow 'scattering' of ashes, not a bad thing as in that wind few would have made it onto his mother's grave. Fortunately, we stood facing the wind away from grave; a hole had been dug for the 'urns' (small oak boxes) and while the vicar was saying his bit, the wind blew extra hard and William over. If we had stood the other side it would have been William down the hole!

I found it difficult to take the occasion seriously, probably Peter's influence. He would have enjoyed the humour of the occasion. I could not think that the small box being buried contained all that was left of him but I had fulfilled his wishes. The family put a plaque on the grave.

AN APPRECIATION OF PETER DASHWOOD

by Colin Cater

I first met Peter in the early nineteen seventies when I moved to Essex. He was a cherubic man of great good humour, seemingly endless patience and considerably more vision than I personally gave him credit for at the time.

At that time folk was booming. Singers and song club audiences were looking to expand their knowledge and active interests well beyond the weekly concert hall into both ceremonial and social dancing. As EFDSS Eastern Area Organiser, Peter knew dance better than song, though he was quick to appreciate the different cultural flavour of the song club and anxious to bring the two together.

On several occasions he came to Chelmsford Folk Club, then meeting at the Three Cups, to run normal club evenings as Ceilidhs. Initially he brought a tremendously gifted musician with him — John Kirkpatrick: later on, he came as an honoured guest as an emergent Bill Delderfield practised his embryonic skills and the club band played. He had returned the dance to folk, extended the tradition and out of his initial patronage and commitment a thriving network of Essex bands and callers has grown. When Lumps of Plum Pudding was formed, he gave us sound advice (which we did not always appreciate!). He also found bookings for us though he must have known that it would take some time for us to develop the subtleties needed to play for experienced dancers.

I also remember Peter in District Committee meetings — a source of endless enthusiasm, guidance, forbearance and desire to bring the two arms of dance and song together, despite their seeming resistance to each other. Peter was one of that full timers (Bill Rutter & Graham Binless were two of the others) who led the Society through a Golden Age of expansion and development of new ideas and forms of folk activity. Twice under his chairmanship, Folkeast ran at Chelmsford, as well as being hosted in Essex on other occasions. Opportunities were provided for countless morris sides, bands, callers and singers to practise their myriad skills in front of larger and always appreciative audiences. Felixstowe, the East's regional festival also owes its existence to Peter's unstinting dedication, as does the folk event in the annual EXPO at Peterborough.

However, the sun did not always shine on Peter. He was forced to endure family hardship which he bore with great courage and fortitude. Though many of its difficulties had been caused by others, it was Peter who was asked to relinquish his post when the Society fell on hard times. I last saw him in Peterborough two years ago when his illness had first been diagnosed. He still chatted and laughed and all his old tenacity was apparent in his cheery conversation. My real memories of him though go back much further. He was a doer, perhaps not always selling himself as well he might, but promoting enthusiasm, fun and togetherness throughout the folk world.

ESSEX FOLK NEWS, Autumn 1990.

Peter with Colin Matthews, Expo 88

A MAN WHO NURTURES THE IDIOM OF THE PEOPLE

Peter Dashwood — Profile by Deryck Harvey

Comparatively few men feel the need or have the courage to change the course of their lives in mid-career, especially when the decision means they will lose a pension and halve their salary, but Peter Dashwood, Eastern Area Organiser of the English Folk Dance and Song Society, did just that and, after eight years, he has no regrets.

Quietly spoken, smartly, soberly dressed, Mr. Dashwood, aged 39, balding, with a full-cheeked black beard, now going white at the point, has been

Cambridge Evening News, 15th January 1973

his society's conscience in the Eastern Region for the past three years. He covers Norfolk, Cambridgeshire, Suffolk, Hertfordshire and Essex. Until he recently moved home and headquarters to 16, Hatter St, Bury St. Edmunds, he was based at the Cambridge Arts Centre, Warkworth St. Cambridge.

The society's declared aim embraces a wide, general principle, that of encouraging the practice and enjoyment of folk music, song and dance and to stimulate interest in and to preserve associated customs and drama. It is to these ends that Mr Dashwood gave up the security of the Civil Service after he had first become interested in folk song and dance at St Helens in Lancashire. "I'll tell you how I really came into this," he said over coffee at the Wagon and Horses, a Newmarket pub. "There was a great interest in square dancing at the time, after the Queen had visited Canada. Suddenly, we had a wave of enthusiasm in this country. I came in on that wave and stuck."

He spent five happy years in Lancashire and then he moved to Woking in Surrey. "It was there that I really took to Morris dancing with the Thames Valley Morris Men." And then he made his decision "It was a 'daring' decision." he admits. "The salary was also daring! but I felt the need to do something... I needed to get out. In a way I was lucky the society were looking for somebody at the time I was available."

A Morris dancer, he admires the "gutsiness" of the form. "It's the sheer 'gutsiness' of doing the thing, the vigorous sort of stepping." Ironically, Mr Dashwood, does not belong to a group now that he's an organiser. "The job means looking after a tremendous number of clubs. I've just started a newsletter called 'Anglian Broadsheet.' In our last distribution this went to about 150 folk dance and song clubs throughout the area. There are all sorts of clubs, of course, folk, dance, Morris and sword clubs. I haven't visited half of them.

The society are first concerned with the English traditional dances and British traditional songs. There has been a great revival in folk songs in the past 15 years, and one of the most joyous things about the clubs is that they encourage their audiences to join in and sing from the floor." Mr Dashwood is delighted that the Crofter's Club, of Cambridge, have introduced a very successful Ceilidh band. "More and more we have dancing and singing in our social activities and it is because of groups like the Crofters that this is happening. It's people like me who are trying to find more people like the Crofter's!"

Bigger occasional events, besides club meetings, are also very well supported. "We used the Maltings at Ely for a Ceilidh in December with the Yetis, a well-known group from Dorset."

Between his rounds of club visits, committee meetings and organising larger events, Mr Dashwood is a "caller" at dances, and he admits: "I'm a good listener. I'm all for a mixture of dance and song. This is, for me, the ideal social occasion." He has seen many young people make a progression towards folk activities. "Most of the folk singers of my era have been in it from the beginning, some of them started in jazz and skiffle, and that sort of thing. People don't, or they didn't anyway, go directly to the traditional scene"

He and his wife, Janet, have a son, Giles, aged two months "which is why I look permanently tired!" at the moment he has no time for other pastimes.

With headquarters in London, Mr Dashwood is one of only six field officers in the country. And the numbers have been reduced over the years because of lack of funds. "Although folk itself has never been in a healthier position the society has always been in financial difficulties, and always will be, I suppose. But the society in a way does not look for a return. It is concerned with promoting and encouraging folk dance and song, and it has done a good job in the past. If it should fold tomorrow," he added, not all that pessimistically, "interest is there. Folk itself would carry on for a long, long time."

CAMBRIDGE EVENING NEWS. January 15, 1973.

The spellings and grammar are as they appear in the paper. Obviously the Yetties were not known well enough! Peter lied about his age, he thought 44 sounded too old to be a new father.

A CONSUMER'S POINT OF VIEW

Article written for Occupational Therapist Magazine

I was diagnosed as having Motor Neurone Disease in August 1988 and at the time of writing, in March 1990, I reckon to have been living with the condition for about 3 years. I have the 'progressive' type of the disease which affected the lower limbs in the first instance and later the hands and lower arms. There have been some breathing difficulties in recent months. No one can predict the pace of the progression but in general it takes about 3 — 5 years. The needs are constantly changing so it is important to have equipment and adaptations when needed, if only for a short period. A month in the life of an MND patient and carer is a very long time. A general observation on all the disablement services is that the initiative to secure information or equipment rests entirely with the patient and/or carer.

Nationwide there are about 6000 sufferers at any one time so we are not very thick on the ground locally. Diane, our local Occupational Therapist, came into our lives some time after diagnosis and I believe this was her first MND case. At that stage I was able to walk with the aid of a stick but climbing stairs was very difficult and getting into the bath was more than a problem. The stairlift saga began soon after she first came and ended much later.

We soon learnt that Diane could produce some items immediately, as if from a hat, bath aids were amongst the first. However, adaptations such as ramps and stairlifts are different and involve many others, including the curse of all progress, a committee. Suffice it to say that in no way can needs be met when needed under this system. One officer with the right authority could do it. It would have been easier for my wife too with only one person to nag daily to get something done! Having just seen the film about Steven Pegg on Channel 4 we were shocked at the lack of equipment in use for someone in the advanced stages of the disease (MND) and for a carer who needs more help. Does this show a lack of proper advice from local Health and Social Services or have the family not taken up offers or shouted loud enough?!

We are very well organised with equipment including items which would have helped Steven Pegg such as a hoist and a powered chair. Recalling our own experiences with equipment I think there was a reluctance in official circles to give advice, possibly because I hadn't reached the stage when particular items of equipment were deemed appropriate. In the ideal world for both patient and carer, situations would be anticipated, so that equipment is on hand at the very time it is first needed. We did follow up some early advice, from the Physiotherapist who visits all MND patients in the area, and purchased a posture bed which rises at head and foot and goes up to nursing height as well as vibrating. The advice was well founded and I believe most patients with progressive MND would benefit from such an investment. OT's should be prepared to recommend such items even though it is not supplied by them and presumably not in the general brief.

The Mangar Booster could be in every OT's brief. Having noted the bellows principle with the bath lift we were delighted to discover that Mangar had also incorporated the bellows into a wheelchair. In no time at all my wife had persuaded Diane and her department that this would be a good investment. It's great value was in putting me on my feet from the sitting position with minimum supervision. It was in use until I was no longer able to stand, inflating higher and higher as my condition deteriorated. Now if only the chair had motors to drive it from A to B, what a versatile machine it would be!

The other most vital piece of equipment is the Wessex hoist which sits above my head between A frames (lucky for us that the manual lift which was offered did not fit under the bed). The hoist was in place at the right time, that is when I could no longer stand. My wife can transfer me from bed to wheelchair or commode three or four times a day without any other assistance, which up to that point had been considerable. So, apart from two or three major items, we have done well from the system and from a caring OT. I think too Diane would acknowledge that she has learnt something from our experiences. Alas, there are many other sufferers of various conditions out there who for one reason or another are not so well supplied. I suspect the old maxim about "he who shouts loudest" still applies.

Peter Dashwood. March 1990.

ESSENTIAL CARE PLAN FOR MOTOR NEURONE DISEASE

The first of many losses for anyone suffering from MND is TIME.

A quick diagnosis. Knowing what one is up against is infinitely preferable to knowing something is wrong but not what it is.

Truthfulness about the possibilities while there is doubt. Having knowledge of the possibility of a dramatic disease gives time for coming to terms with it. To go from being "normal" to terminally ill in seconds causes immense stress.

Honesty about the likely course of the disease, at least to the carer. Sensible decisions cannot be made without full and accurate information, decisions that may be vital to the future of the whole family.

One key worker who knows and understands the problems of living with MND, who makes personal contact with the family within a few days of diagnosis, can be contacted by the person with MND or carer and who is responsible for co-ordinating a care plan between the professionals and patient/carer. It is essential for the family to know there is someone who understands and can help with their problems.

A sympathetic and knowledgeable GP.

A phone line for information and for emergency. See contact list MNDA

Counselling to be offered.

Printed information in short advertisement style incorporating plenty of visual material, covering:

- what one might expect to happen physically, mentally and emotionally; Information on coping with bereavement applies to coping with diagnosis.
- what help there is available, who to contact and where.
- the equipment and adaptions that are available with addresses. Perhaps manufacturers could advertise in and sponsor leaflets.
- Tips, recipes, adaptions tried by MND families. See THUMBPRINT, the magazine of the MND Association.

A more detailed medical description of the disease available to the MND sufferers besides the professionals involved.

The person with MND to have control of care given, ie nurses, home carer and equipment. As physical control of one's body is lost, it is very important that control of one's environment remains.

POSSUM, the environmental control system to be explained and discussed with MND families and installed if required. Not everyone can cope with the upheaval.

Professionals to treat families with MND, or any disability, as they would hope to be treated themselves. Common courtesies, such as making appointments or having a regular time for calling, should be observed. The wishes of the family to be a prime consideration, not what the professional thinks is best.

A small, regular team of carers who know the needs of the person with MND and are available in an emergency. As the progression of MND can be very rapid the District Nursing system cannot cope. Any one of a large number of nurses may turn up at any time; not knowing who or when can cause a great deal of stress to the families. If the nurse does not know the current routine, which can change daily, she/he may be more trouble than help.

Equipment and adaptions to be available when needed, if not before. Situations should be anticipated and prepared for physically and mentally, rather than waiting until everyone is struggling, or it is too late.

Physiotherapy daily and swimming regularly to retain use of muscles and keep joints moving. Water is relaxing and provides support enabling greater movement than is possible when competing with gravity.

A meeting place for MND patients and other people with disabilities and/or terminal illness, without their carers, where there is a reason for the patient to be there other than giving the carer a rest. The assessment at Mary Marlborough Lodge fulfilled this need, briefly. The person with MND should have a useful role and not feel he/she is a burden.

Provision of a computer or word processor which can provide means of expression, occupation, work and frustration. May as well vent it on something other than the family!

Good respite care available, where MND is understood. So carers can have a break without too much guilt.

Professionals who are willing to discuss all aspects of the disease, including it's final outcome, ie death, if the patient or carer wishes and how to prepare for this progression of the disease. When one lives with death on a daily basis it would be helpful to be able to discuss it without fear of embarrassing the professional. A trusted person should be able to guage if a patient or carer does want to talk and initiate subjects. One has the feeling with some that death represents failure, this need not be so.

Appendix IV

ADDRESSES AND CONTACTS

MOTOR NEURONE DISEASE ASSOCIATION
PO Box 246 Northampton NN1 2PR.
Information and support services for families with MND. Employs Regional Care Workers. Equipment loan service. Finances research into MND. Make contact if you have the least suspicion of that you may have MND. It helps to be prepared. Always in need of donations.
MND HELPLINE: 0345 626262
All calls charged at local rate. Was not in existence when we needed it.
OWN GENERAL PRACTITIONER
For access to aids, including wheelchairs, District Nurses, Home Carers. If help is required ASK. May need to pester if GP is unfamiliar with MND.
SOCIAL SERVICES DEPT.
For Occupational Therapist, Speech Therapist, structural alterations and adaptions to the home, Physiotherapy, Home Carers, Meals on Wheels, Orange Disabled Badge Scheme for parking. See local Council address in Yellow Pages Telephone Directory. Make contact with them to find out what is available before you need it.
LOCAL LIBRARY:
Reference Medical: Neurological diseases, for diagnosis. Disability and Benefits for information. Contact addresses for organisations which may offer voluntary help such as Crossroads, Age Concern, we did not try these. May house DIAL Office, see below.
DIAL (Disablement Information & Advise Lines)
DIAL UK Ltd. NADIAS Victoria Buildings 117 High Street, Clay Cross, Derbys. 0246 864498. Books and leaflets on everything from equipment to holidays. Run by volunteers who may not know how to find the information you are seeking. It is worth looking for yourself amongst their literature. See Yellow Pages for local office.
BENEFITS ENQUIRY LINE: 0800 882200
Mon - Fri 8.30am - 6.30 pm. Free advice on benefits available to people with disabilities and their carers. Did not try this.
CITIZEN'S ADVICE BUREAU.
See Yellow Pages Advice on Benefits. I found ours helpful.

DISABILITIES LIVING CENTRE:
Lenton Business Centre, Lenton Boulevard, Nottingham, NG7 2BY 0602 420391. Advice for people with disabilities, carers and professionals.
DISABLED LIVING FOUNDATION:
380/38 Harrow Rd Westminster, London, W9 2HU 071-289 6111
National Information Service on disability aids.
RADAR (Royal Association or Disability & Rehabilitation):
12 City Forum 250 City Rd London, EC 1V 8 AF 071-250 3222. Advice, publications on disability, including holidays. Some books available in W. H. Smiths. Useful.
DISABILITY ALLIANCE.
25, Denmark Street, London WC2H 8NJ
Their annual Disability Rights Handbook is essential reading for anyone applying for benefits, includes comprehensive address list. Buy this.
CARERS NATIONAL ASSOCIATION:
20/25 Glasshouse Yard, London, EC 1A 4JS 071-490 8818
Did not have the time to contact this organisation.
NAIDEX CONVENTIONS LTD.
90, Calverley Road, Tunbridge Wells, Kent TN1 2UN. 0892 544027 Fax: 0892 541023.
Annual Exhibition of equipment and services for the disabled and elderly. Fascinating.
CENTRE PARCS LTD.
Kirklington Road, Eakring, Newark, Notts. NG22 ODZ. For brochure: 0272 244744. For bookings: 0623 411411. Holiday Centre with some facilities for disabled customers.
THERAPOSTURE.
10/12, Fore St. Trowbridge , Wilts. BA14 SUB. 0221 469506 Electronically controlled bed to aid sitting up, raising feet, massage and standing. Can't imagine MND life without one.
MANGAR BOOSTER.
Presteigne Industrial Estate, Prestaigne, Powys LD8 2UF. 0544 267674 Fax: 0544 260287.
Low air pressure lifting equipment, including bath seats and multi-purpose wheelchairs. Very useful for raising when fallen, in the bath, standing and transfers.

MOBILITY 2000 (Telford) Ltd.

Unit 5, Telford Industrial Centre, Stafford Park, 4, Telford, Shropshire TF3 3BA 0952 290180
Wheelchair which can climb some stairs and kerbs up tp 8.5 inches, raises and lowers for user to reach high or low. Highly adaptable but also expensive.

ORTOPEDIA GmbH

Postfach 64 09 D-2300 Kiel Germany 14
Tel: 04 31 20 03 0. Series 935. Wonderfully adaptable wheelchairs for indoor and outdoor use. Investigate if you have the money.

MEYRA Rehab.

Millshaw Park Avenue, 6 B Leeds, West Yorkshire. Outdoor wheelchairs capable of going over rough ground. Expensive but give outdoor independence.

POIRIER.

Usines des Roches-Fondettes 37230 Luynes
We bought our reclining, electric wheelchair second-hand, for £700 in 1988. Not so good as above for outdoor use and cumbersome indoors but was indispensible.

HOIST.

Wessex Medical Services, Romsey, Hants.
A-frame, electically operated hoist for aiding transfers. Without this Peter, or I, would have ended up in hospital.

DISABLED DRIVER'S MOTOR CLUB.

Cottingham Way, Thrapston, Northants. NN14 4PL. Information and useful addresses for transporting disabled.

SCOPE (SPASTICS SOCIETY).

12, Park Crescent, London W1N 4EQ
Monthly newspaper DISABILITY NOW useful to all disabled people and their carers. Disabilility is normal. Reading this newspaper helps to relieve the feelings of isolation as it gives lots of advise, addresses, second-hand sales, jobs, etc.

POSSUM CONTROLS LTD.

Middlegreen road, Langley, Slough, Berkshire SL3 6DF 0753 79234
Environmental control system. A single switch can control up to twenty mains electric appliances per room in up to three rooms. Available free from the Department of Health to patients so paralysed or disabled by disease, injury or congenital defect that they are unable to carry out simple tasks at home, such as switching on a light. Watch installers, they may not be as good as you expect. It can seem as if equipment is taking over the house but it proved vital in enabling Peter to stay at home. See GP or Occupational Therapist.

FOUNDATION FOR COMMUNICATION FOR THE DISABLED.

Foundation House, Church Street West, Woking, Surrey GU21 1DJ 0486 227848

A Charity which gives advise on computers, software and other communication equipment as an alternative to writing and/or speech. Very helpful, tailor advise and equipment to individual needs, not just the disability.

MARY MARLBOROUGH LODGE,

Nuffield Orthopaedic Centre, Headington, Oxford. OX3 7LD
National Health Assessment Centre for disabled. "Patient" usually resident for 2 weeks during assessment. Gives advise and equipment on coping with disability. Useful in being a meeting place for people with a variety of problems. Also provided respite for carer without too much guilt. Provided indoor electric chair adapted to Peter's needs and other equipment difficult to obtain elsewhere.

TALKING BOOKS.

National Listening Library, 12, Lent Street, London Se1 1QH 01 407 947.
Postal service of books on cassettes for those unable to read. Can be cumbersome and requires assistance to set up and operate.

INDEPENDENT LIVING FUND:

PO Box 183 Nottingham, NG8 3RD 0602 290423/290427.
Grants money for care, means tested. Enabled Peter to be cared for at home. More stringent rules since 1993 but worth trying.

SWIMMING:

Try local pool, then Physiotherapy Dept. at either rehabilitation hospital or local hospital, maybe school for disabled children. Water is very relaxing and gives support enabling exercise and walking.

REFLEXOLOGY.

Do not have an address.Very helpful in relieving pain and stress without drugs.

BRITISH HUMANIST ASOCIATION:

47 Theobalds Road, London, WC 1R 4RL 071-430 0908
Advice and help with non-religious funerals.

ENGLISH FOLK DANCE & SONG SOCIETY

Cecil Sharp House, 2, Regent's Park Road, London NW1 7AY 071 485 2206
Exists to collect, research and preserve our heritage of folk dances, songs, music and customs so that they can continue to bring enjoyment.

BRITISH INSTITUTE FOR BRAIN-INJURED CHILDREN

Knowle Hall, Knowle, Bridgwater, Somerset TA7 8PJ 0278 684060.
Gives hope for children with Cerebral palsy, Down's Syndrome, Learning Difficulties, or any of a number of labels given to children